# TERRIBLE
# PERFECTION

# TERRIBLE PERFECTION

## Women and Russian Literature

## BARBARA HELDT

INDIANA UNIVERSITY PRESS
Bloomington and Indianapolis

Manufactured in the United States of America

**Library of Congress Cataloging-in-Publication Data**

Heldt, Barbara, 1940–
Terrible perfection.

Bibliography: p.
Includes index.
1. Russian literature—Women authors—History
and criticism. 2. Russian literature—History
and criticism. 3. Women in literature. I. Title.
PG2997.H45   1987       891.7′09′9287       86–45893
ISBN 0–253–35838–8

1 2 3 4 5         91 90 89 88 87

*For GSS*

Perfection is terrible, it cannot have children.
Cold as snow breath, it tamps the womb

> Sylvia Plath

To fuel her dangerous wish for a pure and terrible perfection. To say all or nothing, and to
hear, unmistakably, inside oneself the echo:
nothing.

> Christa Wolf

# CONTENTS

# ACKNOWLEDGMENTS

I wish to thank Christine Nowakowski, Gerry Smith, Marjorie Stam, and Ruby Toren for typing drafts of my manuscript; Jack McIntosh for bibliographical assistance; and, for their comments on earlier versions, Nina Gove, Richard Gregg, Wendy Rosslyn, Gerry Smith, and Mary Zirin. Other friends in Canada, the US, the UK and the USSR gave the encouragement and set the example I needed. I would also like to thank the many scholars unknown but read whose work constituted the social climate in which this book could be written.

I am grateful to the Social Sciences and Humanities Research Council of Canada for a leave fellowship.

Gerry Smith kept our house, kept his sanity, and kept writing.

Portions of this text have appeared in earlier versions in the following: "Tolstoy's Path Toward Feminism," *American Contributions to the VIII International Congress of Slavists, Zagreb, 1978* (Columbus: Slavica, 1978), pp. 523–35; "Two Poems by Marina Tsvetaeva from *Posle Rossii*," *Modern Language Review*, vol. 77, no. 3 (1982), pp. 679–87; "Chekhov (and Flaubert) on Female Devotion," *Ulbandus Review*, vol. 2, no. 2 (Fall, 1982), pp. 166–74; "Nadezhda Durova, Russia's Cavalry Maid," *History Today*, vol. 33 (February 1983), pp. 24–28. All translations are my own unless otherwise indicated.

# TERRIBLE
# PERFECTION

# INTRODUCTION

To most readers outside Russia, Russian literature is a totally male tradition. It means the nineteenth-century Russian novel, with Chekhov closing out the century, and Pasternak in the person of *Dr. Zhivago* representing the twentieth. To Russians, the list expands considerably, and includes their modernist and poetic tradition, in which two women poets, Anna Akhmatova and Marina Tsvetaeva, hold a place of honor. It is still an almost totally male tradition, but Russian poetry provides a few openings, for which no more than two or three women poets need apply.

In this limited perspective, Russian autobiography is rarely considered. It has not been discussed systematically at all as part of the literary tradition with the exceptional mention of fictional childhood accounts like those of Tolstoy, Aksakov, and Gorky. Here again, women writers are invisible: this kind of autobiography is an extension of a career as writer, serving to illuminate that career. Women's writings about careers as writers face the difficulty that more often than not, their denial of ambitions toward such a career is a prerequisite for its very existence. Nearly all the Russian women writers deny the writer's vocation, even as they practice it. They cite the urging of friends or editors, not their own ambitions, as the impetus for writing.

The Russian women who are known to the outside world are not primarily writers, but rather monarchs or revolutionaries: Catherine the Great or Alexandra Kollontai, whose career ended in diplomatic docility, rather than Anna Akhmatova, whose life was quieter but much more heroic. Admirable studies by Dorothy Atkinson, Gail Lapidus, Richard Stites, Barbara Engel, Rose Glickman and Linda Edmondson[1] document the women's movement in Russia and the condition of working women. They chronicle the tremendous odds women had to overcome in the society as a whole to attain or even to discuss the possibility of social and educational betterment. The greater part of the discussion of women's role originated with men, a not disinterested group. Women were busy, as Glickman's book especially demonstrates, leading lives that precluded anything much beyond survival. How literary models of womanhood might have affected them—through contact with male or female upperclass readers—is an interesting subject for speculation: Nekrasov, Dostoevsky, and Chekhov all touch upon it in their stories of reforming prostitutes.

The task of the literary critic is somewhat different from that of the historian, although, for both, the very fact of discovery and reappraisal of women in Russia constitutes a large part of the undertaking.[2] There is no "women's movement" in Russian writing, no group of writers with the common goal of producing texts that exemplify women's experience or view of self. Such texts exist, however, and collecting and explicating them will be one major goal of this study.

There is no lack of general pronouncements about how women act or feel or think in Russian literature: these, however, have been overwhelmingly made by men. The unflattering have been more than amply "balanced" by the flattering. In fact, in Russian fiction the elevation of the Russian woman is matched only by the self-abasement of the Russian man. His is a long and tortuous road to enlightenment, while *she* grasps the essentials of life, if not immediately then certainly firmly and intuitively when the time comes (to fall in love). For the male writers who dominate the tradition of fiction (including the novel, the novella or *povest'* as it is called in Russian, and the short story), woman is a kind of paradigm or shorthand. There is no novel of gradual female development, of rebirth or transformation[3] as we find in Austen or Eliot; while some male characters learn and grow through intellect or experience, the changes in women are mysterious givens of nature, of Womanhood. The heroines of male fiction serve a purpose that ultimately has little to do with women: these heroines are used lavishly in a discourse of male self-definition.

While works of prose by women writers from the 1830s on have been popular, none has ever gained the stature of a classic: they were not read beyond their own time. This is true in spite of the fact that Russia's classic tradition is realism, the tradition in which English and French women writers excelled. This is true in spite of the even more curious fact that heroines of all sorts are to be found in abundance in nearly all the great works of the Russian realist tradition—heroines with whom the whole world has identified, thanks, in part, to the publicity given to them by critics who felt they were models of womanhood. As Russians in particular are fond of stressing, critics do participate in the reputation of artistic works, and cultural practice (publishing and criticism, as opposed to writing and reading) has generally been male-controlled. In Russian in the mid-nineteenth century Dmitri Pisarev reviewed books for a female audience for the journal *Rassvet*. He began a career of activist writing by telling his audience of mothers and daughters what of literature, often European literature written by women, was suitable reading. His ultimate aim, as he himself wrote, was to enlighten women, so as to make them better wives and mothers.

Between the text and the reader, male critics of various persuasions have interposed themselves over the years. Women's writing has been selectively criticized as a side-current which runs parallel to the male mainstream and its "larger" social issues, among which the treatment of the female character is not central. Women's writing in Russia has proven especially vulnerable to interpreters of a different gender, as men's writing has not been. This creates a peculiar awareness on the part of the female writer. The author's sensitivities then may become part of her writing. There is much here for the feminist critic to unravel. If self-protective irony is a constant feature of women's prose and poetry, might this tone not be the result of the expectation of a different, gender-based reading by her male critics? In Karolina Pavlova's *Double Life*, one of the finest examples of nineteenth-century writing by a woman writer, the modern reader can uncover in the tone of the work ironic layers that protect not just poets in general against an insensitive aristocracy, but young girls against the marriage market, unhappily married or unmarried women against social scorn, and, by implication, the values of the novel and its poetry as asserted by a woman author herself, subject to these various female states, against male critics claiming detachment from them.[4]

Thus, we reach a paradox which, even more paradoxically, has not been perceived as such: all the most memorable heroines of Russian literature appear in works by men. Equally strange is the fact that the most famous feminist novels in Russian literature have all been written by men. Further, the remarkable heroines of Russian literature appear, not in feminist novels, but rather in works generally conservative on political issues pertaining to women. Thus, the shapers of the tradition of prose fiction in Russia have always been men. This is certainly not the case in France, England, or Japan: Russia has no Mme. de Staël, Jane Austen, George Eliot, Emily or Charlotte Brontë, Hayashi Fumiko, or Murasaki Shikibu. It does have some George Sands, women writers popular in their day who took up such themes as social oppression and inequality. But male voices spoke with greater consistency and volume on these issues.

Such facts might seem daunting to someone writing a book on women in Russian literature; actually, they have been an incentive to look further in several directions. Territory worked by Russian critics in the past can be seen entirely differently by a person from a different culture and time. What seems an established hierarchy of writers and their literary creations is in fact the result of a densely woven web of conventional expectations. Russians of today regard "their" culture of the past two centuries as works in a museum full of objects under glass. There is remarkably little disagreement about literature among people who disagree violently about most other things. While scholarship since the Formalists has illuminated questions of period, genre, and verbal texture, only rarely is the authorial vision of reality in the text or the author's rhetorical stance made to interact with these other factors.[5] Yet, only by studying these questions can we hope for a more balanced picture of literary art.

It seems clear that the methods and insights of feminist literary criticism that have evolved in the past decade in the West could be of great value in redefining Russian literature as a series of texts involving gender-based values. Russian feminist criticism is almost nonexistent: the most significant exceptions to this culturally dismal rule are cited in the notes to this book. But the choice between and among the profusion of Western feminist literary criticisms whose diversity constitutes their strengths is exhilarating. Within this profusion of the last twenty years, Elaine Showalter suggests three national groupings:

> English feminist criticism, essentially Marxist, stresses oppression; French feminist criticism, essentially psychoanalytic, stresses repression; American feminist criticism, essentially textual, stresses expression. All, however, have become gynocentric. All are struggling to find a terminology that can rescue the feminine from its stereotypical associations with inferiority.[6]

Using this framework, the present study is "American" feminist in its orientation: it proceeds inductively from texts. It assumes that men and women writers inhabited a shared literary culture (if not always a shared social culture), but that women's writings provide an alternate perspective to literature by men. In Russian literature the strongest expressions of this perspective took place in modes of writing in which the feminine had not yet been defined by men, in autobiographical and lyric rather than in fictional modes. Women writers used different words in different genres to project a different view of self. Parts two and three of this study will analyze these virtually undiscussed female traditions, making this, too, a gynocentric work of criticism.

As for Showalter's notion of the identification of the feminine with inferiority, it simply does not apply to Russian literature in quite the same way. Rather, it was the insistence on female superiority in fiction that set the standard for the Russian novelistic heroine. It was a "natural" superiority, untutored and virgin. Rosalind Coward has noted that in the debates of the nineteenth century "a growing space [was] given to the question of the 'natural'." While the relations between the sexes "became the privileged object of study," Coward asserts that the real subject of the debates was not sexual relations, but rather "speculation about society in general."[7] So it was, appearances to the contrary, for the Russian novel. The "natural" perfection of the Russian heroine exemplified a standard not met by Russian society as a whole, a standard decried in works of fiction and criticism bearing titles such as *Who Is to Blame?*, *What Is to be Done?*, and *When Will the Real Day Come?*

It was, thus, a terrible perfection, frightening to men who could not match it in "manly" action and inhibiting to women who were supposed to incarnate it, or else. (The "or else" is often made explicit, as we shall see in chapter 2.) For women writers, such heroines did not bear children in their own work: they could or would not match the artificially high standard, which was not in any case the real center of the debate. Russian women writers found other forms: the perfection of craft in poetry and the autobiographical voice.

Whether centrally or obliquely, women do have their reality named and appropriated in Russian fiction by men. For example, Zinaida, a young woman whose position in society is ambiguous, is the object of naming in the following four-line dialogue between the narrator's mother and father in Turgenev's novella *First Love*. The woman's hostile naming is based on the fact that she suspects future infidelity on her husband's part, but even though this is true, her attempt at naming is put in its place, deconstructed by her husband:

> " . . . And I can't think what she has to be proud of—*avec sa mine de grisette!*"
> "You evidently have never seen any grisettes," father remarked to her.
> "I haven't, thank God!"
> "Yes indeed, thank God . . . only how then can you form an opinion of them?"

In this passage the wife is attempting to judge her husband by denying social approval to a younger woman who could then only exert her power outside acceptable social boundaries, as a *grisette*. (This is indeed the reality of Zinaida's status.) In order to avert judgment by his wife, the husband lays claim to special knowledge available to all members of his sex but only to nonrespectable members of the female sex. It is the lack of such knowledge which constitutes power for women of the respectable category; but then men can use their exclusive knowledge as ultimate power, because it enables them alone to make judgments about women. Only keeping to her place, which means cutting herself off from other women, even from forming positive or negative opinions of them, ensures the married woman's status. Without this survival in her place, she meets the fate of Zinaida, the subject of

the conversation. Rather than be outcast, she allows a man to mediate between the world she is allowed to know and the half-world of the other
women that surrounds it. In this novella the father's agony results from a
not entirely free passage between the two. This is the plot of many a male
fiction where neither of the complementary pair of women is described with
the inner intensity of a Zinaida. Sexual identity and social identity are syn-
onymous with identity itself. Feminist criticism alone bridges the social, the
individual, and the textual in these and many other instances.

The construction of sexual identity and the exercise of sexual authority
within a text may be difficult factors to determine. But without a feminist
criticism, the discussion of their recurring patterns and voices will continue
to be imprecise and self-indulgent. Ignoring the question of the sexual identity of the text means slighting the human factor to an extent that most works
of art cannot afford to bear. It is precisely in this area of naming that literature
by women, however diverse it may be, can be contrasted to literature by
men. As the objects of male discourse, women do not write their own scripts:
in fact, as we see in the above passage, their scripts are taken away from
them. The fact that they often act their hearts out in scripts written by men
should not blind us to this appropriation of female knowledge.

In the first part of this study, women will be viewed as objects of male
self-interest; in the second and third parts they become the subjects of their
own scripts. They attain perfection of another sort, the perfection of the
writer's craft. Giving up their ideal form, perhaps, but also abandoning the
doom, disgrace, and death that result from deviation from this ideal, women
writers find ways of writing in which male definitions can be resisted. As I
read Russian women's writings, two genres seemed to build from separate
and seemingly unrelated works into coherent wholes: the genres of autobiography and lyric poetry. Many of these works have not been discussed
since their year of publication; a few are famous, often because they have
been used as historical evidence. All need to be given a new, literary context,
that of women's writing. Both autobiography and lyric poetry, as distinct
from prose fiction, are self-mediated. The narrative or lyric voice speaks
directly to the reader. Women and their own consciousness are no longer
primarily part of nature or part of society; they are committed to the exploration of self in, as Luce Irigaray puts it, "a sort of universe in expansion
for which no limits could be fixed and which, for all that, would not be
incoherence."[8] Within autobiography and poetry I found consistency and
evolution in the dramatization of the female self that could be termed a
female tradition of Russian writing, one not discussed before. Texts echo
each other both because their female authors made conscious reference to
their predecessors and because they were part of a continuum within a

culture as it evolved to their day and as it continues to evolve in our time. Russia has had more powerful women poets and autobiographers than women novelists, while in England, France, and America the situation seems to have been the reverse. The tradition, once established, has a momentum of its own. When certain modes of literary expression are largely male-defined, women of talent who seek their own voice will work in other forms. These then become the voices other women writers will hear and from which they will seek encouragement.

My first problem seemed to be to define aspects of what I call the male tradition in Russian literature in its most important manifestation, that of prose fiction. Because this is the dominant tradition of Russian literature, no woman writer can ignore it, and a female Russian voice must take it into account in some way. While male portraits of idealized heroines came to be seen as "normal," there is no corresponding female prose tradition of a romantic or idealistic hero which became a norm. Nor did women writers stress perfection in their heroines: rather, they stressed their suffering at the hands of society. The most unfettered heroines in works by women, the ones who provide the best match for the fictive heroines of male authors, are located in the two genres I have named. Hence the tripartite division of my book. Rather than make comparisons within one or two genres, I have focused on writing as a whole. The former choice might have yielded a neater literary study, but it would have impeded the larger aim of understanding why women's voices are heard in a certain way within the Russian tradition. Thus, the focus of this book will be on the image of woman created by men (as expressed in fiction) contrasted with the image of women created by women (as expressed in autobiography and poetry). What women writers made of these two modes of writing will be a central concern of this study.

In defining the male fictions of Russian literature, two main concepts need to be reviewed: the concept of the heroine and the concept of misogyny in fiction. For both, the boundaries need to be altered. They have too often hinged on the dichotomy of flattering versus unflattering, as if male gallantry or male paranoia in the author or the narrator was the sole criterion of judgment. The subjectivity that gives rise to extreme forms of both admiration and disgust is seen in this study as more of a unity than has been apparent until now. In the first two chapters, these seemingly opposed features of Russian literature by male authors are shown to be closely interrelated. Focusing initially on the Turgenevian paradigm, I also bring in other major Russian writers whose works have made their mark on the concept of Russian womanhood in fiction. These range from the medieval to the modern, from writers of fiction to writers of social criticism of Russian fiction. Chapter three is devoted to Tolstoy, who, more than any other writer, made women and family the central issue in his works. The evolution of his writing seen from the feminist perspective, not of women's oppression but of male self-definition, yields a new interpretation of his later, "sexual" writing, one in which it appears more feminist, not less so, than his earlier works. The fourth chapter begins with Chekhov, reputedly the most "balanced" Russian observer of the human dilemma, who centered so many of his stories on female consciousness. Tracing a theme of female passivity, we proceed to examine other writings of the century's end that deal more explicitly with woman's sexuality and offer seemingly new explanations for her nature and conduct. A motif of male voyeurism can be traced in these works, one which has implications for the entire first part of our study. Thus, by the end of part I, I hope to make explicit a central metaphor of male writing about women: the visual trope of woman objectivized and named by man, who is doing the fictive viewing and narrative commentary.

Part I having defined the classical tradition of male fiction and woman's place within it, the next step is to investigate, in part II, a form of nonfictional writing in which women excelled in Russia, the self-creating form of auto-biography. Between 1767, when Natalia Dolgorukaia wrote of how she fol-lowed her husband into Siberian exile, and 1967, when Evgeniia Ginzburg published the first volume of the ordeal of her imprisonment and infinitely more harsh Siberian exile—in those two-hundred years at least—there exist numerous published (and probably countless unpublished) accounts of their own lives by Russian women. These can be seen both as counterweight to fiction and as a tradition in itself, one not before studied as having its own coherence. The woman's world created in these autobiographies ("nonfic-tional narrative accounts are world-creating in the same sense as are works of literature")[9] is permeated with a different view of self and of family and society from that ascribed to women by men. Men are not the central preoc-cupations of women, whose chief concern is to lead independent lives as people. The memoirs of Dashkova, Durova, and Sokhanskaia in particular detail their authors' pride in hard-won accomplishments, not the least of which is freedom from married life and society life, the two givens of the female world in the Russian novel. Dashkova is the only woman president of an academy of sciences in world history; Durova had a distinguished combat military career while disguised as a male hussar; Sokhanskaia forged a career as a writer while living in rural isolation. Each of them inscribed into their autobiographical texts selves quite different from the heroines of male fiction, as did many other women writers. We shall examine the rhetoric of female autobiography in Russia, the styles of self-explanation in various works by women famous and obscure, asserting, as all autobiographies do, what they want the world to see of them.

Another mode of writing is marked by the "I" speaking directly to the audience, unmediated by the sort of narrator we find in works of fiction. The lyric poem was another vehicle for the Russian woman writer to find a true voice, one which transcended gender or social identity, often through the skillful redefinition of these identities. Part III will trace a female poetic tradition in Russia from the female folk lyric to the most powerful poets of the modern age, Akhmatova and Tsvetaeva. This tradition, whose strength in Russia is undeniable, is an alternate voice with the power to be both female and universal.

The poetic and the autobiographical writings of Russian women bypass the need for perfection within a fictive world: they proceed directly to the world of reality or to a world composed of words arranged with the precise perfection of craft (the latter word is echoed from Pavlova to Parnok to Tsvetaeva). Direct, unmediated by narrative other than self-narrative, immediate, and self-defining, the lyric and the autobiography freed women writers to say something which proceeded from the female self and which elaborated its own self-creativity, the perfection of verbal art in the service of that self. In autobiography the words expand into the space of an entire life. In lyric poetry they compress timelessly into density of craft. What are women's contributions to these modes of writing in Russia?

It is high time we began to speak of these traditions of female writing not as exceptions to a "basic" literary tradition in which women's place is at best peripheral, but rather as a particular and a vital instance of the whole writing tradition. If this study separates the two canons into male and female in order to make certain things visible, one can also envision future criticisms written with a view to an eventual reintegration, one markedly different in its gender-awareness from what has gone before.

# PART I.

# The Fictions of Russian Men

The form of her in something else
Is not enough

Wallace Stevens, "Bouquet of Belle Scavoir"

# 1.

# THE RUSSIAN HEROINE
## Where to Find Her and
## Where Not to

In describing the male context of Russian literature within and against which the women writers of Russia were obliged to find their own forms of expression, it is most useful to begin with the concept of the heroine. The Russian heroine is generally taken as a marvelous given of nature, a being in whom not only her own and her family's future, but the future hope of Russia resides. The feminization of virtue in the late eighteenth century and throughout the nineteenth has been noted by feminist scholars of the past fifteen years in all its ramifications in Europe and America. It is a compensatory ideal: as women's work grew ever more tedious and harsh outside the home, the myth of the pure (untouched by society's evils) keeper of the hearth gained strength. The Russian variation on this theme takes it into areas of national consciousness that are unmatched in Europe, although not, perhaps, unrivaled in America.[1] In Russia, however, it is the interaction of male and female within a work, not the heroine alone, which gives the myth a curious twist.

The inadequacies and weaknesses of some male protagonists find their complementary awesome strengths in the young heroines of Russia. This theme emerged with obsessive frequency in Russian writers of the nineteenth-century realist tradition, appearing in all genres: the novel in verse, the poem in prose, the short story, the novella, and the novel itself. Given the number of authors and genres dealing with these unresolved love plots and the span of years with their specific literary and political subtexts, not too many critics and readers give in to the temptation of stressing similarities between these characters while ignoring differences in each work. Their first great publicizer, the radical critic Nikolai Dobroliubov (1836–61), in his essay "What Is Oblomovitis?," made distinctions even between the Byronic progenitors, Pushkin's Onegin and Lermontov's Pechorin. Turgenev, who gets the prize for the greatest numerical contribution to these types, was the one who gave them their name of "superfluous men" (in a story of 1850). His heroines, after Pushkin's Tatiana, are the prototypes for all the others, unto the Soviet era,[2] but they have no name that has caught on: they are just Liza, Natalia, Marianna, etc., and every Russian reader knows their names as well as that of the girl-next-door.

Historically, one should stress the differences between the Byronic types (Onegin, Pechorin), the superfluous men (in Turgenev, Goncharov, and Ostrovsky) and the underground types (in Dostoevsky and his successors, Andreev, Sologub, and Garshin). The one thing they all have in common is that they manage to attract a spirited young woman of marriageable age, and then, whether they play games of superiority or belittle themselves before her and the reader (often both, because it is the same thing), they flee the scene, leaving the heroine standing alone and superior. The heroine and the reader are left in a sort of mutual hand-holding: I-told-you-he-was-no-good, but it was an interesting experience for life (or plot for a fiction) nonetheless.

Many readers, both Russian and Western, have dwelt on the female of the non-pair as if she were the equal of the male in fictive fullness, as well as his superior in moral qualities. We will argue the opposite. If all these works were measured purely for the number of words used on only the male or the female, clearly the female is considerably short-changed. Sometimes the story is written as a monologue of the male, so that the female never speaks to the reader directly. Often she is a mere episode in a longer story concerning the male and how he came to be that way. (How *she* came to be that way is simple: she just lived at home.) These are works written by male authors, and their protagonists, also male, differ in varying fictive degrees from their creators. The very attractiveness of the females described is a sort of "What if?" for the hero: What would my life be if I had the perfect life's companion? Or, for the more sociohistorically minded Turgenev: How could I live as a citizen in Russia, were even a true marriage a reality? For Dostoevsky's anti-hero of philosophical bent: How can I live with myself even with a woman who (like Liza the prostitute in *Notes from the Underground*, Sonia in *Crime and Punishment*, or the woman in *The Meek One*) has known greater suffering than I and still isn't such a swine?

Leaving biography, history, and philosophy aside, we will argue on literary grounds that this Russian female character, ubiquitous and always more nearly perfect than the male, is often literarily the least interesting of Russian heroines, because she is a mere foil for the male and his larger preoccupations, not a true heroine on whom the events of the plot center. She does not fit Tomashevsky's definition of the hero: "the character who receives the most pointed and vivid emotional coloration . . . that person whom the reader follows with the greatest intensity and attention."[3]

Consider, by way of exception, Nastasia Filippovna in *The Idiot*, orchestrating the scene (part I, chapter 16) where several men desire her, but some desire money, respectability or peace even more: she sorts them out by throwing a packet of many rubles (her "dowry") into the fire. Consider Anna Karenina, directing her own "death scene," when she gives birth to Vronsky's child and orders her husband and her lover to embrace and forgive each other (part IV, chapter 17). Tolstoy describes her every word and gesture as utterly false ("But there is another in me as well, and I am afraid of her. She fell in love with that other one . . ."); yet it produces an effect of rightness in both the men. These are examples of real womanly force; but their male authors shrink from eulogizing such power. An even better example can be found in Turgenev's best work, the novella *First Love*, in which Zinaida is the third point of a triangle with a father and a son (the narrator), both of whom love her. Their lives are joined forever at the end in memory and throughout the narrative in willed and passive interactions, alternating continually both in action and in consciousness. Zinaida is a captive princess in squalid surroundings. She maintains her freedom by exerting her will over her "suitors." She is both powerful and powerless, déclassée, and, by society's rules, compromised. But she exerts her will freely, parodying the male homage paid to her. One suitor gives her a present of a kitten and asks to kiss her hand in return. "Both hands," she replies (chapter 4), taking the initiative and mocking the convention. The father, like her, is economically dependent (on his wife). Both are compromised even more by their love, their loss of mastery. The boy-witness gradually understands and, when he has reached the age that his father was, relates the story as a completed event in the past that has an enduring psychological future. Zinaida is presented as neither better, nor worse, nor "different." She is like the men in alternating love with "control" over passions. When there is loss of control through love, and of love through death, all lose. This is Turgenev's most balanced work: the woman is incapable of either saving or destroying the men, though at times they would have her do both. She is one of the agents of the plot, and her life is described on a par with that of the men. Not a political, but only a family background is given in all cases. The family (hers, the narrator's and husband-wife relations) prevents love, but at the end of the story the (grown) "boy's" love for Zinaida and his father transcends and prevents what Tolstoy called family happiness.

The preceding examples of truly "strong" heroines of Russian literature all have independent power to move events within the fiction; they do not merely embody complementarity to a male in a male-centered work that inverts male nonvirtue into female virtue. The works we will now proceed to examine are of interest as studies not of females but rather of female/male interaction of a certain kind, with overtones of disillusionment, impotence, and terror. In these works, where one female is always more "perfect" ("whole" is a favorite Russian word) than the male, other female characters, invariably older ones, may be grotesquely imperfect. All the works are structured so that the hero is center-stage; the heroine approaches for a falling-in-love section, followed by a dramatic confrontation in which the hero will bolt, defeated by her moral superiority.

Certainly Pushkin and Chekhov had their moments of irony about such maidens. Tatiana grows wise under the narrator's ironic tutelage. Chekhov consciously avoided the Turgenev heroine, as we shall see. But critics and readers have not proven as critical as these authors. Whether it is because they sympathize with the plight of life under the autocracy or because they love loving beautiful maidens (the men, that is; the women may just be searching for relief from descriptions of women as monsters)—for whatever reason, one strains hard to hear a Russian critic speak of this more conventional Russian heroine in any tone other than reverential. Russians put their hope in the glory and strength of Russian womanhood-in-fiction, echoing the question the authors seem to be asking—"If even a woman is ready to perform feats of heroism, why cannot a man?"—without seeing the irony of the *even* a woman or of the *ready* to perform, as if the readiness were all. Heroinic performance is rarely if ever shown. Seemingly it is unnecessary. These heroines are heroic only in declaring their love and their willingness to action.

The only Russian critic who has written with wit and accuracy about the female counterpart to the superfluous man is Abram Tertz in his mock-essay, "What Is Socialist Realism?" Giving a serious parody (a genre he almost invents) of the central preoccupations of nineteenth-century Russian literature, he finds that it "contains a great multitude of love stories in which a defective man and a lovely woman meet and separate without any result."[4] Tertz, of course, glosses over these love stories, from Pushkin's dreamy Tatiana to Blok's Beautiful Lady, making only superficial distinctions in keeping with his comic tone ("sometimes the hero yawns; sometimes he kills his beloved"). But the main point he makes is that: "The woman in this literature was the touchstone for the man. Through his relations with her he exposed his weakness . . . , compromised by her strength and beauty." And further: "For indeed, from a familiar standpoint, woman is a sort of vague, pure and lovely thing. There's no need for her to be more concrete and more defined, it is enough for her (does one ask much of women?) to be pure and lovely to save man."[5] This passage, perhaps the best piece of feminist criticism ever written in Russian, is part of Tertz's ironic discussion of the movement from the Russian hero to the Soviet hero, who is allowed no such negative qualities. Tertz has shown that one need not ask much of these women beyond what they symbolize for the men in the story. The reasons for the strong heroine's appeal to the ordinary reader are obvious: We men cannot act in autocratic Russia; the women will be there to inspire courage till we can, and nurse our wounds when we have failed (or continually remind us of them by their strength, if we are masochistically inclined). But obviously these heroines are not merely symbols of the motherland calling her sons to action, as in the famous Soviet war poster, whatever their extra-literary appeal.

Let us examine the "strong" heroine as she appears in the words of some Russian texts. The chief thing we may say about her is that, in comparison to the male, she is underdescribed. We will use the term "underdescribed" to signify various modes of verbal portraiture, such as the reliance on conventional clichés (one example being figures of speech), or the lack of complexity (pointing toward or away from beauty as the sum of the parts) with greater frequency when females are described.

In a comparative study of similes in Pushkin and Lermontov, one critic has found that, in both poets, "similes arising from physical description of female characters are two to four times more frequent than those describing male characters. Thus the simile, a consciously poetic embellishment, is one of the devices used by romantic poets to idealize women."[6] Idealization, in the form of stock similes or poetic embellishment of a nonindividualized type, is one form of underdescription. Romanticism's ancestress of realism's strong woman is the beautiful black-eyed native maiden of the Caucasus that the Russian hero loves and leaves. She often kills herself, for she cannot return defiled to the strict laws of her people; but before she dies, like Lermontov's Bela in the first section of A Hero of Our Time, she exhibits many of the defiant qualities of the strong woman. These women, like Turgenev's heroines, are more alive in speech, in confrontation with the male, than in dreamy solitude. Bela is "beautiful: tall, slender, with black eyes which resembled those of a mountain gazelle" (the eyes of a prized horse are also compared to hers). She resists Pechorin rather effectively at first by not loving him: "I am your captive. . . your slave; of course you can compel me." But when she loves, he loses interest.

The ultimate poetic travesty in underdescription of young females belongs, of course, to Gogol', who can make absence into terrifying presence:

> . . . a young girl of sixteen with golden hair very skillfully and charmingly smoothed down on her little head. The pretty oval of her face was rounded

like a fresh egg and like it shone with a transparent whiteness as when, fresh and new-laid, it is held up to the light for testing by the dark-skinned hands of the housekeeper . . .

(*Dead Souls*, chapter 5)

Every adjective and noun referring to the girl that can possibly be expressed as a diminutive in Russian is accorded that sweetly endearing status in this sentence, unreproducible in English. But if the housekeeper is testing the egg to see if it is really fresh, or indeed what may hatch from it, there is no way of testing girls before marriage to see whether they will remain deliciously blank or whether some terrifying potential will be realized. Girls grow into ladies, that other category of the Gogolian female gender and (as we find again and again in his fiction) "it is extremely dangerous to look too deeply into the hearts of ladies" (*Dead Souls*, chapter 8). Let us therefore not describe females in anything but simile. In Gogol' a screen of words shields us from the abyss of reality.

Portraits which are "romantic" or "abnormal/humorous" are usually separated from the realistic canon. But there are similarities between them which need to be explored. Consider the following introductory description of seventeen-year-old Irina in Turgenev's later novel, *Smoke* (1867):

She was a tall, well-proportioned girl with a slightly sunken chest and the narrow shoulders of youth, with pale lustreless skin, rare at her age, pure and smooth as porcelain, with thick blonde hair; its dark strands blended unusually with other light ones. The features of her face exquisitely, almost faultlessly, regular, had not yet fully lost that artless expression, natural to early youth; but in the languid inclination of her pretty neck, in her smile not quite distracted nor yet tired, was suggested a high-strung young lady, and in the very outline of those faintly smiling, fine lips, of that small, rather narrow, aquiline nose was something self-willed and passionate, something dangerous both to others and to herself. Striking, truly striking, were her eyes, dark-grey with a tinge of green, eyes long and languishing, like those of Egyptian deities, with radiant lashes and a bold sweep of brown. These eyes had a strange expression: they seemed to gaze, attentively and thoughtfully gaze, from some unknown depths and distance.

(chapter 7)

Portrait of the temptress as a young woman. This is the turning point between the seventeen-year-old positive heroine and the older femme fatale, generally considered to be two polarized female types in Turgenev. One recent critic very rightly makes the point that the two have their similarities.[7]

Their essential function as a foil to male impotence is certainly the reason for this blurring of memory when one tries to separate Turgenev's heroines. Yet their portraits differ in detail. The one just quoted of a woman in potentio as well as at a certain time in her life would seem to be both full and subtle.

The face and upper portion of the body are stressed.[8] Skin, hair, neck, lips, and eyes are painted as if on canvas, sheen, shape, color, and expression dwelt on. The sum of the parts as well as their separate details might point to slightly flawed or unusual beauty—but this is a moral portrait, and in it flawed beauty (all the more lovely for being slightly imperfect) is the key to latent imperfection of character. The danger is stated explicitly by the narrator. The artless expression of the Gogolian young lady, as well as the dangerous potential, is translated into terms of moral realism, where each detailed likeness has its correspondence in the ethical scheme of things. The same female "depths" that Gogol's narrator shuns are reflected in the actual "strange expression" of the eyes. The reader is led to understand that Irina will grow to be the temptress she becomes; men who love her (the "others" she will be dangerous to) will be doomed—we know this from the start and we watch it happen, fatally and inevitably. How *she* feels is never made very clear, the fatal beauty of Turgenev seldom being granted motives beyond dominance for its own mysterious sake.

Turgenev's female characters fall into three types on a scale of beauty: the femme fatale, the heroine, and the plain or ugly woman. In all his female portraits, beauty is a primary issue: women who have lost it through age (Lasunskaia in *Rudin*, for example) or who have been ugly from birth (Mashurina in *Virgin Soil*) are pitilessly portrayed by the author when they try to attract men; they are simply ridiculous, and no amount of money, intellect, or cigarette-smoking can change that invariable rule. Yet, by contrast, that hideous male, Lemm of *A Nest of Gentry*, is filled with moral radiance. So is the heroine of *A Living Relic*, but she is mostly a voice, not a woman, and has no prominent counterpart in the novels.

It is the almost plain but potentially lovely young (usually aged seventeen) heroine who is Turgenev's and the compliant reader's ideal. Like Tatiana she grows to beauty, as she grows to womanhood, by falling in love. Her inner beauty will emerge in outer beauty at this moment. Critics of the time in Russia heartily agreed that (as Pisarev said): "in order to give oneself an idea of what woman's capabilities are, . . . study her when she is still full of life and freshness and not when she is crumpled, beaten down and faded . . . ."[9] The girl-woman's energy and beauty contrast with the older (typically aged thirty-five) man's inertia and mixed attractiveness. At first he seems to educate her with words about the latest Byronic or German (depending upon the decade) ideas; but later, in their nonlove scene, it is she who enlightens him—not about German philosophy or the needs of Russia—but about himself. And, parallel to this, except in *Fathers and Sons* and *On the Eve*, she makes her own bitter discovery about the man—how he lacks her deeper understanding because he is incapable of joining emotion to reason.

The hero and the heroine, both Russian and usually of the same social class, are actually from different worlds, the male and the female.[10] The female culture is based on feelings; the male culture is based on ideas. The two may learn from each other; but while the female never loses her emotions and integrates them into a future, informed, clear-headedness that will often include political action, the male has his ideas tested by falling in love, and he crumples. The female, whole and perfect in herself, is to the male a fragment or missing piece of himself, a vital part of him that should exist but does not, a link to a reality he is doomed to break with (in both its womanly and its social form).

Turgenev's *Rudin* is the paradigmatic work for the clash of the male and female cultures. The heroine Natalia is underdescribed in all the above-mentioned ways:

> . . . at first glance you might not like her. She had not yet had time to develop, was thin, dark, and somewhat round-shouldered. But the features of her face were beautiful and regular, although too large for a seventeen-year-old girl. . . .
>
> (chapter 5)

The author makes her a future beauty and her future is love. For now, he vacillates between negative and positive features, but the scales are weighted in an opposite manner from those on which Irina is placed.

Natalia is an important Turgenev heroine; but Rudin is the center of the work. Only in the dialogue of their tryst and in its aftermath is her characterization fully realized. Before that, she is simply contrasted to her unattractive mother, just as the heroine Marianna in *Virgin Soil* does silent battle with her beautiful but wicked aunt. In neither case does the older woman understand the younger, so Turgenev makes it natural for the girl to want to leave home and to believe in men rather than women. Natalia's confrontation with Rudin completes the story, not because of her maturity (it was a given from the outset), but because it solves the enigma of Rudin himself: will he or won't he act, now that he is faced with a girl-woman who believes his words and is herself willing to act? In chapter 9 the reader can actually hear the two speaking different languages. In contrast to Rudin's: "What did your mother say?," "I feel only my own unhappiness," and (to himself after they part) "How pitiful and worthless I was in front of her," we have Natalia's verbal progression from: "You are a man; I'm accustomed to believing you, I will believe you to the end. Tell me, what are your intentions?," to "In future please weigh your words; don't talk idly. When I told you I loved you, I knew what that word meant: I was ready for anything. . . . Now I have only to thank you for the lesson and say goodbye," and through to her final argument of the heart: "Oh? If you loved me, I would feel it now, this instant. . . . No, no, goodbye." Rudin speaks with romantic self-pity; Natalia with inner-directed firmness.

The clash of two cultures results here in a reversal of expectations for both of them. Paradoxically, the man is tied to convention, the woman ready to break with it. She contrasts his words to her "simple" but trustworthy feelings. Turgenev is all on her side, but he extols the woman as a model of *what a man should be*. Women are capable of heroism when impelled by love; men, incapable of loving themselves, cannot love women. Women are rooted in their society because they have stayed home; men have wandered about and no longer know what is Russian, what European. Women are whole in mind and body, acting as one being; men are torn between the words they are capable of using after being highly educated and the actions they are politically prevented from, or sexually prevent themselves from performing. Women, when they are not agents of materialism and the status quo (grasping mothers of eligible daughters) or blue-stockings (talking even better than the men, short-haired, smokers) are earthly representatives of something which men can attain only in their dreams or in a brief moment of reciprocated love. But, paradoxically, even the most revolutionary heroines, Elena (*On the Eve*) and Marianna (*Virgin Soil*) wait for a man's love to galvanize them to action.

Rudin is more icy-hearted than most of Turgenev's superfluous men. He is a sort of reversal of the cold femme fatale, the worthless beloved of much European romantic fiction; his capacity for self-pity, however, is a trait usually reserved for the male. Natalia is more difficult to differentiate from other Turgenev heroines. Like them, she has no background in friendship, education, ideas; she is only one thing: a woman ready for love. She is not so much the "other," or a victim, but rather the missing part of the male identity in the novel, Rudin's longed-for completeness. Otherwise, Rudin could have talked, impressed those around him, or failed to do so, without her challenging presence. Rudin, who responds defensively to every question, is playing his last card, but is not aware of what is at stake. It takes Natalia to make him aware. She is pivotal to the Rudin-centered plot, but she is heroic only in this. She will, in the epilogue, fall into an ordinary marriage, which does not mean the same thing for Turgenev as for Tolstoy; it is an ending in a minor rather than a major key.

A word should be said here about Odintsova in Turgenev's *Fathers and Sons*, whom readers have considered to be a genuine heroine, a mature woman who is cool, independent, intellectual (but not too intellectual), fairly considerate of her aged aunt, polite and philosophical to Bazarov, whose philosophy of materialism she tests and admires, but whose manners she finds wanting. Odintsova reverses our paradigm: she attracts Bazarov, he declares himself (more obliquely than the young maiden) and then *she* withdraws, remaining alone like her name.

But in fact it is Katya, not Odintsova, who is the true heroine of *Fathers and Sons*. Odintsova, mature and sexual, though not passionate, really fits the category of the predatory female. She flirts with more than one man: with Arkady as well as Bazarov. Although she does not actually maul her prey (as Bazarov does Fenichka), her ability to disperse her sexual energy among several men is not in keeping with the single-minded purity of the true heroine.

In the Turgenevian context Odintsova is the most elegant and pleasant of predators, but the results of her attraction are decidedly deadly. Bazarov seeks an absurd death when she has done with him, after pathetically returning to her, spurning his elderly parents, and losing his pride. Katya, the true Turgenev heroine with "rather narrow shoulders," is stifled by her elder sister and comes into her own only through the love of Arkady. When Odintsova remarries, it is once again for wealth and status, not love. She and Bazarov are fellow experimenters who miss out on love and family. Odintsova doesn't even recognize love in Arkady and Katya.

Odintsova's position in the structure of the novel is significant. She appears after Kukshina, the dirty emancipée whom Bazarov is rude to because he likes women to be beautiful. Odintsova is beautiful, but she parallels Kukshina in several ways. Both have conversations of ideas with men. Both are rich and not bound by spousal authority or children. Both recline languidly—Kukshina on a leather-covered sofa and Odintsova on her silk- and lace-covered bed. A combination of sexuality and coldness (symbolized by intellect, which the men in this supposed novel of politics and ideas certainly lack!) makes the women something of a threat. They blight men's lives as surely as the princess with the enigmatic eyes and no brains at all who cauterizes the growth of Pavel Petrovich, Bazarov's seeming opposite but true counterpart. Better the image of Fenichka in the failed photograph, an eyeless face, than the clear eyes of Odintsova.

Gogol', Turgenev, Goncharov, Tolstoy, Dostoevsky, and Chekhov all describe marriages that don't happen, often against a background of bad or ordinary ones that do.[11] Only Tolstoy dares to attempt the portrayal of good marriages. Of course, he also has nonproposal scenes: Varenka and Koznyshev in *Anna Karenina*, two rationally benevolent people in absolute stasis; neither can "take the step." In the other authors there is a curious imbalance. The woman seems the stronger figure in "love," the man passively acquiesces, panics or resists by fleeing. The hero in Gogol's play *The Marriage* jumps out a window to prove his point. Prince Myshkin of *The Idiot* refuses to choose between two women and destroys both of them. Chekhov's best example of a "marriage" is in actuality an adulterous affair. "The Lady with the Pet Dog," with its famous ending, describes this love affair as if it were a true marriage, as difficult and precious to maintain.

Nonmarriage has more novelistic potential in a work of fiction, so marriage is often relegated to a tacked-on ending. But within this larger nineteenth-century theme of love unfulfilled and even punished, female characters often are true heroines, displaying a wide range of behavior. But if they are only heroes of love, if their only growth consists in the realization of the inferiority of the male beloved, their description limited to versions of beauty, their dialogue mere defiance doomed to disappointment—these women characters are not full "heroines" in any but an extra-literary sense. They are not their male author's primary concern, as he plots a novel structured around complex male ways of saying "no."

For years, then, Russian criticism embroidered upon Russian fiction with myths of its own. Belinsky, Dobroliubov, Chernyshevsky, Pisarev, and others less well known, wrote copiously on the Russian woman in fiction because they were interested in the implications that the hidden "male" theme of the plot had for Russian reality. All the famous Russian liberal critics were men, as were their opponents, Slavophils and others, who upheld different political values but also wrote on women's issues. As men debated the interpretation of women characters in works largely by men, in journals published by men, throughout the entire nineteenth-century and into the twentieth, their goals were "larger" than the betterment of the lot of women, and they did not pretend otherwise. If we pick up a book devoted to women in Russian literature published in St. Petersburg in 1914, many things become clear. It consists of a preface followed by excerpts from twenty-eight works of literature by fifteen Russian authors (only one of them female and using a male pseudonym). Its author, M. V. Portugalov, writes in the preface that the question of special interest is "the problem of the female personality, the growth of her self-awareness and liberation, her exit from the narrowly female sphere (of love and family) onto the threshold of the social struggle and civic service."[12] He eventually links the woman question to that of serfdom, as had so many critics before him and, like them, he urges on writers who were not primarily concerned with either of these issues a civic and personal humaneness few writers anywhere have ever in fact possessed:

> The humane thought of the nineteenth-century Russian writers was directed before anything towards freeing the serf and woman from social oppression and every tyranny. . . . The destruction of serfdom and the emancipation of women—these are two phenomena which go hand in hand in Russian literature of the nineteenth century.[13]

This is an accurate perception, except that nearly every major Russian writer (e.g., Turgenev, Tolstoy, Dostoevsky, Chekhov) managed to portray the emancipated Russian woman as a dirty, loud-mouthed, chain-smoking bore—a character, furthermore, quite unnecessary to the plot. The whole threatening issue of female emancipation is negatively evoked with rare wit in Sukhovo-Kobylin's play *The Death of Tarelkin* (1869) in which the anti-hero eulogizes himself at his own funeral in the following words:

> When a standard was borne, Tarelkin marched ahead of the standard; when progress was proclaimed, there he was—in advance of progress—so that Tarelkin was in the fore and progress brought up the rear!—When the emancipation of women came, Tarelkin shed tears over the fact that he was not a woman so that he could remove his crinoline before the public and show it . . . how one ought to emancipate one's self.[14]

Many Russian intellectuals too were ahead of progress, a persistent problem for the Russian women's movement, as men formulated and defined woman's place in society.

There was often little difference between what might be thought of as conservatives and liberal/radicals where the question of women was concerned. Their education was a highly debated problem for both. An *ustav* of 1843 from the Church Synod concerning the education of priests' daughters noted the two following goals:

> 1) to be worthy wives of the servants of the Altar of the Lord, on whom lies the sacred duty of edification of parishoners in faith and morality and who therefore must be distinguished by a preeminently pious life and
>
> 2) to be trustworthy mothers who will return their children to the rules of piety and morality, who will be able to develop talents in them and communicate to them all the necessary early knowledge, and prepare their sons for entry into school and see to the good use of free time.[15]

And D. I. Pisarev in his "radical" treatise "The Thoughts of Virkhov on the Education of Women" (1865) rhetorically proclaims his strategy against opponents of education for women:

> Do you know what a radical transformation must be brought about in the whole system of women's education in order that it should actually provide society with *good* wives, *good* mothers and *good* housekeepers?[16]

Conservative or radical, religious or secular: these appellations matter little when questions of women's future are subordinated to social goals in a society where men rule and men interpret.

Just as the woman question was largely debated by men and cast in the mold of their own ultimate interests, so too the portrayal of women in fiction constituted part of the male domain. One of the specialities of Russian male writers was the convincing illusionistic description of a female character's inner feelings and thoughts. Tolstoy and Chekhov described such intimate female states as pregnancy and miscarriage with skill unsurpassed in any other writers, male or female, until the next century. These two writers will be discussed at greater length in chapters three and four: the general point I wish to make here is that thematic tendencies cannot be neatly classified by gender in a tradition of realism in which writing about women and even about their inner world formed part of the canon. The problem will be, rather, to determine just how the angle of vision of the male eye affects the way in which we as readers are made to see the object.

The most obviously distorted viewings occur in overtly misogynistic texts. The following chapter will work from some of these back into authors considered part of the tradition of Russian realism—Lermontov, Nekrasov and Dostoevsky—writers who incorporated these misogynistic images in a less obvious way. In some of these images the threatening female is silenced by murder; but even silent or dead, she exerts a strange power over the surviving male. The common denominator in all of these works is that Woman, even though mysterious, can be an extension of male knowing and is more powerful when silent than when attempting self-explanation. Silence is another form of terrible perfection.

# 2.

# MISOGYNY AND THE POWER OF SILENCE

It should be possible to speak of misogyny in fiction as another facet of male imaging of women, one which extends from, rather than opposes-itself to, the image of perfection. If not one, then the other. Or, more precisely, where one leaves off, the other begins—even, as we have seen, within a single, developing Turgenevian character. Misogyny in its undiluted form constitutes a none too small and chronologically very persistent stream in Russian literature. It is most often associated with the grotesque, with prose that is nontransparent, nonillusionistic, which calls attention to itself as does its troubled, self-confessing speaker.

The manifestations of misogyny are firmly rooted in both traditions which nourished Russian literature: the oral folklore and the written literature of the Church.[1] The emanations of the male authorial psyche from the anonymous medieval suppliant to the very model of the modern Russian Bolshevik vary little: all displace male malaise onto female malice. The individual male psyche of this sort is bolstered by permissiveness on the part of his society in abuse of women, from proverbial wife-baiting to literal wife-beating. The worst insult for a man is to be called a woman, a *baba*. In the popular Russian song "Stenka Razin," the hero flings his bride into the waves of Mother Volga when his comrades tease him for being so in love with her that he too has become a *baba*. With no such background of societal approval, women writers do not rail against men or depict them as sexually or emotionally grotesque. Their rhetoric was confined to irony.

Antonia Glasse traces a type of "formidable woman,"[2] huge and menacing, from Nestor's late eleventh-century *Life of Theodosius* to Saltykov-Shchedrin's *The Golovlevs*. However, the devouring mother figure, the threatening female, is even more prevalent in modern writers like Zamyatin, Bely, Olesha and Babel'. Death in domesticity, the humiliation of a man by a woman, and sexual pollution or engulfment illustrate a basic but often irresistible fear. These texts are highly poeticized and linguistically intricate. The basic medieval text to begin with here is the thirteenth-century *Petition of Daniil the Exile (Molenie Daniila Zatochnika).*[3] The unknown speaker is asking a prince for support, countering the advice he imagines he will receive with all sorts of protestations:

> Or do you say, prince:
> "Marry (someone) with a rich father;
> There you will drink and there you will eat!"
> It would be better for me to be sick with fever:
> For a fever, having shaken a person, departs;
> But an evil wife will dry you up to death.
>
> As it is said in folk sayings,
> "No bird among birds is the owl;
> No beast among beasts is the hedgehog;
> No fish among fishes is the crayfish;
> No cattle among cattle is the goat;
> No slave is a slave who works for another slave;
> No man among men is one who obeys a woman."
> A debauchery among debaucheries it is if someone takes an evil wife
> For the sake of a dowry or a rich father-in-law.
> So it would be better to see an ox in my house
> Than a woman of evil appearance.
> I have seen gold on a woman of evil appearance,
> And I said to her, "This is hard on the gold."
> It would be better for me to found iron
> Than to live with an evil wife.
> A woman of evil appearance is like a scratch:
> It cuts through here, and the next thing you know you are sick there.
>
> Another time I saw an old woman, of evil appearance,
> Cross-eyed, she looked like the devil,
> Big-mouthed, with a protruding jaw, evil-tongued,
> And peering into a mirror; and I said to her:
> "Don't look at a mirror, rather look at a scab (in a grave)!"
> It is not fitting for an evil-looking woman to look at a mirror,
> Lest she fall into a great sorrow
> Having gazed upon the ugliness of her face.
>
> (Translated by James Rice)

This text speaks for itself. The form is related to a genre in Byzantine literature called *The Bee*, a book of literary proverbs. Proverbs have traditionally been a repository of misogyny in both the oral and literary traditions in Russia—the most famous one being: "A hen is not a bird; a woman is not a human." Here the parallelisms, grammatical rhymes, and far-fetched but striking analogies, all deep in Russian speech, provide a tempting form for the misogynist in question. But, it must be stressed that any surviving text of Old Russian literature would have been copied many times and preserved by a certain number of other men, probably monks, who presumably copied what they liked and wanted to see preserved.

The woman as *baba* (derogatory for female), rather than as *chelovek* (human), in the male imagination appears in Russian modernism in texts similar in style to the medieval. She may take a more attractive but equally dangerous form as the ostrich-feathered female vampire of symbolism. The poet Alexander Blok's longing for Woman is tempered by the fear that she may change into something quite different from her present image. The phrase "izmenish' oblik ty?" in his poem of June 4, 1909, is a constant theme of anxiety undercutting desire. In the poem which is his greatest epic statement, "The Twelve," Blok put the betrayal of the prostitute Kat'ka into a symbolic historical frame: she leaves the Red Guardsman for a bourgeois traitor and is killed by her former lover after his friends taunt him for being a *baba* (line 210: "Chto ty, Pet'ka, baba chto-l'?"), the ultimate and unbearable insult for a man in love, especially if he is also involved in a revolt and in good male fellowship, as Stenka Razin had been, too.

In most of Russian literature sexual union, whether described or only implied, is hideous and grotesque. The twentieth century has more explicitly nasty versions of sexuality. The final lapse of Oblomov into comfortable union with his housekeeper becomes Kavelerov's conquest of the widow Annichka (in Yurii Olesha's *Envy* of 1927), whose belly and whose bed engulf him— the male psychic fear of being replaceable while Woman endures. Kavelerov suspects that the leather strap on his suspenders has been torn off the widow's husband's old suspenders. She smiles as he beats her, saying her husband did the same.

The misogynist regards physical abuse of women as proof of their endurance and of the transience of men. In a short story by Isaac Babel' called "The Sin of Jesus," all males are vanquished by the lowliest of women. Arina, a hotel servant, is beaten and impregnated by any man who happens by. The beatings are described by Babel', through dialogue or narration, as peculiarly remote and almost logical. However, in this story, Jesus Christ answers Arina's prayers for respite by sending her an angel from heaven to be her husband for four years. Nonetheless, clumsy and sluttishly pregnant, Arina rolls over in bed and smothers the angel. When Jesus curses her and leaves her abandoned, she raises her belly to the sky (a woman's counter-curse of life!) and tells Christ, after she begs forgiveness, that *she* will never forgive *Him*. The enduring slob, who absorbs blows and casually drops babies in orphanages, should be pursued as a comic-tragic theme in Russian literature, rage at abandonment by mother producing outrage at "motherly" women. The theme is often connected to the Russian's rage at a passively devouring Russia.

These, then, are a small sample of themes in what must be viewed as one of the most creative streams in the male literary tradition in Russia. Rarely is woman-as-disturbing-force turned to humor and narrative self-parody— one of the features that distinguishes a novel like Zamyatin's *We*, where sex is a comic part of the new technology. After Pushkin who, here as in many other things, must be counted as an eighteenth-century writer for his light-hearted bawdy, sexual love in Russian literature is a serious matter. Women in love are a force to be neutralized in some way, or the results can be deadly. A strategy must be found: Lermontov has his hero conquer by deceit; Turgenev admits defeat by making women superior; Dostoevsky has them choose spiritual wisdom or doom. Except in Tolstoy and Chekhov, women seem always to be complementary opposites to men, defined by this relationship and dangerous when incipiently self-defined. As the dialogue from an Ostrovsky play called "The Dowerless Bride" ("Bespridannitsa") goes:

> Paratov: What is to be done, Larisa Dmitrievna?
>     In love there is no equality, that's not just
>     my idea. In love one must weep at times.
> Larisa: And always the woman?
> Paratov: Well, naturally not the man.
> Larisa: And why not?
> Paratov: Very simply because, if a man weeps, they
>     call him a woman (*baba*), and this nickname is
>     worse than anything the human mind can invent.
>
> (act II, scene 8)

Only Chekhov tries to break out of the bind of making women either better or worse—more suffering or more inflicting of suffering—than men, as he experiments with women's quest for identity in a tradition of realism where identity quests were so prominent and so exclusively a male preserve. But with Chekhov it was already too late for anyone to pursue the quest in any but the most modest and quietly despairing terms. After Chekhov, Gorky gives us a further split into the ideal and the reality within the frame of naturalism, and, as we shall see in our conclusion, modern Russian literature also divides its female characters into materialists or the wise and spiritual.

Russian heroines incarnate perfection in youth or in extreme old age; mature women are presented in a qualified or less flattering light. One might question, then, whether realism is indeed realistic, not with reference to "reality" but with reference to the semblances of reality it constructs with words. A female character may have beautiful hair, eyes, and teeth; to a feminist this is hardly a semblance of anything other than male desire.

Male desire for a certain kind of female informs most fictions of (Russian) men. Women must be perfect, or fall short. The seeing eye is male, and it is a judging and voyeuristic one. Female rebellion in this context is also encoded into male desire. The gestures which encapsulate female rebelliousness (Agafya's straightened shoulders, Bela's flashing eyes) as well as the proud or defiant words of Tatiana, Turgenev's heroines, Dostoevsky's or Gorky's—all are mere moments in the years of male existence. Even during those moments their reception or nonreception by the male within the fiction counts more than the impulse that gave rise to them.

The rebellious heroine (who, needless to say, is a beauty) is best exemplified in Lermontov and in Dostoevsky. Never is her rebelliousness allowed to triumph within the fiction: it is used, instead, as a challenge for the hero to exert his dominance and rightly or wrongly, to interpret his own faults and failures, often, literally, over her dead body.

Lermontov's *A Hero of Our Time* (1840) presents a Byronic hero, Pechorin, who continually victimizes women. Nevertheless, in the context of the book, the women themselves are made to share the blame for being disappointing in some way—boring, unreliable or status-seeking: those who fall into the orbit of the hero "get what they deserve." Pechorin seems closer to Lermontov himself than has generally been officially acknowledged. The attitudes toward women in *A Hero of Our Time* are not dissimilar to those in his early "Hussar" poems which lightheartedly described gang-rape and mistaken identity rape with no consequences of any sort for the hero.[4] The values of pornography are what Lermontov and his class of males shared: no matter how alone the romantic hero feels, he is not alone in this respect.

The four principal female characters are secondary to Pechorin: two of them are exotic and two from the protagonist's own culture. The two "exotic" women are defined by Pechorin with his own squarely Russian imagination that sees danger in and conquest of women as a corollary of the Russian imperialistic conquest and "civilizing" of the people of the Caucasus. The two Russian ones are bred to react conventionally. One, Vera, "understands" and forgives Pechorin; but he cannot incorporate such forgiveness into his world-view. The other, Princess Mary, is duped, in part, by her own snobbery. She has spurned a man of inferior rank who loves her naively in favor of Pechorin, who is playing a complicated game with his own past self as reflected in this man. Pechorin is eloquent in his own defense just as he behaves most callously, in both the Bela and the Princess Mary sections. These two women from two different cultures, Circassian and Russian, have in common an aristocratic pride that delays their ultimate self-humiliation; this delay toward an obvious end is similar to pornography.

Although *A Hero of Our Time* comprises five chapters, the second and the fifth, in which male/male relationships are primary, function less as self-contained narratives than as narrative resolutions to the three sections in which male/female relationships predominate. *Taman'*, the story placed third in the sequence of five chapters that the novel comprises, seemingly stands out as a reversal of the Pechorin-victimizing-women pattern in the other sections. Here Pechorin appears as the tired officer seeking shelter for the night in a coastal town on the Black Sea, who is attracted to what he considers the "breeding" of an exotic woman whom he compares to Goethe's Mignon. She is actually a smuggler whose business he interrupts. She disarms him, both figuratively and literally, and tries to drown him, but he throws her overboard instead. The woman survives—she has been called a mermaid several times by Pechorin; but a blind boy and an old woman are left abandoned. The story is admirably balanced between the pursuits of the smugglers and the officer's desire to survive and leave the place; what changes is his perception of the woman—from exotically unreal to really dangerous in a more familiar sense.

In the other two chapters involving Pechorin and women, "Bela" and "Princess Mary," we find him the superior combatant in all respects. Bela is captured, held prisoner and then abandoned by him. She dances for him and he dresses her up "like a little doll." But when he becomes bored with her company, even his co-narrator, the kindly and obtuse Maksim Maksimich, warns her not to complain if he leaves her or she'll become all the more boring to him. Pechorin's first long monologue admits to this "unfortunate disposition" ("neschastnyi kharakter"). The kindly Maksim Maksimich acts as a voyeuristic go-between who appreciates Bela's beauty and Pechorin's short-lived friendship. Bela is, thus, interpreted by two men of the Russian tribe before she is finally repossessed and stabbed to death by a man of her own tribe.

Lermontov continually contrasts the vast panorama of the Caucasus to the shrunken arena of the town, a spa frequented by Russians into whose society, at the beginning of the chapter, Pechorin literally descends, and from which none of the women characters ever emerges. Rather they rule where they can. The "charm" of the ladies who change their lovers every year is mentioned by the narrator in passing as a threat to be overcome. Responding to a French epigram about hating "les hommes," Pechorin ripostes that he scorns "les femmes." Women characters in the novel consistently inhabit the particular, not the general, human category. Pechorin alone is "man," capable of complicated and interesting sufferings, of paradoxical musings:

One thing has always struck me as strange: I never became the slave of the women I loved; on the contrary, I have always gained unconquerable power over their will and heart, with no effort at all. Why is it so? Is it because I never treasured anything too much, while they incessantly feared to let me slip out of their hands? Or is it the magnetic influence of a strong organism? Or did I simply never succeed in encountering a woman with a stubborn will of her own?

I must admit that, indeed, I never cared for women with wills of their own, it is not their department.

True, I remember now—once, only once did I love a strong-willed woman, whom I could never conquer. We parted enemies—but even so, perhaps, had our meeting occurred five years later, we would have parted differently.

The question the novel poses is whether such a life is fated (either in such times as Nicholas's Russia or in post-romantic perception) to be fatal to women, whether Pechorin is, as Byron's Manfred was, "fatal and fated in his sufferings." We are asked a more complicated question in "Princess Mary" than in "Bela," where an indignant response to injustice can be made. What is to blame: culture or the character of Pechorin? Lermontov shows the two as inseparable; yet the will of the hero dominates the plot. Another among the facile epigrams and paradoxes uttered by Pechorin in "Princess Mary" declares that: "Women love only those whom they do not know." Pechorin is presumably warning the naive other man, Grushnitskii, whom he is actually using as a stalking horse, not to show too much interest in the beloved. But the phrase is also revealing of Pechorin's own fear of being rejected which rules his attitudes and behavior. He carefully prepares a trap for the exposed emotions of the people whom he has targeted; that way his own sensibilities are never ensnared:

I love my enemies, although not in a Christian sense: they amuse me, they quicken my pulses. To be always on the lookout, to intercept every glance, to catch the meaning of every word, to guess intentions, to thwart plots, to pretend to be fooled, and suddenly, with one push, to upset the entire enormous and elaborate structure of cunning and scheming—that is what I call life.

and

Women ought to desire that all men know them as well as I do, because I love them a hundred times better, ever since I stopped fearing them and comprehended their little weaknesses.

Pechorin shows his real emotions only when alone, confronted with the grandiose panorama of the Caucasus, which shrinks all human feeling to its proper size:

There is no feminine gaze that I would not forget at the sight of mountains

covered with curly vegetation, and illumined by the southern sun, at the sight
of the blue sky, or at the sound of a torrent that falls from crag to crag.

The novel's setting gives the reader a choice that is a foregone conclusion:
the grandeur of nature or the pettiness of female-dominated society. There
is no Tatiana to unite the two on a middle scale.

Pechorin continually tests without believing. In the last chapter of the
book, *The Fatalist*, he tests fate and death; but the only explanation we are
given as to why people die when they do is the uncomprehendingly practical
one of Maksim Maksimich, the earliest but partial unfolder of the mystery
of Pechorin. Lermontov is telling us that Pechorin is no mystery: he understands himself as a doubter and despiser of society, but many readers
can go further. In all parts of the novel, Pechorin tests others compulsively
as a way of proving his own existence. His tirades about himself in the past
attempt to impose a meaning on the present. Testing and trapping the other
characters, he gives the present an occupation, if not a significance. It is left
to us to determine whether or not Pechorin's reasoning is circular: A) there
is no significance (in women, in life); B) I will prove nonbelief in these things
by direct engagement (acting as if I did believe) followed by abrupt withdrawal into the isolation I believed in all along; C) therefore isolation exists.
Man creates Woman in his own imagination. Literally or figuratively im-
prisoning her bodily and culturally, he then works on the final spiritual
imprisonment, which can succeed only as long as he pretends to love. But
this pretense is self-debasement, and woman is scorned all the more for
seeming to cause and comply with it. Russian literature has no better example
of woman as metaphor for man's self-entrapment than *A Hero of Our Time*.

Despite the complexity of narrative voices in this work, none belongs to
a woman. They are seen under at least one, sometimes two, layers of narrative interpretation as they play their own disparate games within the tight
restrictions of their culture. Bela, once sullied, must be killed. Mary has
narrowly escaped a defilement which would make her too less than marriageable.

The opposite of the relationship of sexually experienced and predatory
male to virgin and wary female (the one considered a normal prelude to
marriage) also thrived in Russian fiction of the male tradition. In his article
"The Fallen Woman in Russian Literature,"[5] George Siegel outlines a pattern
beginning with Gogol's *Nevsky Avenue* in which an innocent man meets a
"fallen woman," (the usual nineteenth century euphemism for a prostitute)
who is both beautiful and depraved, and attempts to reform her by marrying
her. The finale is usually violent. The original romantic image is modified
by many Russian writers from Chernyshevsky to Chekhov, but nowhere is
the modification so radical as in Dostoevsky's *Notes from the Underground*.

As its epigraph this story uses part of a Nekrasov poem of 1845 ("Kogda iz mraka . . . "), which is quoted by Siegel in a marvellous poeticized English version by Archibald Carey Coolidge (the two last lines of it have been altered by Siegel):

When from thine error, dark, degrading,
With words of fiery persuading,
I drew thy fallen spirit out;
And thou, thy hands in anguish wringing,
Didst curse, filled with a torment stinging,
The sin that compassed thee about;
When thou, thy conscience dilatory
Chastising with the memory's shame,
Didst there unfold to me the story
Of that which was before I came;
And sudden with they two hands shielding
In loathing and dismay thy face,
To floods of tears I saw thee yielding,
O ' erwhelmed, yea prostrate with disgrace—
Trust me! thy tale did not importune;
I caught each word and tired not.
I understood, child of misfortune!
I pardoned all, and all forgot.
Why is it then, a secret doubting
Still preys upon thee every hour?
The world's opinion, thoughtless flouting,
Holds even thee too in its power?
Heed not the world, its lies dissembling,
Henceforth from all thy doubts be free;
Nor let thy soul, unduly trembling,
Still harbor thoughts that torture thee.
By grieving fruitlessly and vainly
Warm not the serpents in thy breast,
Into my house come bold and free,
Its rightful mistress there to be.

Siegel argues, correctly, that Dostoevsky parodies the poem by cutting it short in the epigraph and then reversing its premises in the story of Lisa the prostitute. But one could also argue that the silent unease of the woman in the second half of the poem, which is not quoted by Dostoevsky, who ends with the fourteenth line, is precisely the psychic terrain that interested Dostoevsky most, and something he explored in many of his fictional confrontations. In *Notes . . .* Lisa keeps silence while being "redeemed" volubly and spuriously by the narrator. Dostoevsky saw the promise of marriage by a man such as Luzhin or the husband in *A Gentle Creature* as worse than the usual kind of prostitution.

Dignified silence in place of argument is the hallmark of all Dostoevsky's "spiritual" characters, such as Sonia, Myshkin, or Alyosha and, in "The Legend of the Grand Inquisitor," his Christ. As a method of portraying female characters, this stance may well be traced to more than one of Nekrasov's poems, which present a fairly consistent view of women.

Nekrasov's women have a dignity or pathetic beauty emblematic of their nobility. In his scale of values, noblewomen achieve true nobility in the same way as do female peasants or the urban poor—by self-sacrifice to their men. The wives of the proto-revolutionary Decembrist noblemen became legendary along with their husbands by electing to share Siberian exile with them. In Nekrasov's long poem *Russian Women*, the Princesses Trubetskaia and Volkonskaia follow their husbands on the long hard journey, ensuring that their own lives will be no better. But they go further than mere sharing. One kisses her husband's fetters. An act of symbolic defiance of a husband's jailer consists in being submissive to his prisoner.

Dignity in submission is the stance of Nekrasov's ideal female of all classes. In another famous long poem, *Frost, the Red-Nosed*, the speaker alternately mourns the fate of the Russian peasant woman who must marry and obey a slave and bear the son of a slave, and praises her queenly bearing as she walks through the village.

The personal guilt arising from this dichotomy between nobility and oppression manifests itself in Nekrasov's somber and distraught lyrics, in which the woman is of his own class, and from the narrator's own household.[6] In this situation female self-sacrifice, while still somehow logical and laudable, is also sacrifice to him personally. In the famous poem "Whenever I'm driving down dark streets at night" (1847), the speaker recalls an incident when a woman he was living with, who had left her unlovable husband, in the poem's main section, sees her baby son die of hunger. The speaker comforts her with the thought that they will all die soon. She dresses up and goes out into the street, obviously to prostitute herself, although the distraught speaker claims not to have realized it at the time. "And an hour later you hurried back with a little coffin for the child and a meal for the father." This is the crucial image of female self-sacrifice. The speaker ends with a series of rhetorical questions that relate to the present: Has the usual fate overtaken you? Who will protect you? And he asserts his own "ineffectiveness" (*bespoleznost'*) as he curses either society's treatment of her or his own—which of the two is not clear. How soon after the incident he leaves the woman also remains unclear. Feelings dominate the facts. The more personally he becomes involved with female nobility, the more guilty Nekrasov's male speaker turns out to feel.

The same word for ineffective (*bespoleznyi*) is found in another Nekrasov poem, "Timidity" ("Zastenchivost'," 1852 or 1853), in which the speaker is rendered socially impotent (hands ineffective, words dying on his lips) before a society beauty. Here only the speaker suffers and, by implication, the nonsuffering woman is on the side of his oppressors. The gender-based roots of Nekrasov's identification with the downtrodden are made manifest in this painfully personal lyric.

Nekrasov's overtly misogynistic verse is less well-known. "Husband and Wife" ("Muzh i zhena," 1877) consists of three stanzas in which the husband's voice first begs the wife not to sell one-third of their property, then repents and confesses to being a bad manager. Next, he apologizes for his jealousy (an affair with their son's tutor is suggested) and finally for asking her to stay at home so that he can work peacefully. Between the timid requests and the apology for making them, there is the refrain: "Tears, nervous laughter and fits"—her effective reply to his pathetically reasonable requests.

For Dostoevsky, too, tears in women argue against themselves—although he is a master at showing male hysteria as well. However, Dostoevsky is more interested in bad women, where Nekrasov and other idealists are interested in "The Good Woman." Dostoevsky grants his female anti-heroines the ultimate human status of choosing their fate. In his early fiction, he arouses the reader's pity by underlining the societal oppression of his protagonists, Lisa and Sonia, who are prostitutes from economic necessity; but no dire straits exist in the case of the kept women of Dostoevsky's later fiction. His most thorough consideration of women's status occurs in *The Idiot*,[7] and here the Nekrasov myth is genuinely reversed. "Female" submissiveness is allotted to Prince Myshkin, while the two women protagonists dominate every situation of the plot. After appearances have been dispensed with, they have complete freedom, economic and otherwise, to choose their own fate. They do it very badly. Nastasia Filippovna chooses to flaunt her status as a kept woman while actually living chastely. Aglaia, rebelling against what Dostoevsky shows to be almost nonexistent family pressure to marry, as she calls it, "straight out of the bottle" she was reared in, marries absurdly. Far from needing to be forgiven, or from seeing political powerplay in male forgiveness—although both possibilities are aired in the novel—these women characters are confronted with the most difficult Dostoevskian dilemma, that of having to forgive themselves. No quarter is given to the actual restrictions of their social position as we (not Dostoevsky) would see them.

When she has barred her own way to self-forgiveness, Nastasia Filippovna allows Rogozhin to murder her. Her old oppressor, Totsky, is himself confined in "some place in Brittany." She is given a multitude of opportunities to cast aside her role as femme fatale or fallen woman, she is shown to be capable of living quietly; but she is ultimately unwilling to live. Dostoevsky's conservatism does not allow an abused woman the right to remain angry and alive. Nastasia Filippovna's corpse is described to the reader as it lies in the "dead silence of the room" where earlier she had generated frantic motion in all her entourage. The key images are silence, whiteness, and stillness:

> . . . someone lay asleep . . . in an absolutely motionless sleep; not the faintest movement could be heard, not the faintest breath. The sleeper was covered, from head to foot, with a white sheet, but the limbs were, somehow, only faintly visible; only from the raised outlines was it possible to make out that a human being was lying there stretched out full length. All around, in disorder, on the bed, at the foot of the bed, on the arm-chair beside the bed, even on the floor, clothes were scattered—a white silk dress, flowers, ribbons. On the little table at the head of the bed some diamonds, which had been taken off and thrown down, lay glittering. At the foot of the bed some sort of lace lay in a crumpled heap, and on the white lace, protruding from under the sheet, the tip of a bare foot could be made out; it seemed as though it were carved out of marble, and it was dreadfully still.
>
> (part IV, chapter 11)

Dostoevsky has taken the stereotype of the woman of ill repute and transmuted her into a dead princess dressed in bride's clothes grieved over by men—like Snow White, Desdemona, Madame Bovary, or Lily Bart. Only the tip of her foot conveys a slight necrophiliac touch to what would have been a Victorian painting had the scene been in an English novel.

Aglaia is Nastasia Filippovna's perfect complement, which accounts for the Dostoevskian intensity of their shadow relationship, carried on by correspondence and through other characters. Aglaia begins as a princess, the youngest of three sisters who agree that she will do better in life than any other of them. On the threshold of highly advantaged womanhood, she speaks out for women's rights: as in several other places in the novel, Dostoevsky makes this ridiculous. She wishes to witness executions on an equal basis with men. She imagines herself lying in a coffin with everyone weeping over her (part III, chapter 8), but her fate instead is to marry a Pole and be influenced by a fashionable Catholic priest—an end merely stated on the last page of the novel as a sort of verbal throw-away, and in Dostoevsky's view a particularly low form of self-inflicted entrapment.

Aglaia is often portrayed as a comic figure in her attempts to control her own fate, although her insistent rebellion against her upbringing may strike the reader as more admirable than Dostoevsky intended. But she is, with the Prince, the only person to understand Nastasia Filippovna—although they do so differently. The Prince says Nastasia Filippovna "believes with all her heart that . . . she herself is to blame" (part III, chapter 8). Aglaia sees that Nastasia Filippovna has tried to manipulate life, but mistakenly thinks the other woman has a kind of freedom in her "madness." Nastasia Filippovna mistakenly loves Aglaia as an innocent version of herself. The femme fatale is actually more innocent than the Princess, as Dostoevsky makes clear when he has Nastasia Filippovna write to Aglaia: "You alone are capable of loving not for yourself, but for the sake of him you love" (part III, chapter 10). Nastasia Filippovna thinks Aglaia worthy of the Prince and herself unworthy, but even when she discovers Aglaia to be like herself, she pursues her plan to marry Rogozhin and die. Dostoevsky's conservatism has robbed her both of her abused past as explanation for her actions and of future control over these actions.

In the course of the novel these women are shown pursuing parallel courses of obstinate self-definition in the teeth of bewildered societal (usually male) reaction. Only Prince Myshkin "understands" them, and they both reject him. Finally their parallel courses collide, when Dostoevsky has the two women meet just before the end, through the ancient device of correspondence leading to confrontation. What the two women mean to each other is described not in terms of sisterly compassion for similar struggles, but in terms of rivalry (a female duel over a passive male) and of "perverted" intensity of feeling. In this sense only, "Woman understood woman" (part IV, chapter 8)—a sense far removed from what we find in women's writings. In *The Idiot*, Dostoevsky has enlarged the theme of forgiving the prostitute almost beyond recognition, but he retains the violence of the ending and the ultimate silence of both the unredeemable soul and the ineffectual redeemer.

We will rejoin the image of the prone, silent, yet defiant woman in our final chapter. Dostoevsky's renamings of female experience do not lie at the center of his work and they stem from the misogyny of neoromanticism no matter how well he adapted them to his own concerns about "man" in a society at war with itself. This study sees Dostoevsky not as a great precursor of twentieth-century psychic dilemmas, but rather as the inheritor of the melodramatic pornographic posing that combined terror with infatuation—in other words, misogyny.

Tolstoy, who is generally considered the misogynist and more "naive" than Dostoevsky on questions of the human psyche, is, in our view, the real thinker on the subject of male desire. He defines the old romantic agony of man's "fascination" with woman as not love but something else. Nor can real love be sullied by being called love (i.e., sexual infatuation): "*Net, tut drugoe a ne liubov',*" as Levin says to Stiva Oblonsky in part I, chapter 10 of *Anna Karenina*.

# 3.

# TOLSTOY'S PATH
# TOWARD FEMINISM

L eo Tolstoy wrote about women in their ordinary contexts, home or society. He, unlike our other Russian authors, made explicit his preoccupation with the role women play in men's lives and thus freed himself of the burden of explaining a mystery. He is generally thought, by readers and by critics alike, to have placed his heroines in a subsidiary role to men, that of wife and child-raiser, and to have exalted this role beyond measure, while his freer heroes struggle with politics and philosophy. This argument is misleading. Tolstoy of all Russian writers shows the greatest development from his early to his late fiction. That development is not toward increasing misogyny but toward what we will define as feminism, a world-view which releases women from the burden of male-definition and even shows the latter to be a grave error.

Describing the ordinary in human events with intensity and the extreme with step-by-step logic, Leo Tolstoy could make both the familiar (marriage, courtship) and the unusual (suicide, murder) believable.[1] Tolstoy's female characters share both in the ordinary—their usual association—and in the extreme, as do his male characters. Often Tolstoy's women experience both at once. In his last novel *Resurrection*, a young woman, pregnant and deserted by her lover, runs hopelessly after the train that is carrying him away, intending to throw herself under the next wheels that roll by. But suddenly the baby moves inside her; she renounces death and slowly walks back to life again—although to a life greatly changed. We should marvel not that Tolstoy "knew" what it was like to be a woman and feel life inside oneself, but rather that he convinces us that he knew. Similarly, he has convinced generations of the living of what it feels like to die.

Many who agree that Tolstoy could describe the intimate states of mind of women also feel that too often in his fiction woman's otherness is stressed and that "the familiar accomplice nature" (as Virginia Woolf calls it in *Three Guineas*) is dragged in to clinch an argument. Tolstoy's biological similes are perhaps the weakest part of his writing, and when in *The Kreutzer Sonata* it is stated that a hen doesn't ask herself why her chick died but "cackles for awhile, and then leaves off and goes on living as before" (XVI), we are not convinced that it is unnatural for humans to fret over their children. It is little consolation that Tolstoy applies biological similes to men as well as to women.

If one examines Tolstoy's women not in isolation but in the context of the world they share with Tolstoy's men, one finds a web of interaction and common experience or responsibilities which is far more intricate than many people have believed. Even parenthood, the ultimate domain of women, is increasingly a shared world in his fiction. Not in the bedroom but in the nursery, the two sexes really meet. In *Family Happiness* and *War and Peace* the male protagonist takes only tentative steps into that world; in *Anna Karenina* Levin steps into it fully. But in that novel, Kitty and Levin's marriage is a tiny haven from the growing disintegration of values in the society around it. In *The Kreutzer Sonata* Tolstoy seeks out the causes of that disintegration in the relations between the sexes and finds them not in women's folly but in man's deliberate creation of a certain type of woman. In all three works a deeply-felt fear of sexuality destroys the notion of romantic love, but Tolstoy, while always stressing society's role in manipulating that urge, comes to see that women have nowhere else to learn and no place else to go. When Vronsky ties himself to Anna Karenina, he enters her limited world. Whether in Europe, on his estate, or in Russian cities, he feels its limits. In *The Kreutzer Sonata* women are rhetorically pushed into a corner, and then seen to dominate from that corner. As in modern feminist argument, the more social conditioning separates the sexes, putting each into an unnaturally preordained isolation, the more ruinous the resulting warfare. But Tolstoy understands woman's dominance as illusory, and thus deals with his own fear of it more perceptively than when he had advocated marriage with male domination as a safe haven in his earliest work about women, *Family Happiness*.

*Family Happiness* (1859) closely parallels the ideals of Tolstoy's first serious courtship with a young woman named Valeriia Arsen'eva.[2] It proceeds from the premise that a man may educate a woman for her role in life, that of motherhood, but that only the woman can blend this teaching with her own experience. Tolstoy has made his argument even more logical by making the man, Sergei, older (he is thirty-six) and the legal guardian of Masha, who has been orphaned at the age of seventeen, a crucial time of life when she would have made her début in Petersburg society. Forced to live in the country, she looks upon Sergei as a blend of surrogate father and deliverer, falls in love with and marries him, becomes bored, tastes Petersburg and foreign society, and then eventually returns to the country and a different kind of marriage with Sergei. Tolstoy gives the first person narrative to his heroine, in order to make the change in her even more convincing.

At first, Masha believes that "the proper object of life (is) happiness" (part I, chapter 1). With her girlish fluctuations between romantic daydreams and a feeling that life is passing her by, she is contrasted with Sergei, who is "plain," "decisive," and "honest." She is more than willing to be led by him: "All my thoughts and feelings of that time were not really mine; they were his thoughts and feelings, which had suddenly become mine and passed into my life and lighted it up" (part I, chapter 2). Ideal as this situation might sound to a conventional distruster of women, Tolstoy recognizes its pitfalls: Masha is too willing to adapt her character rather than build it. Symbolic of her failure to live for herself (and therefore for Sergei) is her recurring desire to stop time, so that her summer's love might never turn to autumn, and present happiness never be threatened. The most metaphysically potent of all Tolstoy's lush nature descriptions in this story occurs when Masha and Sergei are strolling in the garden at night, a setting both familiar and magical: "at each step the magic wall closed up again behind us and in front, and I ceased to believe in the possibility of advancing further—I ceased to believe in the reality of it all" (part I, chapter 3). Tolstoy would use this sense of a magical world in Natasha's feeling that she will never again be so happy as she was in the troika ride of *War and Peace*. He endows his heroines with both an admirable capacity for feeling the present and a decided reluctance to relinquish it. But for Tolstoy life must be greater than happiness; and Masha is "afraid of life, afraid of any feeling that might break in on that happiness" (part I, chapter 4). She clings to her closed-in spaces (to borrow an Eriksonian concept): the closed path and her bedroom with its shut door and shuttered windows.

Masha's other feminine flaw is that she dissembles too well. Later on, in *The Kreutzer Sonata*, Tolstoy blames men for making women into dissemblers. Here Masha, successfully affecting a simplicity of manner that is not her own but rather Sergei's ideal, actually improves herself: "Without wishing to deceive him, I did deceive him, and I became better myself while deceiving him" (part I, chapter 2).

Tolstoy hints that Masha has another side, almost a will to power, or at least to equality with Sergei, and the road to power for a woman is through sex. In one of the story's earlier variants this aggressive side of Masha is made more explicit: Masha says, "I needed to show him the power of my beauty and youth."[3] When they go to Petersburg, in the final version, she merely says, "It pleased me so much to find myself in these surroundings not merely his equal but his superior, and yet to love him better and more independently than before, that I could not understand what he could object to for me in society life" (part II, chapter 2). Earlier in the story, though, there is a hint of Masha's power to reduce Sergei to equality (so to speak) in the orchard scene, where Masha catches him day-dreaming about her and thinks: "He had ceased to be the old uncle who spoiled or scolded me; he was a person equal to me,[4] who loved and feared me as I loved and feared him" (part I, chapter 3).

This kind of power play between man and woman becomes more of a central issue in *The Kreutzer Sonata*. In *Family Happiness* Tolstoy puts it aside because in this story he wants to show married life taking the place of romantic love, "a happiness not greater but different." Resuming her role as child-woman, Masha asks Sergei at the end, "Why did you give me a freedom for which I was unfit? Why did you stop teaching me?" Sergei says later, "all of us, and especially you women, must have personal experience of all the nonsense of life, in order to get back to life itself." At the end Masha, who was unable to enjoy motherhood in Petersburg, substitutes for the love of a husband "a new feeling of love for my children and *the father of my children.*" Both her children are male, and Tolstoy is perhaps rationalizing into something natural a husbandly fear of being replaced in his wife's affections by his children.

In exchange for the wisdom Sergei brings to her, Masha brings youth and, in a few scenes which are expanded from the earliest manuscript versions, her eagerness to please but limited musical abilities. On the evening after the orchard scene, Masha completes her seduction of Sergei by playing the piano for him. In *The Kreutzer Sonata* music assumes a more sinister aspect: it is identified with the cultivation of a sexual passion which results in adultery (whether potential or actual) and in murder. One has only to listen to the dialogue between violin and piano in the first movement of Beethoven's great work, in which the violin leads the piano into ever more daring expressions of musical emotion, to realize that Tolstoy chose the piece of music that would perfectly embody the jealous husband's obsession with his pianist wife and her violinist lover. Pozdnyshev says, quite explicitly, "Music only excites, it doesn't lead to a climax" (tol'ko razdrazhaet, ne konchaet, XXIII).

The same sexual attraction which can result in a bad marriage can also end more dangerously, in suicide or murder. In destructive relationships like that between Anna and Vronsky, love is foremost. On her way to suicide, Anna thinks to herself: "If I could be anything but his mistress, passionately loving nothing but his caresses—but I cannot and do not want to be anything else" (part VIII, chapter 30). In *The Kreutzer Sonata* disputes between Pozdnyshev and his wife are always associated with sexual joinings. The sexual act in which Anna and Vronsky engage is metaphorically made into a murder ("he felt what a murderer must feel when looking at the body he has deprived of life"), and the *Kreutzer Sonata* murder is an intensified sexual act, an outlet for sexual feelings. Conversely, something other than love (sexual or romantic attraction) will be the prelude to a harmonious relationship between the sexes. In *Anna Karenina*, as we have seen, Levin describes his feelings for Kitty: "This is not love. I have been in love, but this is not that" (part I, chapter 10).

Between the overly rationalized surface of *Family Happiness* and the abyss of *The Kreutzer Sonata* lies the novel *Anna Karenina*, where many different arrangements between the sexes are given time to form, dissolve, and form themselves anew. Some of the novel's minor characters remark how fundamentally disparate the two sexes really are. Serpukhovskoi, Vronsky's careerist friend, tells him "women are always more materialistic than men. Men make of love something enormous, but women are always terra-à-terre" (part III, chapter 21). Katavasov, a professional flirt, talks in a truly Gogolian sentence about his "very interesting observations on the differences in character and even in physiognomy between male and female house-flies and on their life" (part VIII, chapter 17).

Such glib or humorous remarks form little eddies which run counter to the main streams of the novel. For no matter how relentlessly Tolstoy divides and dissects the different social worlds of men and women, the two sexes seem in this novel to share whatever worlds are real to a greater extent than they ever had or would again in Tolstoy's works. Field work and having and raising children are the most real of occuptions in the novel, and they are shared, perhaps not equally, but nonetheless shared between the sexes. Two newly married peasants, Ivan Parmenov and his wife, work together in the fields. Levin observes them and later, before and after his marriage, finds a new respect for the mysterious world of women with their petty material worries.

This was not so in the earlier works. At the conclusion of *Family Happiness*, Sergei looks only fleetingly at his baby in the nursery before Masha covers him up again (with the words "none but I had any business to look long at him"—part II, chapter 4). Earlier Sergei had sat in the nursery while she went off to a ball—a role reversal used for shock effect. Pierre in *War and Peace* hands his baby back to the nurse as soon as it wets. Yet Levin, in the crucial transitional *Anna Karenina*, not only enters into the nursery but into a state of mind that makes him the true parent of his child. After the birth of his baby, his senses are overwhelmed, and after the storm in nature he takes a further step into fatherhood, that of love (before he had felt only "repulsion," "fear" and "pity"). Levin's responses lag behind those of Kitty to the point of being funny, but Tolstoy endows both parents with true parental feelings. Levin's feelings are a surprise to himself.

The actual social world of the Russian gentry of his time, so thoroughly described by Tolstoy, in no way manages to reunite the sexes in any human or meaningful fashion. Where business is conducted by men—in offices in town or in the zemstvo in the country—they engage in meaningless debate or report-writing, less useful than the all-female household activity of jam-making. The numerous all-male social diversions—French theater, restaurants (where a waiter spoils Stiva's ritual of pleasure by repeating in French what he has ordered in Russian), clubs, army officers' parties, or country hunts which end in dalliance with peasant girls—lose their appeal because Vronsky or Levin has his mind on something else, and even Stiva has his family and financial worries. When women preside over social circles, like Betsy Tverskoi or wield power through their influence over men, like the Countess Lidiia Ivanovna, they are incarnations of hypocrisy and do perhaps even more evil than the men.

Charitable and intellectually worthy activities for both men and women are made unattractive in this novel. Koznyshev's debates seem to be purposely made boring. Anna partakes fully of Vronsky's improvements on the estate, learns architecture, reads serious authors like Taine, excels to the point where Vronsky consults her; but all these activities are performed to fill the time she does not spend with her child. They enable her to avoid self-scrutiny of her personal morality by substituting a more impersonal expertise.

Where there are children to be cared for, there is no question of boredom or meaningless activity, but Tolstoy shows us no simple snapshots of happy family life as he did in *Family Happiness* or *War and Peace*. Dolly often reflects the accumulated cares and worries of years of child-rearing in her "thin, care-worn face" (part VI, chapter 18) and, although more often she loves them, at times she seems to hate her children. No one reading the novel could envy her; but both she and Anna, always in opposite state of being, are enhanced by their bringing together two female worlds that never touch except in friendship. Neither the Shcherbatskii girls' education (learning to speak French and English on alternate days) nor the men's (learning to ride horses or discourse philosophically) prepares for life. Adultery, if committed properly, conventionally, can be carried off by either sex, although certainly Anna has less social mobility than Vronsky in their peculiar relationship.

Anna and Vronsky's mutual passion is made effective and irresistible to the reader partly because it is described in androgynous terms. Vronsky is submissive. Tolstoy writes that "in her presence he had no will of his own" (part III, chapter 22). Both are conventionally feminine responses. Anna's sexual feelings for Vronsky are described in much greater detail than his for her.

Anna's vitality, the essence of her attractiveness, is made up in large part of sexuality, and with Tolstoy sexuality fulfills only itself and leads away from life. Thus we have the paradox of Anna, who is so alive, yet ends her life in suicide. At the beginning Anna is all movement and resolution; it is the way she walks more than anything that attracts Vronsky . Her last action, dropping onto her knees under the train, is also accomplished "with a light movement" (part VII, chapter 30). But despite the gracefulness of her movements she has nowhere to go. Her confused feelings on trains (in Tolstoy's works trains are a speedier way to disaster), not knowing after she leaves Moscow at the beginning of the novel whether she is going backward or forward, are of course a metaphor for the lack of direction in her life, motivated only by love. Vronsky's movements are almost always more abrupt, the most central one being the "unpardonable movement" that kills his mare (part II, chapter 25). Levin, for all his social clumsiness, shares with Anna the sort of physical grace that makes him an excellent skater and able to mow so that his body seems to be moved by the scythe (part III, chapter 5).

When things run smoothly in Tolstoy it signals a shutting-out of life. Anna's well-run nursery in which she plays no part is contrasted to Dolly's chaotic child-rearing, where her daughter may need a coat one day and go to a party dressed as a marquise the next, where children not only consume but also waste what has been provided for them. Life is messy. Absolutes—of color, for example (Anna's black ball-gown, white dressing-gown, black hair, white skin), are also not life-like.

Anna and Levin, the protagonists of the novel, whom Tolstoy endows with the most complicated states of consciousness, embody respectively the sexual vitality that must be killed and the nurturing energy that must be allowed to grow in either sex. There are no acceptable alternatives in this novel, of all those explored.

Anna Karenina, in a symbolic gesture of total isolation, looking at her distorted self in the mirror and imagining Vronsky's kisses, suddenly raises her hand to her lips and kisses it (part VIII, chapter 27). Sexual love which is supposed to be the union of two people is, for Tolstoy, a reflection of the single self. In *The Kreutzer Sonata* a marriage based on sexual attraction is no union at all, but a deadly proximity of two isolated souls. One of them, the narrator, rides one of those trains going nowhere and tells his story. After *Anna Karenina*, Tolstoy shifts his position to show the effects of passion primarily on men, and deals more directly with his own feelings.

*The Kreutzer Sonata* (1889) is often dismissed as an extreme example of Tolstoy's misogyny, without any redeeming artistic virtues. No authoritative text exists for this work; Tolstoy rewrote it at least five times. He had misgivings about publishing it, even after his wife had gone to Petersburg to intercede with the Tsar on his behalf. He speaks of something "nasty" (skvernoe) and "ugly" (durnoe) in it.[5] He seemed surprised at his own conclusions and wrote in the afterword to the story: "I never expected that my train of thought would lead me where it did. I was horrified at my own conclusions, wanted not to believe them, but it was impossible not to."[6] It is increasingly impossible for the modern reader not to either.

*The Kreutzer Sonata* does have an artistic structure, a distinctive one, not easy on the reader. It is an anti-novel, because so many novels have ended unsatisfactorily from Tolstoy's point of view: romance leading to happiness. Far from being misogynistic, it takes men's hatred of women and lays bare its roots, finding them in a social and economic universe entirely of men's making.

Tolstoy accomplished this feat without once sharing the point of view with a woman, as he had done so successfully in earlier works. Pozdnyshev's wife, who never even receives a name, possesses only the motivations her husband attributes to her. She is shown directly occasionally in angry dialogue. She is described and treated as an animal, though less sympathetically. Even on her deathbed, she is no meek angel: she neither forgives nor accepts forgiveness, but expresses hatred and a vengeful desire to take her murderer-husband's children from him .It would seem that misogyny rules throughout. But Tolstoy is attempting a more difficult feat: without giving woman her say (the woman on the train at the beginning needs the lawyer's help even to express her "wrong" modern notions on love and divorce) and without giving us any example of admirable behavior in women, he clearly shows how she has been deprived of her humanity. Part of men's baseness consists of converting women into higher beings; Tolstoy shows the wife as she is.[7]

To do so, he creates a universe that could not be more different from that of his novels. The frame structure is a deception, as purposely artificial as the passions it contains, for this is no ordinary story. Even the literary genre of the madman's confession is used slightly differently, for while we are accustomed to the madman, or in this case the madman-murderer, having an interesting story to tell us to illustrate his estranged view of the world, here the actual plot is the least of it. "Yes, I keep getting carried away," he says (xviii), and the excursuses or digressions at every turn of the story—courtship, engagement, marriage and adultery (whether in thought or deed)—form the actions of greatest interest in this work. What should be the heart of the plot in a novel—the wife's relations with a lover or the murder of a wife by a husband—is a side issue in this story.

Its unity and major interest derive from the rage and the "extreme" views on women of the protagonist. Pozdnyshev's narrative goes on all night, but we never learn whether the dawn brings new understanding to his interlocutor. Pozdnyshev's clothes reflect a change of life, from his Western, well-tailored overcoat to his Russian embroidered shirt underneath. His voice and face also change as he propels himself into his narrative, to the ever-faster movement of the train.

Pozdnyshev ironically credits women with an expertness men don't possess, knowledge of the rules of physical attraction and their practical application. While Levin succumbs with grateful awe to the women's world that takes him over after his engagement, Pozdnyshev understands that women are commodities in a competitive market. Socioeconomic imagery dominates the narrative. Pozdnyshev's second quarrel with his wife ends with her accusing him of trying to control her by means of money. Later, when she is convinced by a doctor not to nurse her first child, a wetnurse is hired: "That is, we took advantage of the poverty, the need, and the ignorance of a woman, tempted her away from her own baby to ours" (xiv). Pozdnyshev continually refers to modern customs within "our class," but claims they are spreading to the peasantry as well.

Finally, the most potent similes in the narrative compare upper-class Russian women to their most unlikely social opposites: slaves in a bazaar and Jews. "The maids (devy) sit around and the men walk about, as at a bazaar, choosing. And the wenches (devki) wait and think, but dare not say: Me, Sir! No, me. Not her, me: look what shoulders and other things I have." Pozdnyshev's interlocutor asks sarcastically if women should propose marriage then and meets with the answer, "Oh, I don't know how; only if there's to be equality, let it be equality. If they have discovered that prearranged matches are degrading, why this is a thousand times worse!" (viii) Women compensate for debasement the only way they can: "On the one hand woman is reduced to the lowest state of humiliation, while on the other hand she dominates. Just like the Jews: as they pay us back for their oppression by a financial domination, so it is with women, 'Ah, you want us to be traders only—all right, as traders we will dominate you!' say the Jews. 'Ah, you want us to be merely objects of sensuality—all right, as objects of sensuality we will enslave you,' say the women" (ix). As a final economic argument, Pozdnyshev maintains that nine-tenths of mankind does heavy labor to produce the various "useless" objects women use and consume. The repeated use of these economic images in a work of fiction increases its leanings toward "reality" and strains at the conventions of the narrative itself.

Though the consequences of inequality between the sexes are economic, Pozdnyshev does not believe that the root causes and therefore the solutions are political or economic: "woman's lack of rights arises not from the fact that she must not vote or be a judge—to be occupied with such affairs is no privilege—but from the fact that she is not man's equal in sexual intercourse and has not the right to use a man or abstain from him as she likes" (ix).

*Anna Karenina* had already made clear that social institutions tend to help neither men nor women; but the issue here is a more fundamental one. Tolstoy comes out squarely against the liberal assumption that education will bring about change: "The education of women will always respond to men's opinion of them" (xiv). He posits the need for the most radical change, "a change in men's outlook on women and women's way of regarding themselves" (xiv). For Tolstoy, chastity would be the sine qua non of this change; but the reasons for its necessity, the description of sexual politics as they exist, are the same as those made by feminists today.

Beside the intensity of Pozdnyshev's arguments, his own story pales and becomes faintly ludicrous. Rather than take this fact as a sign of artistic weakness, I think we should see it as deliberate. Tolstoy wants us to focus on an entire argument about the condition of women and men, not on a single marriage which is repeatedly said to be like all others in its mutual hatred and lack of communication between the sexes. Therefore he comically belittles the mutual attraction of his sleek wife and the musician with the "twitching thigh" (xxi). Pozdnyshev has an almost Dostoevskian obsession with bringing them together. He later refuses to face his dying wife without his shoes on. Pozdnyshev's state of mind before the murder is described rather briefly and rationally, unlike the expanded treatment given Anna's suicide in which her mental state is shown from inside. Paradoxically in this first-person narrative, Pozdnyshev's description of his psychic condition preceding the murder has a certain remoteness. The reason for this split is that Pozdnyshev is already a changed man.

The murder instead could have been a suicide of either party, we are told. Back in 1856 Tolstoy had already contemplated these extreme consequences of a marriage gone bad. In a letter to Arsen'eva, he writes of fearing marriage because he looks upon it too severely; if it turned out badly, he would cut his throat. He says, "I'm staking everything on that card."[8] In "The Kreutzer Sonata," the murder of the wife is not even much of a legal crime; a crime of passion is easily acquitted and soon forgiven. Pozdnyshev is estranged from his fellow men not because he is a murderer, but because of his knowledge: "Yes, it will be a long time before people learn what I know. How much of iron and other metal there is in the sun is easy to find out, but anything that exposes our swinishness is difficult, terribly difficult!" (xv).

If we focus only on Tolstoy's stated opinions of women in his diaries and letters, the examples of misogyny are too numerous to cite. Further, if we treat his female characters in isolation from their world, a world populated by both sexes, we may find little that appeals to the modern mind. Tolstoy came to judge his male characters by the same exacting standards of abstinence and self-absorbed honesty as his female ones. Far from blaming women for men's lapses into temptation, a convenient earlier projection of his own sexual guilt, Tolstoy comes to blame men for creating women in the image that suited them, in life as in art ("Take all poetry, all pictures and sculpture . . . and you will see that woman is an instrument of enjoyment," says Pozdnyshev [xiv]).

In *Middlemarch* (1871), George Eliot described the thoughts of a young man before a disastrous marriage. Lydgate thought he had found the perfect wife "who was instructed to the true womanly limit and not a hairsbreadth beyond—docile, therefore, and ready to carry out behests which came from beyond that limit." Tolstoy would never describe the fruits of such error with Eliot's quiet, knowing irony. In his hopes for marriage, too much was at stake. Tolstoy converted his fear of women as an unknown and unruly quantity into a difficult knowledge of human interaction and shared responsibilities. From a feminist perspective, Pozdnyshev's vituperative rage is ultimately more humane than the nursery scenes of *Family Happiness* and *War and Peace*. Progressing from the belief that a good man can create a good woman to the knowledge that men are too flawed to create anything but a caricature of their own desires, Tolstoy's attitude toward women is never quietly expressed, nor is it ever a side issue. It forms the very core of his writings.

# 4.

## "WOMAN IS
## EVERYWHERE PASSIVE"
### Chekhov and the Century's End

A nton Chekhov gives us such a range of heroines that generalizations with examples, typologies according to periods of writing or social class, need always to be refined down to each particular story. One cannot speak of the Chekhov heroine the way one can of the Turgenev, Dostoevsky, or even the Tolstoy heroine. Few, if any, of his predecessors influenced his fictional heroines except to spur him to polemics. Chekhov confronts the pettiest and the most "puzzling" aspects of women's social behavior; but social theories never dominate his fiction except in dramatic form, and he keeps both biological determinism and double standards well at bay.[1] In his letters and notebooks Chekhov does write down observations about the "differences" between men and women, such as the one in a letter of April 17–18, 1883: "the history of man and woman. Woman is everywhere passive." These observations do not, however, enter his fiction directly. Chekhov's humaneness, his willingness to assume that human beings are basically similar (his *wish* to assume so) should not be questioned. Nevertheless, Chekhov did explore woman's "differentness" in his own terms. The naturalistic story "Agafya" and the grotesque story "The Darling," each with a radically different narration, are two examples of this fictional testing of a societally-held hypothesis in which Chekhov himself did not necessarily believe. Each one confronts woman's sexuality and the relation between female passivity and her sexual aggressiveness in ways seemingly impossible to other Russian writers who departed from more fixed notions.

Chekhov's short story "Agafya," written in the watershed year of 1886, seems simplicity itself and a worthy addendum to Turgenev's *Huntsman's Sketches* in its sympathetic balance between gentry narrator and peasants, as well as in its symbolically realistic outdoor setting; perhaps this explains why it has been so briefly mentioned in any other light. It has only three characters—a woman and two men. Their relation to each other is triangular (but not amorous): each character is affected by the other two and affects them. The two men (the narrator and Savka) in the story's time of evening into dawn of one night, have a relationship of intense relaxation and mutual admiration that excludes the woman. They go through the motions of hunting and fishing, but these traditional male pastimes have no obvious goal: no birds or fish are caught. The woman, Agafya, and one of the men share the same class (they are peasants) and a sexual relationship. We are told in passing that Savka has the features of a woman, and he receives other women in much the same manner as he does Agafya. The third and most obvious side of the triangle—the line between Agafya and the narrator—provides the reader with a view on the story. The word "view" is used here to mean both opinion (point of view) and visual focus, for much of the story involves watching and it exists on various visual planes.

The story (like Turgenev's "The Singers" or Chekhov's later work "In the Ravine") has a symbolic locale, a static landscape through which, in this case, only one character moves. The events, the meeting of the three characters, take place across the river from the village. All three have come to escape its constrictions. The gentry narrator wants to eat and sleep any time he pleases. Savka is an outsider in general: he can stand motionless for hours and commune with nature, he lives on the charity of the married women who visit him, bringing food and clothing in exchange for sex. (Chekhov, unlike Turgenev, makes this explicit and deromanticizes it, but, unlike Tolstoy, he does not disparage it.) Savka despises women in proverbial peasant language, but accepts their visits. Agafya, a young woman of nineteen or twenty, is called "a new one," and it is her crossing over from the village to the other side of the bank and especially her crossing back that constitute the drama of the plot which ultimately focuses on her, as the title suggests.

"Agafya" is one of the rare works by men that treats female sensuality not as an object of titillation for a male audience nor as a pretext for moral condemnation, but purely for its own sake, as part of life. Agafya is first recognized by the narrator breathless "probably from fear" after having forded a river in the dark. Having become aware of the narrator's presence, she tries to pretend she has come on an errand. She begins speaking in the respectful tones appropriate when addressing a person from the gentry, but Savka cruelly makes the situation clear: "The *barin* knows why you've come." She begins to drink vodka and Savka remarks how a woman (baba) always brings something to eat. Her sensuality has thus been despised, a third party allowed to remain at the tryst, and her gifts mocked. As the narrator tells us later: "Savka despised women." He posits this as an explanation for why they like Savka, then explains it as their impulse to mother a failure—two contradictory explanations which cancel each other out. Savka's good looks and a need similar to that of the men to escape seem to emerge as the primary cause for a married woman, who will be beaten by her husband, to take such a risk. But "reasons" figure less in the story than the simplicity of action and the courage of a risk-taking decision.

Agafya at first is humiliated in front of two men, then later further insulted when Savka goes off, leaving her awkwardly alone with the barin. She drinks some more and gets what she wants, only after deciding to stay so long that her husband will surely find out. "That's it, I'll wait," she says simply. Agafya's husband is a signalman: his life, measured by the arrival and departure of trains, represents the village's organized society, from which the three temporarily escape. Chekhov only states this occupation, leaving the reader to deduce the rest. The narrator tactfully leaves, and when he returns, Agafya doesn't even notice his arrival, wrapped up as she is in her own sensations. Both men urge her to go before it is too late. She laughs, both with pain and with determination. A peculiar image follows—not one of sensual coarseness, but of tenderness and innocence. The narrator walks to the river and feels a flower brush his cheek, "like a child that wants you to know it's not sleeping." He has caught nothing on his line: his pursuits are as inconsequential as those of his male counterpart in the peasantry, Savka, who insists on catching birds with his bare hands. Both men are "artists" (Savka is called one). Chekhov often sympathizes with men of this type, because they do not actively cause harm.

The story takes a different turn at the end, as Agafya (but not the men) must return to the village to face her husband, who now knows and can punish her. Savka also anticipates punishment for his philandering.

The visual levels become primary as the two men watch her cross the river. A third man, her husband, is also watching her as she moves towards him. He has been waiting a whole hour, "motionless as a post." Characters lying down in this story are sympathetic, lust and drunkenness, as well as sleep, being preferable to rigid authority. At first Agafya's body expresses indecision, helplessness and fear. It undergoes convulsive movements (as if—again this is only implied—she were already being beaten). But at the end, after more peasant misogyny ("the cat laughs, the mouse weeps") from Savka, and sympathy from the narrator, we have the final two sentences: "Agafya suddenly jumped up, shook her head, and with a bold step walked toward her husband. She, evidently, had pulled herself together and made her decision."

Words meaning decisiveness or decision are paradoxically applied to the character who is the least free of the three in the story: married, a woman, and a peasant. While the two men lead a timeless and passive existence, the arrival and departure of the train define Agafya's free time. She has broken out of time and place for reasons of pure sexuality and not love (she gets none) or empathy: each of the two men "understands" her in his own way. Their lazy pastoral, in a whispering, caressing landscape, their listening to birds and catching no fish, located away from social reality, is interrupted by Agafya, although she seeks similar escape. Her immediate drama is shared by them. Outside society as well as in it, however, women belong to a different world. Chekhov presents Agafya's decision to gratify her own needs as a heroinic act.

The animal and bird imagery of this story often metaphorically reflects the human world: Agafya is twice compared to a tortured animal;[2] and the village huts are compared to "frightened young partridges huddling together." Chekhov's humans are never deprived of choice, but freedom is more readily available to men than to women in the pastoral if not the village world. Agafya accepts what the two men spend their time trying to avoid— the commitment to pleasure and escape within heavily defined limits. In terms of the story's imagery, the characters choose to see what they wish. "Lying down, I could not see the river," the narrator says towards the beginning of the story. At the end, the men see both river and village. They make the comments, but the extent of their perception depends upon their understanding, which the reader perceives as partial, making the final identification with Agafya alone.

There is an opposite movement in our other story: gradual estrangement from its heroine who is not a heroine in the usual sense, but rather a travesty on the nineteenth-century woman-who-loves. Olenka, the protagonist of "The Darling" ("Dushechka," written in late 1898), escapes the setting of her story to become a kind of archetype: the passive female who lives only for those she loves. Olenka's hyperbolized passivity paradoxically dominates everything: her surroundings, the weather, and all other characters in the story. This has led many readers to ignore the story's detail and to make confident statements about Olenka's character. Olenka is a recognizable heroine, a woman men think they know, although she seems to be differently familiar to different readers.[3] A "simple" heroine, her relationship to her own psyche is clear: she desires one thing and reacts to events with a consistency usually found in comic types. In his correspondence, Chekhov refers to "The Darling" only as a "comic story";[4] nevertheless it is something more. Chekhov deliberately structures his narrative not merely for comic effect but in order to foster a fake confidence in the reader about the identity of the heroine: No one seems to feel uncertain about his attitude toward Olenka and yet attitudes differ so sharply. Chekhov has given us an outline of a character that we fill in as we like. Olenka's consistency of motivation has only pseudoplausibility; we supply the rest from our own experience and wishes.

There is a curious inconsistency of authorial voice in the story which has led readers in their various directions. It can generally be called comic with sinister overtones. Whether we laugh, feel outraged or ultimately take fright depends upon ourselves, upon how devoted we are to the idea of female devotion. I would like to suggest a reason why Chekhov leaves us so much to our own reactions. The "we-all-know-Olenka" reaction befits a comic type and compensates for the outrageous lack of plausibility in the structure of the story and in the character of its heroine. We don't bother to question our stereotyped reaction to conventionally understood "female" behavior (Chekhov's passive males, like the "man in a case," don't live for love; rather the opposite). We join in Chekhov's locker-room joke; like all such jokes, it's on us, but it's still funny.

Like that of many of Chekhov's protagonists, the tenor of Olenka's existence ranges from quiet desperation to palpable disaster; but Olenka also experiences bliss. The alternation of despair and joy in her life occurs with mechanical regularity in the story even though its cause is human: the absence or presence of a man for Olenka to love. In the course of the twelve-page story Olenka falls in love and lives with a beloved four times. She is married twice, to a theater-manager and a lumberman, lives with an already married veterinarian and finally with his nine-year-old son Sasha. It is both the frequency and the subject of the changes that make the story humorous. The *idée reçue* of love and marriage is that it happens once or twice in a lifetime but normally not three or four times. Too much of a good thing can be disturbingly comic. Plurality underlines the passion and trivializes its object. Furthermore, Olenka quite naturally forgets her former lovers completely. She lives in an emotionally intense present that totally obliterates the past. The narration itself continually reminds us that Olenka is a "repeater" in loving.

English translations often gloss over Chekhov's use of diminutive endings in the story. Its title ("Dushechka") and its first word ("Olenka") already refer to the heroine, Olga, as childish and endearing, for the nicknames sound somewhat ridiculous for a fully grown woman. Her tragic loss of three-and-a-half men (the boy may be taken back by his mother and resists Olenka in his dream at the end; so he will certainly be lost to her as well) is undercut by their own names as well as by their appearance. The three grown men are called Vanichka, Vasichka and Volodichka, diminutives as interchangeable as Tom, Dick, and Harry. Olenka's affection trivializes her loved ones, small men in any case.

The narrative, with a strange inconsistency of tone, trivializes Olenka while seemingly making her heroic. This process has an additive progression, a change within each set of repetitions, and a cumulative effect. As the story opens, rain-clouds gather and Kukin (soon to be husband number one) tells Olenka his business troubles. She listens with Desdemona-like sympathy. The scene is repeated three times: Kukin rails against the rainy weather and the Philistine tastes of the public. So far Olenka says nothing: she listens and loves. Kukin is described in repulsive physical terms, small and thin, with a yellow face and a thin falsetto voice, while Olenka is antithetically soft, full, and rosy. The first of several narrative declarations tells us: "She was always in love with someone and could not live without this."

People love her too. Throughout the story, when Olenka is on the upswing, a choral exclamation of townsfolk, "Darling!" regularly occurs. At her lowest ebb, the townsfolk look at her differently and do not smile. Olenka's moods totally dominate the story's environment.

After she marries Kukin she speaks with his words, and she grows fatter while he grows thinner and dies. She learns of his death in a garbled, punning telegram. Chekhov juxtaposes the dehumanizing with the grandiose: Olenka laments her late husband in a Russian lament, as do the townsfolk, until, three months later, she "happens" (the inevitable coincidence) to meet husband number two, the lumberman. After that she talks and even dreams of lumber (her dream is comically surrealistic). The implacable narrator tells us: "What thoughts her husband had, she had too." Nothing remains of her first husband; since the lumberman is religious, they never attend the theater. The narration assumes a chronicle tone for these middle-class people: "And thus the Pustovalovs lived quietly and peacefully, in love and in full harmony, for six years." The husband's inevitable death from the minutest of causes, a cold, sends Olenka into her second cycle of depression from which she is seen by the neighbors to recover when she suddenly speaks of veterinary matters. Chekhov has introduced us to the veterinarian in question earlier, so we know more than the neighbors or than Olenka herself. As readers, we now seem to be getting ahead of things. Chekhov wants us to feel that we understand: "There were no mysteries in her life" ( vse bylo tak poniatno v ee zhizni ).

At this point there is a subtle change in the story. Olenka's possibly scandalous relationship with a married man, although once again the antithesis of her previous staid marriage, is not the cause. The neighbors condemn nothing about Olenka. It is the vet himself who berates her for talking about his professional matters ("Volodichka, then what am I to talk about?") and finally leaves "forever." By now the reader senses that the pattern of Olenka's mindless devotion has been seriously disrupted and we anxiously prepare for a downward spiral. Chekhov gives us several long, descending sentences for this time of emptiness, punctuating them with ironic exclamations like "How dreadful it is not to have any opinions."

Olenka's final, seemingly maternal relationship with the boy has impure overtones since we liken it to her other, marital, attachments. The boy fights Olenka's smothering mothering in a dream in the last words of the story. The dreaming cry to "Get away" is in the masculine singular past tense, but Sasha has just previously begged Olenka to "Leave me alone," so the connection, too obvious in English, is made in Russian in dream-language. We are all the more disturbed that Olenka has affected the boy's psyche to the point where his sleep becomes a repeated scream. This is how Chekhov ends the story.

Tolstoy and others may have liked Olenka, but Chekhov did not. Nor, in the end, does he expect us to. In some ways she resembles that incarnation of middle-class evil, Natasha in *The Three Sisters*, who also changes her environment until it reflects her soul. He had even more comic scorn for the men from whom she takes her existence and, ultimately, *their* existence. His chorus of approving neighbors are faceless everybodies who lag behind the reader's awareness at the end: they will approve anything. The long-time bachelor Chekhov must himself have been aware that everybody loves men and women best in couples, a fact all too worthy of satire.

How did Chekhov come to write this travesty of the hallowed theme of woman's endurance through love? His correspondence and the memoirs of his friends give no clue to the genesis of this story which is so different in tone from others of Chekhov's mature years.[5] Its distinctness may be explained in part by the echoing of another short story by an author well-known in Russia. Flaubert's "Un Coeur simple" (1876), with its mixture of compassionate and ruthless naturalistic detail, also has a qualified effect upon the reader. The servant character who lives only for others, who lives for more than one other and who outlives the ones she lives for, is ironically named, like Dushechka ("darling," "dear soul," "dear heart"), for her cruel life. Olenka's analogue, Félicité, follows a pattern of devotion which includes, in turn, as its objects: the children of her mistress (she loves them more than their mother does, as Olenka loves Sasha), her nephew, a dying old man and, on the very day he dies, a parrot named Loulou, finally a worm-eaten corpse who becomes, at the end, the Holy Ghost.[6]

There is more substance to the Flaubert story; the outlines are all filled in. We see Félicité briefly as a young girl, but mostly as an old woman. The story is sombre instead of comic, for no one is attracted to Félicité. She gives but doesn't get. She loves undemandingly and asexually, while Olenka is not satisfied with her cat's love and needs, demands, a comprehensive, overwhelming passion for a human male to "warm her aging blood."

Both "Un Coeur simple" and "Dushechka" make us queasy about cyclical female devotion, passivity raised to the intensity of an active force in the stories. Félicité, as a servant, is at once removed from our capacity to identify with her; nevertheless, she is part of human death and rot. Olenka's devotion has an endurance that goes beyond the limits of the story. Ordinary and middle-class, she is closer to the reader in an obvious way. While predictable in one way (women are supposed to live for love and, given a lack of anything else to live for, they often do), her need to feed her emotions with some man, any man, makes us question the value of the emotion. When it fails to occupy her, she experiences "so many years of silence and emptiness of thoughts." Her thoughts depend on her emotions. They are one, much as with Tolstoy's Natasha or Turgenev's heroines. Olenka's "wholeness" is a round zero, and our set ideas about how good it is to love (especially for women) come back to haunt us.

Chekhov has first made us like Olenka, made us anxious for her continued ability to find an object for her love, and then made us question our initial reaction of cheering her on as do the townsfolk. Then Chekhov, who always goes out of his way to be absent from his stories, leaves us alone at our very moment of realization (the end of the story). As we depend more and more upon the narrative for our opinion of Olenka, it leaves us to our own devices, having given us too much positive encouragement of a very ironic sort.

Chekhov has left us in the lurch, much as the veterinarian leaves Olenka. Our reaction that we-all-know-Olenka is safely comic, and we are quite free to be content with reading the story on a purely humorous level. On the more sophisticated level of sexual politics, we can also add the knowledge that women, conditioned into cultivating their capacity for devotion, use men in a peculiar fashion, one that is destructive of the man's own sense of self.

Russian writers since Chekhov have lacked the confidence of irony. They seem to return to the search for the right answer about women, the playing out of the old themes of mysterious otherness. Not only her spiritual goodness but also woman's sexuality has crucial significance for writers from the century's end until the Soviet era, when a sanitized neo-Turgenevian ideal began once again to prevail.

The years 1899 and 1900 seemed symbolically significant to writers of the time, in Russia as elsewhere. Like Shaw's *Man and Superman*, a 1900 play by Nikolai Minsky and an 1899 short story by Maxim Gorky, Minsky's opposite in just about everything, were permeated with a sense of the need for radical change in the old order and the human beings it oppressed. Woman, in both these works, stands apart from Man—she is different, insisting on being herself and not what men make of her. Although Minsky, the first well-known Jewish writer in Russian literature, and Gorky, considered the father of all proletarian Russian writers, belong to different literary schools—presymbolist and naturalist—they both mix the two streams in some of their work: the use of character and setting in a sort of symbolic realism to illustrate burning questions of the day. Bodily disintegration symbolizes the spiritual depletion against which the future-oriented soul must struggle. And as for Woman, her beauty (and, as always, its effect on Man) seems to be the battleground on which the struggle occurs. Man is a voyeur, an observer of woman's sexuality and, perhaps thereby, of some mystery not evident in the male world.

Gorky's "Twenty-six Men and a Girl," which in its Russian title, "Twenty-six and One," carries its gender opposition in number alone, was subtitled *poema*, pointing to the fact that it is written in a poetic prose different from those romantic narratives with which Gorky began his career. It is more akin to Chekhov's mature style, in which no word is superfluous and the narrative line leads to a seemingly inevitable conclusion. It bears some resemblance to "Agafya" in that the central issue revolves around an all-male subworld (here a negative, antipastoral one) which includes a female only briefly and disruptively.

Gorky can also be seen as descending from the Nekrasov school, where "pure" women can bring disillusionment and prostitutes are often more comforting to men, like the kind Natasha who shelters and "kisses" the young narrator under a boat in Gorky's short story "Once in Autumn"—kisses that cost him nothing, unlike later ones, he tells us. "Twenty-six and One" provides brilliant insight into the disillusionment and rage felt by men when the purity of woman fails them. Like *The Idiot*, it can be seen as a parable of male love exceeding its object. The story's setting dominates from the first paragraph and a naturalistic determinism sets all other forces in motion. Meaningless, mechanical work in an unhealthy setting produces an extreme reaction in the men; the twenty-six act as a single character. In this story the lowest of men try to interfere with the life of a woman, to make her live according to their desires: even though they themselves are too lowly to possess her, they want no other man to do so. The men, unhealthy, called "living machines," knead dough in a damp cellar, whose windows, covered with flour-dust, do not let in the sun. The men's singing is their only free expression described just before the appearance of Tanya, a girl of sixteen who works on a floor above them in the same building embroidering in gold. The men, enslaved to their monster oven, look up to this princess-apparition wearing her hair in a braid (the sign of virginity in Slavic cultures) who appears at their door, four steps above them. The men separate her from their usual "coarse, shameless talk" about women "who, we knew, perhaps deserved no other kind of talk." She takes rolls from them; when one of them asks her to mend his shirt, she replies with scorn. Though the men agree that she is above them, the fact that they feed her and give her advice already foreshadows the tyranny of a love greater than its object. When a young dandy appears, in good health and wearing bright colors—sexually outclassing them, but speaking the same way as they do about women—the men actually want him to seduce other women, as their surrogate; but Tanya is theirs. When they make a bet with him that he can't seduce her, they are testing the strength of their idol. The narrator, who interprets and explains, as a voice for the mute men, uses these words. The inevitable conquest takes place, while they watch. Imagery of dirt and rain surrounds the act of betrayal, and Tanya, like Agafya, staggers with uneven steps to her post-sexual punishment by men who feel they own her. They form a circle around her and begin to abuse her verbally. Gorky explicitly states that they do not beat her (fiction being kinder than reality) and focuses instead on the men's pain as they return to their cellar, now sunless and godless. Tanya walks away contemptuously. Here, as in Tolstoy's later stories, attention is concentrated on the men, with women a symbol and a catalyst for their own suffering—not heroines, in any sense.

Our other work of the period, the play Minsky called *Alma*[7]—its protagonist changes her name from plain Russian Alya to that exalted one—also uses woman symbolically, but gives her a Nietzschean superman quality.[8] She has the power to lead men; but first she must lead herself to a perfect freedom beyond any social constraint. She is already rich and beautiful—and, we are told, accustomed to hold sway from childhood—but the curtain opens with Alma in a totally vulnerable position, lying unconscious on a couch, having attempted suicide, as a man reads her diary. The image conjures up so many pictorial ones—like the frontispiece of the midnineteenth century journal "Dawn," that used a Psyche-like reclining woman about to awaken, as acceptable pornography with a progressive message. Here the fact that a doctor (one of a long line of violators of women's bodies, as Tolstoy pointed out repeatedly) is reading her intimate thoughts aloud to the audience (and her uncle) constitutes a double violation and an interesting coup de théâtre. The doctor characterizes her disease as "erotomania," the cult of love fearing its own satisfaction, which afflicts one woman in ten. Her diary proclaims her desire not to be equal to men, for men lead a coarse and ugly life. The doctor explains that contemporary woman takes revenge for her past life in a harem, at no risk to herself and at great risk to men.

Alma regains consciousness and the doctor declares his hopeless love for her, although he is a married man, as the situation reverses itself into the sado-masochism often found in symbolist literary works: she will inflict "pure suffering" on him. Alma proclaims her right to freedom of choice, and tells the doctor's wife (also a doctor) that she does not want him, but asks her to write a prescription for poison so that she can be free to die when she wants. She will marry an artist and announces that her room is no longer a temple and her portrait no longer an icon. She opens the window-sash and looks out at the street, at reality.

Act II takes place in the real world three years later. Alma has organized a home for children, and has put her own daughter in it, substituting another child to bring home. Her aim is to prove that humanity should love all children as their own and to vanquish the maternal instinct. The other mothers know they will never recognize "their" children again, but some husbands (Alma's, and an absentee husband of another woman) cannot see the point. A famous male pediatrician proclaims that maternal instinct is the strongest force in the world. One child dies, an event precipitating conflict, as Alma reveals it is not "hers" but the one she had substituted without her husband's knowledge. Instinct has been vanquished, Alma proclaims: "Either everything must remain as before, or else a new light will shine, without sun but also without shadow."

Act III takes place three years in the future, in a leper colony. It juxtaposes three women—the doctor's wife, Alma (now coworkers) and Alma's sister—to a chorus of lepers who speak graphically of their illness, in full knowledge that their future will be even more horrifying than their present state. It is a hell on earth that Alma has now deliberately made herself part of, for she has kissed the lepers and infected herself. She wants to be able to freely love beauty by coming to terms with disfigurement. The final instinct—the will to live—has been vanquished. Alma, ahead of all the other ordinary women and men in the play, has conquered first love, then the maternal instinct—the two elements out of which, and out of which alone, the image of woman in literature had been fashioned—and finally the fear of death itself. The play incorporates all the era's clichés of perfection: woman's symbolic beauty and spiritual leadership. It combines the use of social questions with the love-goddess image, giving the audience social uplift and sensationalism at the same time.

It was this combination of feminism with sensationalism that made a woman writer, Anastasiia Verbitskaia (1861–1928), so popular from roughly 1907 to 1918, that she would advertise the huge printings of her book at the end of each new volume.[9] Her novel, *Keys to Happiness* (1908–1913) came out in six volumes, and Verbitskaia managed to include in it both feminist meetings in Paris and the rise and fall of a heroine whose loves rather than career determine her life. Verbitskaia's style was accessible: her sentences were brief and her paragraphs often consisted of a whole one of these sentences. Nonetheless, after lasciviously demonstrating the unhappy loves of her heroines, she gives them monologues of self-understanding. The heroine of the novella "Our Mistakes" proclaims, in similar tones to Alma:

> One wants to believe . . . that the new age will not see these tragedies of love . . . one wants to believe that the cult of love will disappear, as many fatal prejudices and medieval delusions have already done. And our descendants a hundred years from now will look with surprise mixed with pity at our literature consecrated to love. 'What erotomaniacs they were,' they'll say, 'all this is the result of a falsely sentimental upbringing and the absence of a broad and intense social life. . . .

Thus the sexual theme—sexual freedom passing for the sort of freedom men enjoyed for centuries—merely made obvious what was latent in the theme we began with: perfection of the heroine. Social issues once again loomed large behind the stated importance for women of changing their lives. Women either adapt (and therefore, through their passivity, become part of the general evil of society) or conquer (and lead the way for men). Let us juxtapose this Verbitskaia passage to one written in a famous feminist novel, Alexander Herzen's *Who Is to Blame?*

> . . . the barrenness of the young girl's environment did not squelch her development. On the contrary, her petty surroundings were conducive to the acceleration of her powerful growth. Therein lies the secret of the feminine soul. Either from the very beginning a girl adapts to her environment so that already at the age of fourteen she flirts, gossips, makes eyes at passing offices, notices whether the servants are pilfering tea and sugar, and prepares to become an honorable housewife and stern mother, or, with extraordinary ease, she frees herself from the surrounding dirt and trash, and conquers her environment with an inner nobility. Through a kind of revelation she comes to understand life and acquires a tactfulness which protects and accompanies her. Men hardly ever develop that way.[10]

Herzen's novel of 1841–46, along with Druzhinin's *Polin'ka Saks* (1847) one of the first male feminist novels of Russia, proclaims the same message, minus its "erotic" theme, as Verbitskaia. Woman's self-understanding, her inner perfection, will lead the way to a new era—unless she gives in to the norms of the society around her (which often include those of her mother in Russian novels) and becomes a female boor. Either . . . or . . .

Beginning with the so-called "George-Sandists," the women writers of Russia's nineteenth century had concentrated their efforts on the attempts of their female characters to determine their own "fate" in the narrow sense: not vis-à-vis God or history or Russia (as for male characters in the fictions of Russian men), but merely within the family or in the shrunken arena of their acquaintance. These tales,[11] whose heroines often represented the only positive moral value, rarely ended happily, as the reader guessed from such titles as Elena Gan's "Society's Judgement." The heroine either submitted to her "fate" or was crushed. Women's lives were in any case socially defined, the moral and social dimensions collapsed into one. This is a different kind of either/or from most of the men's fiction we have been discussing. As the most perceptive critic of nineteenth-century Russian woman writers has put it:

> Beginning with E. A. Gan and ending with Evgeniia Tur, our women writers have always restricted themselves to certain particular plots that concern, on the one hand, the spectacle of the unequal struggle waged by a highly gifted woman who is searching for freedom and independence against high society and its prejudices, and against the family and its despotism; and on the other, plots that expose the treasures of mind and heart that are buried inside the female personality, and the absolute worth of this personality. The themes and characters of this second category continue the series of ideal female images in "male" literature.[12]

Socially limited, but morally superior—women have a double burden within a tradition of fiction which focused on self-definition, but excluded women from the self to be defined. Women were predefined by most male writers whether liberal or conservative (Turgenev/Herzen or Dostoevsky/Sukhovo-Kobylin). Deviation from superiority resulted in woman fallen or stridently attempting self-definition in a context of futility. The expectation of perfection, when disappointed, led inevitably to a terrible opposite.

The metaphors of voyeurism we have traced in several works are all related to woman in her perfectionized state, one which is also most vulnerable to the male eye. Nastasya Filippovna laid out in death, Agafya crossing the river to her brutal husband, Tanya dazed in the rain, and Alma unconscious on her couch—in all we see both seeming vulnerability and actual latent or nascent strength. There is a progression in disregard for and defiance of the observing males on the part of the heroines; nonetheless the reader stands closest to the male consciousness. The woman is distant, preoccupied, unconscious or dead. At great cost, she advances into an independent existence. The paradox of a male author creating a female character, itself necessarily an act of voyeurism, results in much Russian fiction not in an attempt to integrate the image of woman into a human model transcending gender, a *chelovek*, but rather to isolate her from men, as she acts out her "fate." A heroine's insistence on self-definition is usually violently punished, for whether as objects of desire or as objects of male self-definition, their striving toward self-naming has dire implications for the men who do the naming:

> Women . . . are considered merely as the *objects* of desire, and as the *objects* of the question. To the extent that women 'are the question', they cannot enunciate the question; they cannot be the speaking *subjects* of the knowledge or the science which the question seeks.[13]

The kind of voyeurism which sees women characters performing their female activities, focuses on the male observer. The main, male fictions of Russian literature in which one female character observes another are of a different sort altogether. These are not usually interactions of a positive nature, but rather ones involving jealousy leading to the murder of one woman by the other, always in a rage of repressed sexuality that is male-oriented—as in Leskov's "Lady Macbeth of Mtsensk," Zamiatin's "The Flood" or Aleksei Tolstoi's "The Viper."

The fictions of Russian men tended to isolate female characters from one another, attending to their interactions with men under a male observing eye. Women's writing in Russian prose fiction was reactive, substituting irony for admiration, but rarely willing or able to break free of the idea that women constituted a separate but better model of behavior. In order to make themselves heard at all, women had to use the discourse of their cultural tradition, its language in the broadest sense. In Russian literature it is a discourse in which the political can be found just beneath the surface of the family novel or the novel of love. These politics are the politics not of women, but of men: they involve struggles for power and for free movement in arenas which largely reflect the male aspirations. Lermontov's homage to Pushkin in "Death of a Poet" is concerned with the limitations on the poet's political freedom. Women's freedom, circumscribed by their duties to men, seemed less important, more elusive to write about. Women's oppression seemed a lesser theme than that of the entire nation.

Self-definition was achieved by women writers in different genres from those of prose fiction. What might have been novelistic themes—complicated interactions between woman and woman, between women and family or society, and between woman and herself—all appear as crucial themes in female autobiographies. Rarely do these dwell much upon romantic relationships with men. In autobiography and in lyric poetry, Russian women writers found their most congenial modes of self-expression. These, then, are the forms of female writing to which we now turn.

# PART II.

# Women's Autobiography in Russia

But this she has made. If it is
Another image, it is one she has made.

Wallace Stevens, "Bouquet of Belle Scavoir"

# 5.

# PUBLIC AND PRIVATE
# LIVES

A utobiography, as opposed to fiction, is written as an exercise less of
the imagination than of memory; but that is to say very little. For
fiction can be composed from memory, with only the pronouns changed to
protect that most innocent of innocents—the self. The other extreme, in the
most confessional of autobiographies, the exposure of self complete with
blemishes and guilt is often a "lie," an elaborate narrative pose. Impersonating another *and* impersonating oneself can be either autobiographical (as
Gertrude Stein has shown) or a device of fiction.

The autobiography or memoir, with its polished self-reflexive writing, its
awareness of a public self as well as a private one, remains a category apart.
Among texts presented to the reader as autobiography, striking dissimilarities
exist on both the individual and the national levels. Russian autobiographies
differ from those of the more familiar nations of Europe in their greater
concern with social or political reality, with Russian reality in particular.
Yet, of the recent spate of writings on autobiography, almost none have
mentioned any Russian texts. Theories have been built upon an accepted
canon, from Augustine to Rousseau, usually culminating in a French or an
English tradition which becomes the basis for a new theory.[1] Russian scholars
themselves have given us no comprehensive or selective history of autobiography in Russia to which Western scholarship could refer. The Russian
bibliographies of memoir literature of historical interest and descriptions of
archival holdings contain few listed writings by women.[2] The memoirs of
women who had no careers outside their family or who were not associated
with well-known men may well be lost or invisible, remaining outside ar-
chives or catalogued under a male family name. Thus, Russian women who
wrote autobiographies remain doubly invisible to us: as Russians they are
obscure, and as women they are often completely lost or ignored.

Feminist critics of female autobiography are beginning to search for the
differences in how men and women write about their lives, and to formulate
a study of autobiography which takes these differences and their origins into

account. The best recent essay on the subject, while it comes to no hard conclusions of the sort that have been less than useful in autobiography theory in general, nevertheless raises some of the same questions about the female self that have informed our study:

> Because of woman's different status in the symbolic order, autogynography . . . dramatized the fundamental alterity and non-presence of the subject, even as it asserts itself discursively and strives toward an always impossible self-possession. This gendered narrative involved a different plotting and con-figuration of the split subject.[3]

The theme of the split subject will be a central one in our next section, for it recurs in the female lyric in Russia. In this section the autobiographies we have selected for extensive analysis all display some sort of conflict as their different plotting. They present a self in the making, a self that stresses the conflicts of a life rather than their harmonious resolution, a self that expresses this life in formation in prose whose texture interweaves the com-plexities of past and present selves into powerful patterns of self-expression.

When we view a number of these texts, certain thematic groupings become evident, themes which may also be found, of course, in memoir writings of a more superficial nature. The themes that seem to repeat themselves in numerous women's autobiographies in Russia are: the public versus the private life, mothers and daughters, and the woman emerging as writer. Each chapter will exemplify its theme by the detailed analysis of one au-tobiography in particular and discuss others in less detail for purposes of support and comparison. Within one nation, as feminist critics are beginning to demonstrate, women autobiographers often write differently than men (we will discuss some of those differences in this chapter), but in similar ways to women of other nations. These themes in the Russian tradition would seem to lend support to that hypothesis.

Our three pivotal autobiographies—those of Dashkova, Durova, and So-khanskaia—are as dense in character, plot, setting, and theme as most Rus-sian fiction; nevertheless they remain (with the exception of Dashkova's) unpublished in full in book form and unavailable in English.[4] They and other autobiographies we will discuss, those of Labzina, Vodovozova, Liubov' Blok, and Tsvetaeva, embody images of women not highly visible in Russian fic-tion, autonomous beings rather than heroines in search of a hero. The either/ or of perfection or doom is not at issue; rather we see the emergence of a female self who exists independently, who is neither destroyed nor redeemed by love, and whose own words build the reality of her inner and outer worlds. In the conclusion to this study we will trace the strength of the female autobiographical tradition in Russia into the post-war era in the writings of

two of its greatest figures, Nadezhda Mandelstam and, in particular, Evgeniia Ginzburg.

At least two truly prominent Russian women, Ekaterina Romanovna Dashkova and Sofiia Kovalevskaia, have written autobiographies that prove what
one feminist critic has asserted: "The identity of public performance may
cause its female possessor to experience intensely, or at any rate to reveal
emphatically, preexistent uncertainties of personal identity."[5] Sofiia Kovalevskaia (1850–1891), a mathematician of world rank, wrote one of the best
Russian childhood memoirs—as if the isolation of her later life in Europe as
a woman surmounting professional difficulty at great personal cost made her
wish to recall her closeness to her sister and to Russian family life in the
country. Hers is one of the few Russian female autobiographies to receive
due attention, and we can refer readers to two admirable works about her
in English.[6] Most of our female autobiographers experienced isolation over
many years. Any fame was short-lived if it existed at all.

The three works I have chosen to discuss amount to extended self-
creations, autobiographical versions of the Russian female heroine. The first
autobiography, that of Princess Dashkova, president of the Academy of Sciences, is well known, but regarded chiefly as an appendage to the history
of Catherine's Russia. The second, that of Nadezhda Durova, who fought in
the Napoleonic wars disguised as a man, is known only in Russia. The third,
that of Nadezhda Sokhanskaia, a minor mid-nineteenth-century author, was
published after her death, in 1896, and has not been published or written
about anywhere since. These autobiographies all convey a sense of purpose
in deviating from the common path. All three women lived lives of celibacy
or isolation for most of the time. They kept their inner selves apart from
their surroundings. Two of them—Dashkova and Durova—experienced extremes of renown and obscurity and learned to deal with both. In all three
autobiographies the uncertainty, loneliness, and partial failure that accom-
pany the search for a self-defined female existence are perceptively set forth.
Isolation from female "normality" can be postulated as a prerequisite for
most of our female autobiographies, and this isolation is usually self-chosen.
This, too, is not a topic of the Russian novel.

These autobiographies by Russian women, many not published in their
own lifetime, comprise a full expression of self that that is rarely seen in
fiction. Their stylistic linkage to their fictional era—Dashkova to classicism/
sentimentalism, Durova to romantic war tales, Sokhanskaia to regionalism/
realism, Blok to psychological symbolism, Tsvetaeva to fragmented, subjec-
tive modernism—these linkages serve to reinforce the differences in women's
writing.

The very act of writing an autobiography, for a woman, was audacious.

The almost obligatory apologies are contained within the text: a prominent life unsought (Dashkova), an unusual life explained (Durova or Sokhanskaia), a life close to an important writer justified in its own terms (Blok, Mandelstam), a life of imprisonment made characteristic of others in Russia (Figner, Ginzburg)—these and not self-promotion are the reasons given for writing at all. These are not the "real" reasons; they are embedded in the very shape of the text itself. The female self emerges as a paradox: confidently modest, self-describing.

Confidence in oneself seems to be the hallmark of all women in Russia who wrote their autobiographies—but it was not a confidence rewarded by a long government career, a string of medals, or a body of writings that placed them at the center of Russian letters as was the case with male autobiographers like Derzhavin or Herzen. For women, the public self, the calling, can be motivated by anything from family affairs to the writing of the lives of others, and their own only secondarily. It is a different public life from that of most male autobiographers born into a class and gender where they could easily or uneasily associate problems of selfhood with those of national self-identity.

Men and women autobiographers differ greatly in articulating a conception of selfhood. The autobiographies of men do not generally discuss their own families: their wives and children. They dwell at length on themselves as children, whether in autobiographical fiction (Tolstoy, Aksakov, Gorky) or in autobiography per se (most recently Joseph Brodsky). Remembering themselves as children, few writer-fathers discuss themselves as parents. This does not prevent the concept of family from assuming paramount importance in their work, on the contrary. Augustine and Rousseau seem, in this respect, to be the progenitors of unmentioned or barely mentioned children in the male autobiographical tradition. From Dashkova to Ginzburg, by contrast, children are very much present in women's autobiography, even when physically absent from the mother. Men who define themselves by a career, official or antiofficial, nonetheless articulate their views of life, of their country, and (needless to say) of Woman.

The professional censor Alexander Nikitenko complained in 1841 of "drowning in paper work," wrote of "the deep, dismal awareness of (his) insignificance," of not "doing something real";[7] but he nonetheless made confident pronouncements against equality for women: "It is an irrefutable fact that a woman is weaker than a man. Doesn't she, therefore, need his protection? If she does, then the question of equality is out. The need for protection means dependence."[8] These are the views of a man in the Russian government who was praised by (male) writers for his liberal stance.

The "unofficial" Russian liberal Alexander Herzen takes a more generously understanding view of woman's "plight." It is only partly nature-based; part is socially induced:

> Yes, while considering this theme it is for woman that I am sorriest of all; she is irreparably gnawed and destroyed by the all-devouring Moloch of love. She has more faith in it and she suffers more from it. She is more concentrated on the sexual relationship alone, more driven to love. . . . She is both intellectually more unstable and intellectually less trained than we.
> I am sorry for her.[9]

This view of woman as victim (of love rather than of men: "Who is to blame?") producing a feeling of resigned pity in the male observer takes us back to the novelistic tradition. In none of the autobiographies reviewed do women describe *themselves* as slaves of love for even part of their lives. Liubov' Blok focuses on her *own* sexuality; other women writers scarcely write about men at all. One major difference between the two may well be that while men feel compelled to write about Woman in their own autobiographies, women rarely write about men as sexual beings and never write about men as Man.

There is a genre of "official" autobiography by women, however. In these the public self eclipses the private, and all conflict is resolved and explained. There is a clear sense of mission, as in much male autobiography. The memoirs of a female monarch, Catherine the Great, and those of a professional revolutionary, Vera Figner, are characterized by an official self that never wavers. These women feel no need to disguise their achievements, since they always felt certain of being on the side of progress and history. They easily put their public selves at peace with their private selves. When any disturbing recollections occur, these then become moral lessons on the path to right. When Catherine fills her time with card-playing and dressing during her early years in Russia, it is so as to "be a Russian in order to be liked by Russians."[10] When Vera Figner speaks of her early wish to become a tsaritsa because, as a pretty child, she was flattered by men who visited the family, she says she later became the tsaritsa of the prison, a title proudly accepted.[11] When she recalls seeing her mother praying in front of the icons, she asks rhetorically:

> What could mother have been praying about so long and so earnestly, those many years ago? Her life flowed along evenly, without great joys or disturbing sorrows. . . . Life, especially the life of a woman in the provinces, was confined within the boundaries of petty interests. . . . Then, too, in those times, the human soul was not so complicated, so subtle . . . as it later became.[12]

This quotation tells us neither about Vera Figner's mother nor about the times in which she lived; it imposes too rigid a theory upon a human life.

These completely "public" autobiographies, which have won similar acclaim to those by men written with a public aim, are less interesting than the many more searching documents of female experience, written by women unafraid of showing that they made mistakes, or who hesitated between the lesser of two evils, or who experienced conflict and loss.

The most interesting autobiography by a Russian woman blending the public and the private selves was written by the Princess Ekaterina Romanovna Dashkova, née Vorontsova (1743–1810). Originally she was thrust into historical prominence as part of a court intrigue: she was an ambitious young woman used by an even more ambitious older woman who bore the same name of Catherine. The future Catherine the Great used Dashkova's loyalty to seize the throne from her husband. Although Dashkova certainly exaggerates her own importance in the coup, her feelings of love for Catherine were genuine. The rewards for such loyalty were by no means consistent: Catherine's favor could be withdrawn as easily as it was bestowed. The Empress's most famous reward to Dashkova, naming her director of the Academy of Sciences, gave Dashkova a unique place in women's history. Dashkova herself founded the Russian Academy and became its president. For eleven years she successfully headed the two academies. After that she held no official post and was persecuted after Catherine's death by Paul I, who undid as much of his mother's work as he could, establishing the law of male primogeniture. Dashkova lived out her life in seclusion and obscurity, ignored both by famous friends and by her own children. Nevertheless, her busy private life continued unimpaired. This side of her would be lost to a posterity generally unconcerned with the tending of estates and friendships, were it not for the memoirs she wrote, between February 1804 and late 1805. She called them *Mon histoire* (they were written in French and subsequently translated into English, German, Russian, and then back into French from the English).[13] They are the writings of an old woman looking back on an entire lifetime—a woman who always felt herself a representative of her country and its culture and learning, but whose family and friendships occupied much of her time and thoughts. Few women have achieved such political and intellectual status in any country, or lived through such seesaws between fame and oblivion. Fame such as the immensely rich Russian court could grant; oblivion to which the isolation of the Russian countryside and the immense distances between neighboring estates and towns could condemn its citizens. Dashkova's life veered between the very public and the extremely private. Her capacity for work and reading steadied her through both extremes. Her recognition of her own strengths in her autobiography is accompanied by candid admissions of failure in spite of them, occasionally perhaps because of them.

The memoirs and the legend of Dashkova's life have been interpreted and used in various ways by historians to supplement their picture of happenings in high places or to generalize about Russian society. Extraordinary as she was, Dashkova is often mentioned as a typical specimen of the nobility under Catherine or Paul I ("In almost all respects, the nobleman was as subject to the arbitrariness of the Sovereign and his agents as the lowliest serf was to that of his master"[14]), or used to illustrate the paradoxes in the Russian aristocracy of the eighteenth century (having mastered her native language only after her marriage, Dashkova later became a great patron of Russian learning and culture).[15] The most famous Russian historian V.O. Kliuchevskii, relates an anecdote about Dashkova intended to reveal the seamy underside of Catherine's enlightenment and the fragility of Russia's Westernization:

> When Dashkova finished her brilliant career, she isolated herself in Moscow and there revealed her true nature; she received almost no one, grew indifferent to the fate of her own children, quarrelled unceremoniously with her servant, but concentrated all her maternal feelings and civic emotions on rats, which she succeeded in taming. . . . Only people of Catherine's time could begin with Voltaire and finish with a tame rat.[16]

This view of Dashkova, which regards her as willfully self-debased, is held by a minority. The most famous words about her in the nineteenth century, Alexander Herzen's essay on Dashkova, first published in 1857, cast her in the well-known role of Russian heroine and reinforce the nurturing images "perverted" in Kliuchevskii's account:

> Above all, Dashkova was born *a woman* [Herzen underlined the word] and remained *a woman* all her life. The aspect of the heart, of tenderness, of devotion, was unusually well-developed in her. For us this is especially important.[17]

It was important for Dashkova, too, but not quite as simplistically as that. No one has actually treated the *Memoirs* as an autobiographical entity, examining how Dashkova chose to define herself in all the roles she played, public and private. The *Memoirs* comprise a record not so much of historical truth as of self-explanation.

Dashkova is never unaware of her female status in both its unusual and its ordinary aspects. She is both scholar and daughter, conspirator and bride, Russian representative abroad and mother, administrator of academies and of estates, counsellor and friend. Her autobiography repeatedly stresses the double nature of her life—at times with gratitude, for when things go wrong in one sphere, she compensates by tending to matters in another. A balance, the classical symmetry she seeks, is almost never realized at any one time, but over a lifetime this balance does exist. Her sense of duty is typical of her time. But duty as civic obligation (the male neoclassical ethos) is complemented by duty as motherhood (a female ethos). The narrative of her life alternates passages in which one or the other usually dominates, but their chronology is often simultaneous.

While other people, generously praised or reluctantly blamed, appear in great numbers in the *Memoirs*, all are secondary characters. Dashkova focuses upon herself from the first pages (and on one of her major "enlightenment" themes, education). She sees herself as someone who stands alone, different from others—learned, unlike other Russian women: apprenticed to no one, unlike Russian men. Her mother dies when she is two, and her uncle educates her along with his own daughter:

> The same room, the same masters, even dresses cut from the same cloth, all, in fact should have made us into two perfectly similar individuals; and yet never have two people been so different at all the various periods of their lives. (P. 24)

She points a moral for people who think they know all about education. Nothing is ever simple, as her experience as an educator of her own children will prove. Her own childhood, however, reads almost like an intellectual Saint's Life. At first she is given an aristocratic girl's education: the perfect knowledge of four languages, dancing and drawing—but soon she begins to be different, set apart. She gets the measles and, while recovering, reads Bayle, Montesquieu, Voltaire and Boileau.

Pride gratified shows between the lines when Dashkova speaks of her passion for reading serious works; but wounded pride and thwarted affection are equally present in her early memories:

> I have a proud nature, allied in some way to a sensitive and inordinately affectionate character. Ever since I was a child I craved for affection, I wanted the sympathy of those I loved, and when at the age of thirteen I began to suspect that I was receiving neither, I was overcome by a feeling of loneliness. (P. 25)

She writes of these feelings as forebodings of what she would have to suffer in life. We may assume that she did not rewrite her childhood to conform to later trials; rather that she always felt unique and different both in her difficulties and in her ability to use books and intellectual curiosity about politics and philosophy to create a second and better life.

Catherine the Great, then the Grand Duchess, knew exactly how to flatter the girl of almost fifteen when they met in 1759, as is indicated by the often-quoted lines from the *Memoirs*: "as there were no other two women at the time . . . who did any serious reading, we were mutually drawn toward each other" (P. 28). Reading and politics intertwine in her relationship with Catherine, whose friendship with Dashkova introduces another major theme of the *Memoirs* (a common theme of the time), that of friendly affinity between equals. Dashkova's friendships with other women are important to the *Memoirs*. In two separate scenes, Dashkova climbs into Catherine's bed, the better to conspire—though she relates the ensuing dialogue in the formal tones of a neo-classical tragedy. On the eve of the overthrow of Peter III, the two women disguise themselves as guardsmen, so as to have greater mobility. It would be inconceivable to think of a male ruler elevating a woman to official prominence. In fact, Dashkova was the first woman in Europe to hold a governmental office.

At first Dashkova, with her Petersburg education, spoke Russian badly, but her Muscovite in-laws could speak no French, and she resolved to study Russian for their sake. Her marriage in 1758 at age fifteen, in a way completed her childhood education, which had been foreign and had done nothing for the spiritual side of her life. She loved her husband very much; he was her own choice. His early death, in 1764, left her inconsolable but determined to bring up their children as she assumed he wanted. The decisions were now all hers: she soon took over the trusteeship of the estate, paying off all outstanding debts in five years:

> Had I been told before my marriage that, accustomed as I was to luxury and expense, I should be capable, after becoming a widow at twenty, of stinting myself for several years of everything save the simplest clothes, I should never have believed it. But I wanted to be as good a steward of my children's property as I was their governess and their sick-nurse, and no price was too high. (P. 112)

Dashkova's children were born soon after her marriage. Parallel to her mention of court intrigues and palace revolts is the memory of the room her small daughter occupied. These transitions do not seem sharp in the *Memoirs*. Dashkova continually passes from the court to the home, from famous people to her friends, from high administration to estate and household management. Personalities must be dealt with and arrangements made on both sides of the ledger.

In her career as courtier, Dashkova knew when to feign ignorance, as on the occasion when Peter III tried to get her support in his plan to divorce Catherine in order to marry Dashkova's sister. "On this occasion I pretended not to understand what the Emperor had said, and hastened to take part in a game of *campis*" (P. 46), she remarks. Dashkova multiplies examples of Peter III's malevolent stupidity, and plotting against him increasingly occupies her time:

I continued to visit my family as frequently as ever and, during post days, was fully occupied writing voluminous letters . . . during the rest of the week I spent the entire time, except the few hours needed for sleep, working out my plans and reading everything that had ever been written on the subject of revolution . . . (P. 59)

These multiple activities usually result, in the *Memoirs*, in a breakdown of health from which Dashkova always recovers. A leitmotif of illness and depression, nerves and mental agitation, ripples across the events and the dialogue. Sometimes the causes are major, as when her husband dies: "I contemplated the future through a shroud of death" (P. 110). Sometimes the depressive times are recuperative, leading to a kind of gathering of female strength against male enemies, like the hated Prince Gregory Orlov or Paul I. The theme of recovery—from political and maternal setbacks—is a persistent one.

Just before Catherine's coronation, Dashkova's son dies—the only time this particular child is mentioned. But her surviving daughter and son preoccupy her into her old age. Motherhood, a theme conveyed largely in terms of duty, seems to bring her little peace or rewards. Still, her travels, ostensibly on behalf of her son, further her own education and her international renown. The first trip she undertakes with both children, to Kiev, deepens her knowledge of Russian culture and she writes defensively: "learning had traveled from Greece to Kiev much earlier than it had to many a European nation now so quick to saddle the Russians with the name of barbarians"(P. 114).

Her two trips abroad feature prominently in her *Memoirs*. They parallel an estrangement from the court that she underplays. The first, in 1770, inaugurated her friendship with an Englishwoman, Mrs. Hamilton, to which she accords an importance even greater than her meetings with the most famous men of her time. She had four long meetings with Diderot, lasting from five in the afternoon to midnight. She claims to have refuted all his most cherished ideas with her more conservative arguments about freedom having to be preceded by enlightenment: "When the lower classes of my fellow citizens become more enlightened they will deserve to be free,"she claims, and supports her argument with a long metaphorical analogy (P. 123). Dashkova, thus, relates more of what she says to Diderot than vice versa. Less is said of her meeting with the ailing Voltaire. In several places, reflecting an aristocratic view of things, she calls Rousseau eloquent, but dangerous. Upon her return she gives Catherine a painting by the most famous woman artist of the day, Angelica Kauffmann, who was not yet known in Russia.

Her second trip to Europe was more extensive (1775–1782) and had as its purpose the education of her son at Edinburgh University. Dashkova wanted a Scottish education for her son; achieving and supervising this goal, she played the role of both father and mother to him. She lived in Scotland for several years,[18] a period she characterized as "entirely outside myself—that is, wholly for others and for the sake of my love for my children" (P. 147). When she meets the Queen of England in 1780, they exchange compliments on their respective excellence as mothers: " 'I have always known,' said the Queen, 'that there are few mothers like you' " (P. 151).

But Dashkova made a serious error as a mother and, although it may have seemed more normal in her time to educate a son and marry off a daughter, Dashkova did so with blatant and contrasting haste. In her own words:

> I married my daughter off to Brigadier Shcherbinin . . . who had a melancholy though gentle disposition. Thanks to a certain physical defect, she was not yet fully developed and I could not expect a younger and more dashing husband to remain loving and submissive. The consideration that decided me on this marriage was the nine, or perhaps ten, years that my son's classical and university education abroad would take. It may not have been the best I could have wished for my daughter, but at least it offered me the inestimable advantage of having her with me and being able to keep an eye on her while she was so young. (P. 142)

By giving her daughter little education and a loveless marriage, Dashkova denied her the things she herself had cherished in her own early life. Almost predictably, her son would later disappoint her, by marrying a shopkeeper's daughter and asking for his mother's consent after the fact. Her daughter grew somewhat closer to her, but is mentioned largely in connection with her habit of contracting debts which had to be paid by Dashkova.

Dashkova's failure to remain close to her children must be seen in the light of her mentioning them at all, since most autobiographies of prominent male figures say nothing at all of their offspring. Certainly the recurrence in Dashkova's *Memoirs* of protestations of her keenly-felt obligations as a parent (misguided or not) distinguish her autobiography from those of eighteenth-century men of civic and literary prominence like Benjamin Franklin (whom Dashkova met in Paris in 1780), and Gavril Derzhavin (1743–1816). Derzhavin's memoirs concentrate entirely on his service career and are unified by a tone of what one critic calls "boundless self-certainty."[19] Dashkova, too, has remarkable self-confidence, and she exhibits the same tendency as Derzhavin to divide her world into friends and enemies. Nevertheless, her dual definition of herself as stateswoman and mother gives a dimension to her writings lacking in male autobiography.

Dashkova could well have merely catalogued her achievements on behalf of her country. The second (and briefer) part of her *Memoirs* begins with her arrival in Petersburg in 1782. Catherine makes her son a junior captain in the Guards and gives Dashkova property and 2,500 peasants (167 fewer in actuality, as Dashkova points out) as well as a house in town. Then, at a palace ball, the ruler tells Dashkova that she wishes to appoint her director of the Academy of Sciences. Dashkova protests "that God himself, by creating me a woman, had exempted me from accepting [such] employment" (P. 204), but she does accept and devotes several (but proportionately few) pages to her services to the Academy. She is an active administrator, immediately and successfully occupying herself with the finances of the Academy, which the previous director had neglected. Soon afterwards, in 1783, she presents a plan to Catherine for a Russian Academy. It is approved by Catherine, and Dashkova thus becomes the head of two academies and the founder of one. She holds these offices until dismissed from them by Paul I in 1796. Her achievements are more than administrative: she contributes to the preparation of the first Academy dictionary of the Russian language by collecting words under three letters of the alphabet. She was also asked to define words "bearing upon morals, politics and government" (P. 235), words like "friendship."

Dashkova is indeed more interested in morals than the Russian court of the time would have required. Her enemies knew how to cause her outrage, as when Prince Orlov, himself Catherine's ex-lover, tells her son that he would be a good candidate to become Catherine's next favorite. Dashkova constantly averts her glance from her ruler's private life. She describes herself as a "simple, unaffected woman" (P. 159) and maintains that she eschews frivolity of all kinds—from powdering her face in the fashion of the day to living in high style. She seeks isolation in the country in 1785, even before it is thrust upon her by Paul. She describes her favorite estate, Troitskoe, as the fruit of her labors and supervision. She attests to the prosperity of her peasants by the increase in the number of women, "whom we never reckon in our calculations" (P. 254), since none wanted to marry outside the property. After Catherine's death in 1796, Paul eventually exiles her to an estate of her son's in Novgorod Province, where she had never even visited previously. She mentions several women as comforting friends in her most extreme months of grief. But the best friends of her later years are sent to her by another woman friend from England. They are the two Wilmot sisters, Martha and, later, Catherine. Martha persuaded Dashkova to write the *Memoirs* and eventually smuggled them out of Russia to England.[20]

After Paul dies in 1801, Dashkova describes herself at Alexander I's coronation as "a simple old rustic" (P. 286). She sees Petersburg as a somewhat ridiculous masculinized society, full of "drill-sergeants, because from private to general every individual was occupied solely with the handling of arms"

(P. 287). The people around Alexander disparage Catherine and instill "in the young monarch the idea that a woman could never govern an Empire" (P. 286).

The last words of the *Memoirs* praise her two female friends, obscure and famous, Miss Wilmot ("I wrote these memoirs because she earnestly desired me to do so") and Catherine—"justly called the Great" (P. 288). They speak of "the intrigues and slanders of which I have been victim," and once again balance duty with a sensitive heart:

> . . . my heart was honest and my intentions pure and I was thus able to bear with bitter sorrows to which, but for the comfort of my own conscience, my excessive sensitivity would have made me succumb; and lastly, . . . I contemplate the approach of my own dissolution without fear or apprehension. (P. 289)

Fearlessness and determination indeed seem to be the predominant features of Dashkova's character. A ruthless maker of decisions, she nevertheless continually presents her initiative as a reaction to adverse circumstance or persuasion to take on responsibility. She underplays her decisiveness in favor of stressing a tender heart and a devotion to family duty. Duty fulfilled in solitude, the constant theme of her life both private and public, cuts a channel between the classical (duty-oriented, self-sacrificing) and the sentimental (meditative, emotionally self-pitying) streams of contemporary Russian literature.[21] Dashkova often uses the vocabulary of sentimentalism, from her early words about being lonely in childhood to those just quoted about her old age.

The feeling of isolation cultivated by the sentimentalists was real in the case of the young Dashkova. Acutely remembered in old age, it becomes a paradigm for her description of her entire life. Even when not physically in isolation, she felt so in her unique responsibilities as parent and stateswoman. Since her reaction to duty was to meet it squarely and fulfill it, her account of her life is, paradoxically, one both of an undiminished sense of loneliness and of incessant activity. Although she punctuates her story with accounts of depression, she is hardly a sentimentalist. Her bookish and solitary education and her identification with a ruler of her own gender (and name), whose cultural policy she supported, enabled her to achieve more in the public sphere than any other Russian woman ever has, without losing a womanly ideal of friendship with women or a sense of the complexities of motherhood. The themes of isolation, of female friendship, and of family responsibility will reappear in other autobiographies by Russian women. The mother and daughter relationship seen now from the side of the daughter is important enough to warrant a separate discussion.

# 6.

# MOTHERS AND DAUGHTERS

The mother-daughter relationship, which is often written about extensively in Russian women's autobiographies, has a complexity rarely found in works of fiction. The Russian novel, so rich in fathers and sons, has few mothers and daughters occupying center stage. Usually the mother is a figure of limited understanding, and her appearance in the novel is also limited. The scene between Natasha and her similarly intuitive, understanding mother in *War and Peace* is unique. More common is the failure to communicate. As the Turgenevian narrator remarks in chapter 5 of *Rudin*: "rare is the mother who understands her own daughter." The long monologue of Vera's mother in chapter 1 of Chernyshevsky's *What Is to Be Done?* ends with a plea to live by deception, in the old way, because the new order has not yet arrived. The words sound fairly human and believable, even though in Chernyshevskian terms they are heresy. Vera hates her mother (more, perhaps, than the reader does), and breaking with her is a prerequisite for a new life. This is a common pattern in fiction, which also traces the fate of daughters doomed to live like their manipulative mothers (as in Karolina Pavlova's *A Double Life*). In life, however, one historian has found that the radical female intelligentsia, at least of the 1870s, was characterized by strong mother-daughter ties.[1] In autobiographies of both the eighteenth and nineteenth centuries, daughters also write about mistakes of their mothers that damaged their own lives, but they do so with a far greater understanding than one may find in any work of fiction. Understanding one's mother is, for better or for worse, the preface to self-understanding in many Russian female autobiographies. To balance the positive account of radical women's relationships with their mothers, the three autobiographies presented here—those of Labzina, Vodovozova, and Durova—are chiefly of the "for worse" variety. In the case of Durova, self-definition proceeded from assuming the opposite identity from that of her mother.

The memoirs of Anna Evdokimovna Labzina (1758–1828), written in 1810, and those of Elizaveta Nikolaevna Vodovozova (1844–1923), published in 1911, are unusual in revealing painful intimate memories of the period of late childhood and early womanhood—in both cases the result of maternal impotence or negligence. Yet, neither of these women curses her mother; each has an understanding of the guesswork and pressing urgency involved in marrying off a daughter. In a later marriage she was allowed to choose for herself, each of the authors made up successfully for a dreadful past. Neither was unloved by her mother; rather the mother was helpless in protecting her daughter.

Labzina's memoirs cover the period 1763 to 1819. They begin with the death of her father when she was five and center on the results of her marriage at thirteen to a debauched man of twenty-eight. (He died in 1791 and her second marriage to a man eight years her junior was a happy one.) Her mother began to have visions that her late husband visited her in her room, and she refused to go out or speak to anyone, even her children, or else, she felt, her dead husband would no longer speak to her. She finally recovered from these delusions and became herself again, but died a few years later. Labzina's love for her was equaled by that for her nurse; in nearly all Russian gentry families the nurse was closer to the child than were the parents, and the inevitable separation from her caused great pain. In this case Labzina's marriage when still a child (but a cautious and forceful one) brought on separation from both beloved women. Her mother, who was then dying, married her to what seemed an intellectual and charming man, so that she would be cared for. The future mother-in-law was her friend, but she too proved powerless against the conjugal rights of her son. Labzina's account of her fears and their realization is punctuated by words of advice from female relatives that have a common theme: suffer in silence. On the day of the wedding her mother told her: "Even if he were evil to you, you should bear it patiently and please him, and complain to no one: people will not help you, and you will only advertise his vices and bring shame upon him and yourself."[2]

After that Labzina described her life as one of successive separations: from her mother, who dies shortly after her marriage, from her nurse and relatives, and from Russia as her husband decides to pursue a career in Siberia. Every decision is made by him. He finally begins philandering with other women in the same house (this, we remember, was what caused Dolly's outrage in *Anna Karenina*, when all else had to be tolerated), and even within his wife's hearing. Finally, he asks her to have a child by another man (selected by him, of course, so honor could be maintained secretly). She tells him she has reached the limit of her obedience with that suggestion. Between the lines of the narrative we hear outrage, silent protest, and the seizing of small opportunities for companionship rather than acceptance of humiliation. There is a sense of her own self-worth that never fails Labzina: the very act of writing pages that dwell on misery testifies to an ability to confront shame and horror. The entire autobiography of some one hundred pages, broken off in the middle of a sentence, consists of this confrontation.

Elizaveta Vodovozova's sizable memoirs (published in 1911) have frequently been cited as social history, for she herself points to the social significance of her life. Vodovozova became a writer for children and on pedagogy, was married twice, and was a member of Petersburg populist circles. Her first article, written in 1863, was entitled "What Hinders Women's Independence?" and constituted an answer to *What Is to Be Done?* The family ties she describes in part I of her autobiography, *At the Dawn of Life*, give a female child's vision of her life from the point of view of the grown woman's professional interest and detachment. The narrative distance does not, however, diminish the remembered feeling.

Part I begins with her childhood in the country in the late 1840s and early 1850s. The second part describes life at the Smolny Institute, that exclusive boarding school for girls. Part III describes the fervor of the 1860s. Vodovozova continually demonstrates awareness of social institutions and classes and how they function; nevertheless, she too goes back to the life of her mother and even her mother's childhood as it was told to her for fuller understanding. The first section of her autobiography details the suffering caused by the socially prescribed willful blindness of women to each other's fates and to horrors within the family when its absolute ruler is a male whose behavior borders on or crosses the border of tyrannical mania.

She begins with the story of her mother, whose own father had been remarried to a woman only four years older than his daughter while she was away at school. A natural, intimate friendship developed between the two young women out of sight of the older man who, when he discovered it, insisted angrily that relations between them be the extremely formal ones of upper-class stepmother and stepdaughter. When the young stepmother is almost beaten by her husband, she blames herself: "I was obligated to bring you closer to your father and myself stand closer to my husband's heart, restraining my own feelings. . . ."[3] After her stepdaughter's marriage, the unhappy woman begged to be sent to a nunnery. Instead, she was beaten and exiled to a remote village surrounded by swampland where she died six years later at the age of twenty-eight. She was afraid to see Vodovozova's mother, fearing even worse punishment. Vodovozova draws the conclusion from this story that upper-class women were no better off than serfs.

Vodovozova recalls hearing her mother say "Let her die" when she was ill during a cholera epidemic and describes how she can still feel pain at those words even though she now understands that they were produced by a great fear of another death in the family. Vodovozova's brothers and sisters grew up living separate lives, while their mother, widowed and responsible for the estate, was in the fields soon after sunrise and saw her children only at dinnertime. There was a beloved nurse who acted as mother, but the real mother made the decisions. One of these was to marry one of her daughters to a madman who physically and psychologically tortured both his wife and Vodovozova (then a child). The family shame remained hidden, like the scars on the sister's body. "No one harms each other as much, no one carries in their hearts such deep scars as people tied to one another by blood and a feeling of love."[4]

The estrangement from family at the Smolny Institute, where bedwetting was punished by tying the wet sheet around the girl's neck for the next day, and where hunger and cold prevailed, caused another permanent scar in Vodovozova's soul. At the end of her memoirs she returns to her family just as her mother gives all the inheritance to her favorite son, leaving her other son and her three daughters with nothing. There is no sense of abandonment by any mother of a daughter in a Russian novel as cruel and as developed as the one that exists in parts of Vodovozova's memoirs. The mother, nevertheless, supported her daughter's aspirations, and was a wholehearted advocate of women's equality. Her shouldered responsibilities, however miscarried, set an example for Vodovozova's life.

Our next writer chose the most unconventional life of all—in part to escape her mother's destiny. Nadezhda Durova (1783–1866) decided to live part of her life as a man in male company. She changed identity completely, sloughing off a skin in which she had felt uncomfortable throughout her childhood, adolescence, and young womanhood. Her memoirs tell both of the painfulness of being forced into the world of ordinary womanhood and of the escape into the rigors of military life during the Napoleonic wars, whence she emerged triumphant and proud, only to find relative defeat in the salons of Petersburg, where she was treated as an interesting freak until people lost interest in her. Even now her memoirs which originally appeared in 1836 are published in Russian only in excerpts,[5] although they present a fascinating picture of childhood, of battle conditions, and of a grown woman in perpetual masquerade as a young man. If Durova is referred to at all, it is usually as a minor writer of short stories, in whom the great Russian poet Aleksandr Pushkin briefly took an interest.

Her unusual activities began in September, 1806, when she donned men's clothes, fled from her parents' home and joined a Cossack troop which was stationed in the area and about to move West. Durova became a professional soldier, calling herself by a man's name (Aleksandrov; in Russian, women's names end in -a), and fought through the Prussian campaign. In the War of 1812 she was wounded at Borodino and then became orderly to Field Marshal

Kutuzov, retiring in 1816. She had served in the cavalry all these years and was awarded medals for bravery and for saving officers' lives on two occasions.

Durova/Aleksandrov lived the next fifty years of her life in the provinces, in Sarapul and Yelabuga, except for a stay in Petersburg in 1836–37, to arrange for publication of her memoirs. There she was briefly lionized and eventually ignored, a sort of amusing oddity in men's clothing. She referred to herself in masculine grammatical forms. These are more pervasive in Russian than in English; all verbs in the past tense, for example, show the gender of the speaker. Later, she tried writing fiction as a profession, and saw her collected works in four volumes published during her lifetime (*Povesti i rasskazy*, St Petersburg, 1839). Pushkin admired and published her, and Belinsky and other critics wrote articles about her. Her short stories, novellas, and one novel form a minor part of the literature of the 1830s, but after 1840 she wrote nothing at all except for an article on Russian women in 1858. It was never published but was partly described and quoted in the introduction to the 1979 Kazan' edition of her memoirs. In it she urges the women of her time, bored and inactive, to take up active labor for the sake of their country. Her own feminine childhood education, so unsuited to her true nature, seems to have convinced her that women should seek the opposite of the decorative domesticity they were being trained for.

In her memoirs, Durova makes a significant contribution not only to Russian letters, but to our understanding of what women might have been capable of historically had the military life not been off-bounds to them. They also demonstrate that the peculiar middle to upper middle-class domestic upbringing of girls constituted perhaps a greater perversion of natural capabilities than a freer, more active life. Durova dichotomizes her perception of the free, masculine world of her father and the restricted petty world of her mother. Her choice of the former seems inevitable, even though it had to be made in disguise.

She asked that her book of memoirs be published under the pseudonym "A Russian Amazon, known by the name of Aleksandrov." The separate book edition which appeared after the periodical publication carried the heading: "The Cavalry-Maid: It Happened in Russia" and had no author's name at all. Soviet editions call the book *Notes of a Cavalry Maid*, the genre of *zapiski* or "notes" being one that crosscuts fiction (like Turgenev's *Notes of a Huntsman*) and reality. It implies casual writing, but often the literary finish is high. In her memoirs Durova describes first her childhood and then her military service. There are numerous accounts by men of the 1812 war; they almost form a separate genre. And, of course, descriptions of battle from Tolstoy to Babel' in Russia have their narrators detail the dirt, fatigue, horror, and bravura of war. Durova's account is no different because she is a woman; in fact, she underplays this aspect, thinking of herself completely in her role as a younger male, daring but less hardened. She does use feminine grammatical forms throughout. From her childhood as a girl to her military activities as a man, she is the same person. That fact forms the central interest of her writings.

Durova describes her childhood as tense with frustration at being forced into a woman's role when she wanted to be a man. Her effort of understanding herself involves trying to understand a mother whose difficult female life made her try to impose the same sort of life on her daughter, the oldest sort of parent-child tragedy. The mother had run away from her own despotic parent, her father, to marry her husband. "My mother's deed . . . was so contrary to the patriarchal customs of Little Russia [i.e., the Ukraine] that my grandfather in the first flush of anger laid a curse on his daughter." According to Durova's account of things (which must have been told to her either by her mother or others) her mother dreamed of having a son:

> My mother passionately wanted a son and all through her pregnancy indulged in the most seductive daydreams; she would say: "I will give birth to a son, handsome as a cherub! I will call him Modest, will nurse him myself, will bring him up, and my son, my dear Modest, will be the consolation of my whole life . . ."

Durova was rejected at birth: "Mother pushed me from her lap and turned to the wall."

Durova describes herself as masculine in looks even as a newborn baby— large, with thick black hair and a loud cry. From the outset all her self-descriptions are teleological: she was made by nature to be a man, a military man. She refused the maternal breast. In one most telling incident, her mother threw her from a moving carriage when she had a crying fit, and the baby was rescued by hussars and carried home in her father's saddle. Her rejection by the enclosed sedentary women's world and her miraculous rescue by males who then nurtured and protected her began at infancy. Her father, according to her account, refused to give her back to her mother for a while. His fellow hussars seated her on their horses and gave her their pistols and swords to play with. Durova calls this early experience the root of her passion for the free and military life.

Periodically, however, her mother's world would reassert itself. She would force her daughter to embroider or make lace, sitting indoors for hours. This was less as punishment than as instruction in femininity: her mother, despising her daughter's hussar upbringing, "would sooner have seen me dead than with such tendencies." At ten, Durova was already hatching plans for escape. She learned to appear outwardly submissive, saying she feared nothing except her mother's anger. But parallel to her submissive life, she not only imagined but acted upon her escape. Her father had bought a horse named Alkid whom Durova loved, fed and tamed. At night she would steal out to ride him, and it was this horse that she used for her escape, keeping him throughout her military life until his death.

The outdoor world, the world of night, the world of the sex to which she was not born became the subject of her most intense descriptions. She writes that, had her mother not shown her the worst of the female world, she might have been different. She also writes of an attachment to a young man whose family broke off their relations because she was dowerless. She does not write of her actual marriage and the birth of a son. In fact, Durova ran away from her parental home when she was older (she falsifies her birth date by five years) and had first run away from her husband and child. Do these omissions make her story more romantic? Certainly in all girl-and-horse stories, those adventure tales so perennially popular with young girls, the heroine is always young, an "appropriate" time for adventure. Later, she grows up. Durova wanted adventure as a way of life, when she was already mature. Her memoirs are the ultimate girl-and-horse story.

> With each day I became bolder and more enterprising, and, except for the wrath of my mother, I feared nothing on earth. It seemed very strange that girls my age were afraid to be left alone in the dark; I myself was ready to go out in the depths of midnight to the cemetery, the woods, into an empty house, to a cave, underground.

Durova shows understanding for her mother even as—or perhaps because—she chooses the opposite of her mother's life. The daughter's sympathy begins unmistakably to assert itself when she finds that her beloved father was maintaining another household with a younger woman. Her mother, thus, "was fated to be deceived in all her expectations and drink the cup of bitterness to the dregs." Her mother falls ill as her father goes from one woman to the next, and she dies at the age of thirty-five. Durova blames herself for being the earliest reason for her mother's decline, and comments: "even her unusual beauty did not save her." Durova considered herself ugly, the opposite of her mother in everything, and even this becomes a saving feature of her destiny.

When she was sixteen, her father began to treat Durova like a son, giving her a Cossack outfit and his horse Alkid. "He said that I was the living image of his youthful years and that I would have been the support of his old age and the honor of his name had I been a boy." Durova was determined "to become a soldier, to be a son to my father and forever to separate myself from that sex whose lot and eternal dependency were beginning to terrify me." Yet she feared her mother's curse and her father's sorrow when she actually took the step of escaping.

The sections of her memoirs dealing with her military campaign were concerned not with the establishment of her identity, but rather with its fulfillment through a disguise that became her real self. "I was certain that it wouldn't come into anyone's head to have suspicions about my sex." Apparently at first it did not. It is difficult to believe the story the author maintains—that throughout her military career she was taken for a very young man from the gentry who had left his father's house without his knowledge or permission, a young man who had never tasted wine or sat in a stuffy room in an inn "smoking pipes from morning until evening, playing cards, and talking nonsense" like the other officers. Durova admits to being teased for girlishness, but never to being discovered. The only contradictory accounts were written *after* the fact of her self-disclosure. Denis Davydov, the poet of the war of 1812, wrote to Pushkin on August 10, 1836, that he had met Aleksandrov during the war and that there existed a light-hearted rumor that he was a woman. He remembers Aleksandrov avoiding society as much as possible. Indeed, male forms of off-duty relaxation seemed to present a more trying ordeal for Durova than actual battle conditions.

The memoirs give few place names or dates. One section begins: "*Grodno*. I am alone, completely alone! I am living in a district tavern." An uhlan teaches her to use heavy weapons each morning, to whirl a pike or sabre above her head. She is given a greatcoat and silk epaulettes. Finally she begins to feel like a soldier and rejoices in the feeling; but she has not yet experienced war, only the freedom of being outdoors and living alone.

The next section is dated May 22, 1807, *Gutstadt*, and it describes her first cavalry battle, during which she saves the life of a wounded officer of the Finnish dragoons. On May 29 and 30, a shell explodes under her horse, who tries to rejoin what turns out to be a regiment of corpses. She experiences extremes of hunger, fatigue, and cold. Her limbs ache from sitting in the saddle for hours. "My eyes are open, but objects are transformed as if in a dream." Fear seems to be the least of her emotions, although she notices it in others: "I see many people white as sheets, I see how they bow when a shot flies past as if they could bend away from it." In June, 1807, half her regiment is killed.

Her notes on the War of 1812 are more apocryphal. She meets the commander-in-chief, Kutuzov, and there is extended dialogue between the two. Some of her descriptions prefigure those of Isaac Babel' in his *Red Cavalry*, written a century later. She is dragged by a horse while in a state of wakening sleep. She inadvertently falls asleep next to a corpse.

A practical sense of survival, of maintaining her own bodily integrity and privacy, informs the account of her military life. Two examples, translated by Mary Zirin, occur in chapter 8:

> I honestly never thought to find a use for the two winecups of liquor that are distributed every day to us as well as the soldiers. But obviously nothing should be disdained. Yesterday, passing through a hamlet, our squadron had to cross a narrow dike. The leading detachment met an obstruction of some kind and brought the squadron to a halt; others, still coming on, jostled us from the rear, and our horses, jostling and bracing themselves to keep from falling into the wide trenches bordering the dike, became frantic and began kicking and rearing. In this chaos I was pressed into the middle of my platoon and so squeezed that, although I could see that the horse standing in front of me had every intention of striking me with his well-shod hoof, I was powerless to do anything except anticipate and suffer the blow with courage. The sharp pain brought a gasp from the depths of my soul! The worthless horse had both the will and the opportunity to smash my leg to bits, because I was caught as if in a vise. Fortunately, as he made ready to repeat the blow, the squadron began to move and order was restored.
>
> When we made camp, I examined my leg. I was horrified: it was bruised, bloody, and swollen, and it ached unbearably from the sole to the knee. For the first time in my life I would have been glad to get into a carriage; riding was torment, but I had no choice except to bear it. We have had no vehicles for a long time. Now the liquor has proved itself useful. Every day I wash my sore leg with it and every day, to my alarm, I see it turning a darker purple, although the pain is diminishing. The foot of the injured leg has become as black as coal. I am afraid to look at it, and I cannot understand why the foot has turned black when the blow was midway between it and my knee. Kornilovich, our regimental doctor, says that my leg should be amputated. What nonsense!

From stoicism to relief a few pages later:

> We are still standing in the hemp. The weather is insupportably hot. Captain Podjampolsy asked me if I would like to bathe and, when I replied that I would like it very much, he ordered me to take command of fourteen uhlans he was sending to fetch water from a nearby river, which is also not far from the fighting. "It will give you a chance to bathe," said the captain. "Be careful, though. The enemy is nearby."
>
> "Why aren't we fighting them then?" I asked, dismounting from my horse for the walk to the river.
>
> "As if we can all fight! Just wait, you'll get your share. Be off now, make it quick! Yes, and please, Aleksandrov, watch out that your falcons don't fly away."
>
> I ordered the sergeant to lead the way, took up the rear, and in that order conducted my men to the river. Leaving the uhlans to fill their pots with water, wash, drink, and refresh themselves as best they could, I walked half a verst upstream from them, undressed nimbly, and plunged with indescribable pleasure into the fresh, cold current. I could not revel in this bliss for

long, of course. After ten minutes I got out of the water and dressed even more rapidly than I had undressed, because new shots could be heard quite close to us. I led my refreshed and heartened men to bring the salubrious liquid to their comrades.

Occasionally, in all these years of being someone else who is really, in a deeper sense, herself, Durova finds her past image: once, a fellow-soldier tells her of his sister's unhappy, confined life. Durova remained happiest as an outsider. She lived in isolation, keeping the man's name she had given herself in 1806 for sixty more years, even insisting that her son call her by that name. She had loved what war could give her, for her alienation from death paled in significance before her alienation from being a conventional woman. She makes this alienation plausible in her memoirs; it was, after all, shared by many women who took less actively heroic remedies.

Sandra Gilbert writes of changing costumes as a different phenomenon for women and for men in the modernist tradition, a "utopian ceremonial androgyny whose purpose is very different from . . . ritual transvestism."[6] Durova was not a transvestite but rather a woman who preferred an uhlan jacket and an uhlan life to satin and feathers and a sedentary life. She created herself anew, not in the image of her mother but in the image of her father. Just as Dashkova disguised herself as a man to enter the palace, Durova took on a disguise to enter a space that would have been barred to her. All women autobiographers have a chance to create selves in words that compensate for what most perceive as a lack of experience in deeds. Durova did both.

# 7.

# THE EMERGING WRITER

O ur final three female autobiographers all exemplify eras of writing in Russia that were defined and dominated by male writers: realism, symbolism, and modernism. Yet all three rebel against male namings of these eras and against the image of the Russian heroine of her time incarnate in male-defined love and marriage. The provincial realist Sokhanskaia chooses not to marry, but to write. The woman made icon in her husband's poetry, Liubov' Blok, rebels against the dominant symbolist image of Woman and finds peace in widowhood. The modernist poet Tsvetaeva redefines the male myth of Pushkin by evaluating the true role of Pushkin's women in order to understand her own role as a major Russian poet of a different era. She too must come to terms with the stifled creative life and death of her mother in order to assess her own creativity.

Dashkova and Durova led an isolated life in the provinces after the heat of battles at court or at war; Nadezhda Sokhanskaia (1823–1884) did so without such preliminaries and for an entire lifetime. They were married briefly, Sokhanskaia never was. She led a life of independence on an utterly modest scale. She wrote stories under the pseudonym Kokhanovskaia, beginning in 1844 and into the 1870's. Her last collection was published in 1863. For a hundred years she has received virtually no critical attention for any of her writings. Sokhanskaia's autobiography was published only after her death, in 1896, in serialized journal form.[1] Of all the works we have discussed, it seems the most deserving of rescue from oblivion. It is the sort of unremarkable life that historians rarely notice, written in an arresting prose of which literary critics of the nineteenth century should take note. Sokhanskaia is one of the good writers who do not set out to dazzle or reveal hidden depth, but rather to find the meaning of life in its simplicity, where dramas which go unnoticed emerge as truly dramatic. Hers is an ordinary woman's life, the only difference being that she became a writer.

Sokhanskaia wrote her *Autobiography* in five chapters and a conclusion between June 26, 1847, and October 7, 1848, at the age of twenty-five. It takes the form of being addressed to someone in particular, and refers to this addressee, the man of letters Petr Aleksandrovich Pletnev, throughout.

Pletnev (1792–1865) was a friend of Pushkin and of Gogol'. He edited the leading journal *The Contemporary*, after Pushkin's death and until it was bought by Nekrasov in 1847. When he was no longer editor of the journal, he encouraged Sokhanskaia to write a short autobiography and, as she sent him one notebook after another, he was unstinting in his praise. He had set her to this exercise without any thought of publication. Her own laudatory interruptions to the text, in which she praises him, can be seen as an ironic commentary on their respective set roles. The author, a young woman of the provinces, has no particular claim on the attention of the great man of letters. Yet, she holds his attention by the quality of the writing. She gives a fascinating picture of her life, then disparages it: as a woman, she must remain modest; as a writer she knows better. For one thing, we learn in the course of the narrative that she was inspired to write stories precisely when she began reading the literary journals of the time and felt she herself could do better than half of what was in them.

A provincial girl, almost past marriageable age (though well-wishers might still try to marry her off), poor, but of the gentry class, living alone with her widowed mother and her maiden aunt for company, educated, but cut off from reading matter—this sounds like the heroine of a Victorian novel. Instead, she is the author of her own autobiography and she repeatedly answers the novelistic question of what will be her fate with an anti-novelistic answer: reader, she did not marry him. In fact, "he," the potential fiancé, plays an insignificant role in the autobiography of Nadezhda Sokhanskaia: the only significant characters besides herself are other women. In them the good and evil of human nature is sufficiently of interest to be brought to the reader's attention. The starring roles are reserved for the Russian steppe and for the author herself, as befits an autobiography. Her controlling sensibility guides all the reader's perceptions, both in its modesty of living and in its pride of authorship. Neither highly-placed, nor rich, nor acquainted with such people, Sokhanskaia is merely herself, made noteworthy by her ability to write of what was, even to her contemporaries, remote and somewhat mysterious—the lost Russia of the steppe, the backwater visited at best only occasionally by city-dwellers, and the female world which they inhabited only in childhood, if at all.

The only immodest quality of the autobiography derives from its author's relentless protestations of modesty. Informed by her culture that modesty is woman's chief virtue, Sokhanskaia realizes that writing anything, but above all an autobiography, is an act of paramount immodesty. We may assume that she uses the device of writing to a single person rather than to a reading public in part because women can and do write private letters. She states flatly on the last page: "a woman should not write." She calls writing "her fate," like God's will, a convenient resolution, a resignation both to fame and to oblivion that we see her prepared to accept throughout her life. But she does call the act of writing "artificial" and even dissociates her body from such an unclean practice: "I write something every day; but my hands never have even the slightest mark of ink. I would sooner allow them to be in muck and tar than in ink." Clean hands, a pure intent, female modesty ("[a woman's] first feeling and merit"), and the pretence of writing to one person only—these are the shields behind which the young woman stands; but the individual spirit she describes is, in fact, free of most convention and determined at a very young age to remain so.

The author's prehistory, the story of her parents, is presented exclusively in financial terms. Her father, Ukrainian and propertyless, was honest and therefore failed to provide an inheritance; her mother got sucked into the judicial system with a series of lawsuits, and Sokhanskaia does not even bother to explain the all too probable outcome, failure to win redress. She launches immediately into her first memory: she, her mother, and her aunt sitting at the table reading a fairy-tale. Growing up between two brothers (the younger one died in childhood), she enjoys active games rather than playing with dolls. (Throughout the autobiography the author stresses, without insisting, but much in the fashion of Durova, her nonmaternal impulses and her differentness from what was expected of girls.) Her early reading was neither encouraged nor discouraged: their library consisted of books other people no longer wanted and handed down. Bits of parental dialogue enliven the description of this haphazard reading habit. The family is presented as quaint but lovable, just what the nonprovincial reader would expect; but things change.

In the second part, the author has something to say, not just about her family but about a social institution, the institutes for young women, usually their only educational opportunity between home and marriage. She enters one at the age of ten, and she presents her life in the Kharkov Institute as being divided into two parts. The first she sees as a trial sent her by God. There is no other way to account for the brutality and gross injustice of her treatment. Power is concentrated in the hands of the directress, who rules despotically. She has her favorites, the daughters of the rich, who bribe her with presents of rugs and shawls, presumably learning the ways of their parents early. The children of poorer parents are mistreated in proportion to the favoritism shown the others. As penance for such crimes as smiling in class (called "immoralité, indépendence [or] la mauvaise conduite sans nom") they have to make two or three hundred deep bows, and if they falter, a few more are added. Pedagogy is a farce. If a lesson is not learned, bows or prayers are substituted—the ultimate use of "religion" to reinforce woman's place in an unjust social order. There are seven geography books and five arithmetic books for forty students, and the rich, who can buy textbooks and other supplies, are provided. Nadezhda learns her lessons by reading textbooks over the shoulders of her more fortunate classmates, who are placed in the front row as a sign of their goodness. As in schools for young ladies everywhere, decorum and posture are stressed—in French, which has phrases for such things as "vous ne tenez pas les pieds comme il faut." Such French expressions have provided generations of Russian writers with verbal acts of rebellion in Russian. Tolstoy was obsessed with "comme il faut." Tolstoy was given an education in other things besides decorum and foreign languages—young women were not.

Sokhanskaia learns to be, as the Russian proverb says, "tishe vody—nizhe travy," quieter than water, lower than the grass. Her basic stance of outward conformity and inner independence is the only possible one. There are only four free hours in the entire week. Tears and prayer give the only emotional outlets, and gradually even the comforts of a loving home are forgotten and the Institute becomes her only world. Sokhanskaia calls this "strange," but we may see it as part of the psychology of survival.

A few of the teachers, those who teach Russian subjects, are kind to this obviously good pupil and encourage her in her studies. In the second half of her "Institute life," as she calls it, the headmistress is deposed, and what Sokhanskaia considers the best time of her life begins: her independence and intelligence are rewarded and she begins to read literature as an equal with her teachers. A conservative story called "The Woman Writer" in a Russian journal, meant as a cautionary tale illustrating the dangers of writing, has the opposite effect: Sokhanskaia begins writing verses ("stishonki," as she disparagingly calls them). Women with the intelligence to read critically and rebel against what they read have, with some small encouragement from somewhere, always done so.

The rest of Sokhanskaia's life mostly takes place at home, and its theme is a monotony as overwhelming as that of the Institute, and hardship almost as intense, but also a boundless freedom within her own self and in nature that only her independent, unmarried status can ensure. This status is threatened periodically, but always ultimately retained, for the author is determined to keep it.

In the third section of the *Autobiography*, she is sixteen to seventeen and has just left the Institute, where she has lived for six years. It is a period of change and decisions, and she enters it with the expectations of youth, but describes those expectations with the cool voice of her older self: "It seemed to me that I would be either very happy or very unhappy, just one or the other, that is to say, the definite opposite of what was in store for me."

She endures a twenty-four hour journey from Kharkov; the "estate" is a hut in the fields, consisting of four rooms. In a digression, she enjoins writers about the gentry to see how the lower gentry live. There is a kind of pride and love for the house and its sand floors, on which the traces of her footsteps linger as they wouldn't on parquet. This is one of the images of her identity. Her whole autobiography asserts this identity in the midst of nothingness. Her first weeks are spent playing, like the child she could not be at school. And suddenly a letter arrives offering her a position as governess. The theme of so many Victorian novels asserts itself in life, from which it was drawn. A rich countess offers the girl seemingly her only way of making a living. But this is no novel, full of virtuous hardships ending in marriage or early death (or both). She writes to the family using the name of her mother (who seems to be a totally compliant figure throughout), asking if she will be free after lessons and have a room of her own. The answer is that governesses are always free: after lessons they walk with the children, share their games and spend the night in their rooms. "What other freedom could you possibly need?" replies the Countess. The offer is refused.

Later on, her aunt falls sick and dies in the next room. Perhaps they had not loved her enough. A lyrical digression follows, an extended metaphor which begins:

> Let life give, when it calls, what it has to give. It will give; it has to . . . I have opened my eyes wide to it . . . but, my God, how they wanted to be closed, in order not to see and not to hear, and not to feel my heart tremble! A shallow, dirty rivulet, and it didn't even flow, but crawled around me, clouding everything with silt, mire, ancient mould. So—is that the sea of life? And not one bit of spray, not one drop of living water, to splash on one's face, to fall like dew on the soul! Yes, it's more like a dead sea! And to plunge into that mud, drown in that deep place, like a sparrow up to its knees . . . I cannot, I cannot! . . .

This passage is typical of several digressions in the autobiography. They provide a commentary on the events which, being so few in number, could not otherwise make up a narrative in themselves. The reactions, ironical and lyrical, give a better idea of the life of these people, and especially of the inner life of the heroine, than any "events" could. In her world, every tree and shrub is familiar, and not even a wolf appears near the house to threaten the family of women.

Eventually, however, suitors appear, including an uhlan. There is a dance, which she compares to a bazaar at which young women are on display, one is chosen, and all the others scorned. She describes men metonymically as "the whole gathering of epaulettes and whiskers." She enters into dialogue with herself about whether she can really "love." Finally, she rejects a proposal of marriage by a man with money whose wife has died and left diamonds which she would acquire. She laments the fate of woman in traditional Russian proverbial cadences: "One sews a warm cap for winter; another takes it." She did not want to inherit another woman's goods. In the following paragraph she employs mocking rhythms to describe the man: "He's limp, he's old, he's silly too; he's just this side of stupid." She refuses him and incurs society's wrath for being "proud." She has seen the economics of marriage clearly and has found the norms of her society impossible to accept.

A position as governess or a marriage is typically the only option available to a penniless young woman. Rejecting them, she chooses a life of solitude and poverty in a house dark in winter on the steppe, which she often compares to her soul: a sad landscape, but one unlimited in its boundless freedom. The two people whom she describes at greatest length in the remaining chapters are both women. One is evil and the other good: Sokhanskaia sees their virtue in proportion to their noninterference with the freedom of others, most notably herself.

The first, Maria Ivanovna, is a rich recluse living on a beautiful well-managed estate, the empty rooms of which echo her footsteps "like thunder in the forest." She is a snob, but becomes attached to the author and wants her to live there, bribing her with a huge library. Maria Ivanovna takes any favor done her as her due, and the two proud women soon come into conflict.

At this time, Sokhanskaia begins to write, being dissatisfied with half of what she reads in the journals of the time. She reads her own writings to her brother, on visit from Kharkov, and he yawns. She sends her first story to an editor, who never replied to her letters, even after publishing her story!

Not earning enough as a writer, she accepts a post, paying twelve hundred rubles a year, as governess to a ten-year-old boy. On her return home, the job having ended, her house is completely destroyed in a terrible fire. She describes the confusion, fully aware that life exceeds anything she has described in her art. Her hopes for a separate room to write in, which was being built for her, are dashed, and her independence totally threatened. She finds refuge with another woman, the antithesis of Maria Ivanovna, who also lives alone. Anna Konstantinovna, with whom she lives for eight months without a single book or visitor, relieves the boredom and remoteness with kindness and three or four kinds of home-brewed vodka, drunk at a sitting with her maid Dunyasha, who gets very egalitarian treatment. This is the third all-female household we are shown in the *Autobiography*, one isolated by a combination of choice and circumstance.

The *Autobiography* concludes with the story of how the heroine becomes a writer for *The Contemporary*. Encouraged by the fact that they publish women authors, she writes to them. Letters, of course, take a month to arrive, and even trying to find a copy of the journal is a major undertaking, comically described.

In the final pages her interlocutor is invoked more often, and a self-conscious literariness begins to appear; for example, in the overdrawn description of a samovar, or the musing about how Gogol' would have made fun of her "tenderheartedness." We learn she is a vegetarian who smokes and drinks a lot of tea, a person who loves quiet and who cries a lot, but *to herself* (difficult when one is writing for an audience). She says she cannot tolerate the idea of getting married for marriage's sake and does not fear to utter the fateful words: *old maid.* She thus wards off all pity for herself. She has chosen her life. She gives a list of things she loves, which includes autumn and rain. Her writings give us the impression that her life is strongly centered, that her fatalism is a good rationalization for doing things as she wants, and that she totally identifies with the immediate world around her—less with people (though other women provide companionship) than with nature. Speaking of herself, she writes:

> She sees nothing ahead of her; but this is only distance and not darkness. . . .
> It is her steppe—the bright Ukrainian steppe: it stretches far away and its
> end cannot be seen; for the nearsighted there is nothing on it; but meanwhile
> it is all in bloom and shines modestly with the grace of heavenly dew and the
> rays of the great sun.

Being one with her immediate surroundings and finding writerly power in what appears to others as insignificant, Sokhanskaia symbolizes the life of the woman writer in obscurity by her own metaphor.

As far as we know, Dashkova, Durova, and Sokhanskaia led celibate lives for the time described in their memoirs, and this by choice. These women came from three different generations. Conveniently, they were each born forty years apart: in 1743, 1783, and 1823, respectively. Their lives represent a kind of female self that defined itself independently of a male partner. As an opposite extreme, it might be useful to examine the memoirs of Liubov' Blok (1881–1939). The wife and then the widow of a famous poet, the symbolist Aleksandr Blok, whose visions of woman, idealized and degraded by turns, influenced and epitomized the female image for an entire generation of Russians who used this poetry to rebel against what they saw as the materialism of their parents. Liubov' Blok's father, the internationally famous chemist Mendeleev, discovered the periodic table of elements. His daughter's name means "love" in Russian, and from the age of sixteen she was an object of intense poetic and life-symbolizing attention by her future husband, a young man already sure of his poetic vocation. His best friend, Andrei

Bely, equally talented, competed for her "love." Both wrote about her and used her as a testing ground for their poetic images of womanhood. Thus Liubov' Blok's memoirs (unpublished until the late 1970's) have the unusual task of defining a self already defined for the majority of Russia's reading public. They accomplish their goal in the face of these heavy odds by providing what previous memoirs lacked: an explicit account of the conflict between female and male sexuality, resulting in, at best, an uneasy partnership. The entrance of sex into Russian writing in the form of worshipful preeminence has been noted in the first part of this study in fin de siècle literature. Liubov' Blok's memoirs were thus very much of their time.

She gave them the title *What Happened and What Didn't (Byli i neby-litsy)*,[2] which refers to a series of columns published by Catherine the Great in the Academy periodical of 1783–84. Just as Catherine's reign as ruler had a record that she felt needed setting straight, so too Liubov' Blok's reign as the poet's wife had witnessed the creation of certain myths to the detriment of both her own reputation and her own sense of self. Her entire late childhood and early womanhood had been transposed into poems that were known to all of Russia's reading public. Though succeeded by images based on other women, the early pattern she had inspired remained the primary one: that of a pure vision of a woman who, as reality, impurely mocks the high ideals of the poet, who had awaited her, half fearing just such an inverse incarnation of his pure desire. The ideal and the reality, both in feminine guise, remained the dominant image of the poetry of Aleksandr Blok. Apparently this image also dominated his life.

Liubov' Blok's memoirs also have an achronological, spiraling structure. They return often to her main reason for writing: "If I should begin to write frankly, it won't come out the way the reader expects the memoirs of Blok's wife to be. That is how it has been my whole life." She feels her reader would want, as a prerequisite to her writing at all, an expression of unqualified devotion to the memory of her husband. She had been an object of devotion in his poetry, and in turn she should be devoted to him in his life, and beyond. The reality was not the same for her as for him. Her struggle to express her feelings to him during their courtship and their marriage seems to have been overpowered by his need to imagine her as she was not. He was persuasive: "I believed in Blok and not in myself; I lost my self." Yet she persisted, and her attempts to make her real self visible through the screen of a male-defined psycho-sexually poeticized interrelationship amounted to a feat of heroism within its limited arena. In her generation she was certainly not alone.

She describes her feelings and sensations as those she knows to be the emotions of all girls who are allowed to make the transition slowly from the hazy romantic images they have been presented with to their own bodily sensations. In spite of reading the somewhat risqué fiction of the day (she cites only male authors like Maupassant, Zola, and Loti) and catching glimpses of their brothers' pornographic photographs, they saw and understood "nothing except some anatomical strangenesses." As she explains, "A girl can read everything on earth, but if she is ignorant of the details of concrete physiological occurrences, she understands nothing and imagines unbelievable nonsense, as I well remember."

All autobiographers protest to the reader that they are speaking openly, often offensively so. In this case, the author is well aware of the taboos against frank discussion of female sexuality: "And I will speak of the sides of life which it is unacceptable to mention, knowing almost for certain that I will be accused of cynicism." The Russian word *tsinizm* has sexual connotations. In her memoirs she describes her adolescent awakening in the spring of 1901 in terms of a love for her own body as a link to the beauty of the world and to her own future:

> I spent hours in front of the mirror. Sometimes, late in the evening when everyone was asleep and I was still sitting at my toilette, arranging my hair in different ways or letting it fall, I took my ball gown, put it directly on my naked body and went into the drawing room to the large mirrors. I closed all the doors, lit the big chandelier, posed in front of the mirror and felt disappointed that one could not really appear this way at a ball. Then I threw off the gown and for a long, long time admired myself . . . thus, long before Duncan, I was already accustomed to the mastery of one's unclothed body, to the harmony of its poses, to sensing it in art, analogous to paintings and sculpture I had seen. Not the weapon of "temptation" and sin of our grandmothers and even mothers, but the best thing in myself that I could know and see, my link with the beauty of the world.

The image of the mirrored female self recurs in Akhmatova's poetry: it amounts to a repossession of her own body, the opposite of the male voyeurism in those fictional works discussed previously. Armed with her own developing sense of self, Liubov' was ready to confront life, aware that Petersburg sunsets, candle-lit churches, and imminent courtship might form the continuation of her own outwardly aestheticised inner sensuality.

It did not turn out that way. Her courtship with Blok on those streets and in those churches became instead a ritual involving male worship of a feminine image. Candles flickered before the image of her as woman, as they did before icons of the Virgin in church. She had become the "Beautiful Lady" of Blok's poetry. She protested that he was placing her "incomprehensibly high":

> You look at me as if I were some sort of abstract idea; . . . and because of

that fantastic fiction residing solely in your imagination, you have not noticed
or seen into me, a living human being with a living soul. . . .

These words are from a letter in which she attempts to break with Blok, a
letter that was never sent but was incorporated into her autobiography. Her
words evince full understanding, her actions were more conventional. She
began to assimilate herself into Blok's family and into Blok's ideas. She used
her sensuality to other ends: "the mysterious secret of long kisses insistently
awakened me to life, subordinated me, turned a powerfully proud virginal
independence to an enslaved female submissiveness." Such was the romantic
pornography of the daughters, a different unfreedom from their mothers, to
be sure. Lack of irony toward this assimilation causes Liubov' Blok to hold
the same unenlightened view of Chekhov's "Darling" that we saw in some
of his contemporary readers: "Chekhov makes fun of 'The Darling.' Is it
funny? Isn't it one of the wonders of nature, this capability of a woman's
soul to. . . find a new harmony?"

The inevitable history repeats itself. Feeling she has done her duty, the
woman is astounded at a continuation in the man of precisely those qualities
which had annoyed her most and at which she had protested either only to
herself or after the fact. She expresses annoyance at Blok's continued theo-
rizing after their marriage. Their sexual relationship is unsatisfactory to her:
she describes their encounters as "rare, brief, malely egotistical." She understands the causes as partly social: Blok had known only "paid love" and
had contracted venereal disease. He was never able to reconcile the two
kinds of women—wife and whore—his male social circles had contact with,
having first defined them. Liubov' Blok states that only one woman, his
"Carmen" (Liubov' Delmas, a dancer) "conquered all traumas and only with
her Blok achieved the desired synthesis of the one kind of love with the
other." For the author to penetrate this "region of silence," as she calls it,
is fairly remarkable. Her description of her real-life revenge is totally honest.
As Tolstoy outlined in "Kreutzer Sonata," women, defined by men, use this
definition with a vengeance. Defined as a goddess, Liubov' Blok used her
powers to seduce the man her husband respected most of all his contemporaries, his fellow poet, friend and passionate believer in "brotherly" relations, Andrei Bely. Thus she sought to confirm her view of herself and,
as she says, to gain her husband's attention by the kind of passionate interaction he worshipped her for being capable of, but refused to reciprocate
except (chiefly) by words. Blok "always grew completely indifferent as soon
as he saw me leaving him when some new infatuation occurred."

Liubov' Blok's attitude toward herself as a priestess of bodily self-expression also conflicted with the reality of her only pregnancy. She describes

with disgust the changes in her body: "With repulsion I saw how my body became monstrous, my small breasts coarsened, my stomach's skin stretched." After her baby son dies, she is happy with her recovery: "My son died, and not I." A few pages later, she regresses, as it were, into the tale of her own birth. Then, by another of the associative links that form the structure of her memoirs, she passes to a description of her husband's fear of aging, one far worse than hers. Blok

> very much liked and valued his looks; they were far from being the last joy of his life. When approximately one year before his illness he began imperceptibly to worsen, his hair to thin, he no longer stood quite so straight, his gaze was less clear, he would go up to the mirror bitterly and softly, as if literally not wishing to confirm by any sound what had happened, he would say in a half-whisper: "it's not the same, in trams no one looks at me any longer."

Blok was only forty-one when he died in 1921.

Liubov' and he seem to have reached some sort of reconciliation in later years. Towards the end of her memoir, Liubov' Blok expresses great affection for her dead husband. Significantly, the memoirs were written only after his death. During his lifetime she had a limited career as an actress, which failed because of the lack of determination she recognizes in herself. Even in this sphere, being married to Blok must have been something of which others were all too aware, for Liubov's memoirs claim proudly that she never used her husband's influence to advance her career and even reproaches herself for not having done so—the eternal conflict of retrospectively assessing choice between bad and worse.

Her own old age seems to have been her most peaceful time, for all such limited female "choices" had disappeared. She closes with an interesting discussion of "normalcy," based in part upon her reading of Freud:

> It was no coincidence that my basic good health was such a longed-for haven of inspiration to him. There is no hint of the pathological in me. If I have been at times hysterical and overly sensitive, the reason for that was the same as with all female hysteria: a sex life that from the outset was abnormal in the extreme. And the proof of the normalcy of my nature is that I painlessly made the transition to the state of being an old woman . . .

That Liubov' Blok refers to Freudian theory is most appropriate, for she is a woman of exactly the milieu (in another country) and the eager cast of mind that Freud knew and described. Freedom from sexual repression brought her little freedom from her basic dilemma: that of failed self-definition. Neither the scientific world of her father nor the poetic one of her husband could provide a proper home for a girlish self-image that would mature only in the solitude of widowhood. There, she describes her lodgings as "reflecting my soul . . . the walls are bright and do not limit space." To use the image with which she begins her memoirs, her function in the equation "the poet and his wife" had often equaled zero, "and since I had ceased to exist as a function, I went out of my mind into my own human existence." Perhaps in a different sense from the Decembrist wives and the widows of Stalinist terror, Liubov' Blok, hothouse creature that she is, should also be termed a survivor.

A final word about the female tradition of Russian autobiography should be written about Marina Tsvetaeva (1892–1941), who did not survive the political ordeals of her life, but who is arguably Russia's greatest modern writer. She will appear prominently at the end of our next section on poetry. One of the two or three greatest Russian poets, she took to writing prose especially in the last decade before her suicide, because it would sell and she needed to feed herself and her family. All of her prose is, in a sense, autobiographical; but in prose Tsvetaeva writes not of the pain of the instantaneous, present self as she does in poetry. She writes primarily of the past: her past family, her past friendships, and of past reactions to people— all stylistically transformed into the passionate subjectivity of the present. Our sense of the author's self comes to us directly through the style; there is no coherent exposition of a life-view as it developed, something we have found in other, nonmodernist autobiographies. Rather, the past is judged by a self already formed and in a uniquely acute tone of voice. The text itself becomes the only truth.

By choosing a style of highly-mannered subjectivism when *not* talking ostensibly about herself, Tsvetaeva is declaring her freedom from conventions of objective narration while still retaining the right to historicity (the family chronicle) and to critical judgment of her fellow poets. She establishes her own identity through her evaluations of other poets, as well as through her juxtaposition of self with family. She is alternately epigrammatic—as in her judgment of two symbolist poets: "All that is not Bal'mont is Briusov, and all that is not Briusov is Bal'mont"—and digressive, as we will see. Simulating anti-logic, she makes judgments whose logic then becomes inescapable.

Tsvetaeva's writings often concern women, those of her family and of the Moscow of the twenties. She describes a half-sister in a room of red plush, an aunt alone in a room after the revolution, and (like other women autobiographers) her mother:

> The mother. She was a mother to her son, not to her daughters. May her shade forgive me and may it see that first and last of all I do not judge.[3]

Later, in the same prose piece, *The House of Old Pimen*, she uses spatial imagery and the *softness* of masculine domination to describe her mother's marriage:

> Meanwhile life ever so gradually was reshaping the beautiful woman. When you know that never . . . nowhere . . . you begin to live right here. This way. You adapt to fit the enclosed space. What from the threshold seemed madness and arbitrariness becomes the measure of things—while the jailer, seeing submissiveness, softens a little, gives in a little, and there begins a monstrous alliance, but a real alliance of the prisoner with the jailer, of the unloving with the unloved, the molding *of her* in his image and likeness.[4]

In another memoir, called *Mother and Music*, Tsvetaeva traces the painful link between her mother's thwarted musicianship and her own poetry. She sees her mother buried alive inside her (an image she also uses in her poetry).

Tsvetaeva's most extended prose work the *Story about Sonechka* awaits detailed stylistic commentary and translation into English. Once again, a textual autobiography—describing the self as words used to describe an "other"—it takes the form of a digressive expression of love for another woman, a farewell to the Moscow of 1918–1919 and to youth. It was written in France in 1937 after her friend had died. Sonechka, an actress who could only act herself, becomes a facet of Tsvetaeva's personality: many of her friendships, male and female, explored the other and separated the I from the non-I. This exploration of self and other occurs in everything Tsvetaeva wrote: letters, memoirs, poetry.

Tsvetaeva's most important self-definition through prose, in memoir-criticism, comes (logically for the poet Tsvetaeva) in her various discussions of Aleksandr Pushkin. As a remembered child, she recalls her earliest memories of the poet. As a woman, she deals directly with the three women of the Pushkin myth: his unfaithful wife, his devoted nurse, and his most famous female creation. As a Russian poet, she must identify with her greatest predecessor; but, as a Russian woman poet, she must also separate Pushkin's maleness from his meaning as a poet.

Anna Akhmatova, when she wrote on Pushkin in his own city of Petersburg, took the scholarly path: holding her subject remote, she traced sources in his work and life. One of her posthumously published "remarks" about Pushkin contains the interesting idea: "How does 'Onegin' end? With Pushkin's marriage. The married Pushkin could still write Onegin's letter, but couldn't continue the love affair/novel."[5] But in her completed articles on Pushkin, Akhmatova rarely developed such insights. She begins one such article, called "The Death of Pushkin," with the following words:

> However strange it may seem, I belong with those Pushkinists who think that the theme of Pushkin's family tragedy should not be discussed. By keeping it off-bounds, we undoubtedly would be carrying out the will of the poet.[6]

Akhmatova is attracted by and to Pushkin's restraint. Tsvetaeva is attracted by and to the other side of Pushkin: his freedom. Tsvetaeva is not a Pushkinist, a scholar. In her prose she pays homage to Pushkin's selective attention to his ancestors as well as to his freedom to digress. Her prose style may be uniquely her own in its widened parentheses, which can occur at the level of the sentence or in the space of several pages. The fact of digression is eminently Pushkinian, creation following its own laws.

The most enormous detour taken by Tsvetaeva occurs in a 1929 essay about her contemporary, the artist Natal'ia Sergeevna Goncharova (1881–1962). It concerns Pushkin's name-associated wife, Natal'ia Nikolaevna Goncharova (the artist was her grandniece).[7] The digression is a radical departure from the tenor of the many either scholarly or *biographie romancée* versions of Pushkin's marriage to the "wrong woman," a central episode of the Pushkin myth. The myth is teleological: Pushkin was a great poet and died brutally and senselessly (although not as brutally and senselessly as Tsvetaeva was to die); therefore, the women in his life and art are part of a chain of circumstance, half-willed by him and leading to this finale. Usually the young flirtatious wife of Russia's greatest poet is blamed directly or indirectly for events leading to his duel and death. But Tsvetaeva shifts the blame to the older, experienced husband and to cosmic forces. Ironically included in the latter is the beauty of woman in its role as cosmic force to man.

The argument proceeds by analogy and contrast. Pushkin, having many women to choose from who read his poetry, married one who did not. Pushkin married Goncharova knowing more than she: "Pushkin, a man who had known many women, could not help but know more about Goncharova than Goncharova herself, who had never yet been in love . . ." "From the very start the blame is removed from Natal'ia Goncharova." Tsvetaeva stresses Goncharova's "apathy in giving birth, apathy in naming her children, apathy, very probably, in conceiving them." She was no more of a coquette than her contemporaries, only more beautiful. "There was only one thing about her: she was a beauty. Only a beauty, simply a beauty, without the corrective of mind, soul, heart, talent." Like Helen of Troy, she is a fatal woman. Tsvetaeva, in another parenthetical de-mythology, calls Helen "the pretext for, not the cause of, the Trojan war." War and marriage occur upon the initiative of men. Pushkin "wanted a cipher, for he himself was everything."[8] The idea of the death-wish pales before the physical attraction of matter to nonmatter that Tsvetaeva posits as the explanation for Pushkin choosing Goncharova.

In Tsvetaeva's notebooks of 1931, unpublished by her, is the kernel of all these reflections: she wrote that of all Pushkin's women she would most like to have been his nurse. "For Pushkin (like all his breed) scorned when he was a lover, respected when he was a friend, only he didn't scorn Goncharova (the notion of the wife!)."[9] Except for a separate category of "wife," notional rather than real, Pushkin denigrated women as a sexual (inferior) category. The only real closeness lay through friendship; and his best woman friend was his nurse. Pushkin's nurse, chronologically first in his affections, is our second woman of the Pushkin myth. Pushkin was reunited with his old nurse, a peasant woman who used to tell him fairy-tales, when he was exiled to his country estate in 1826. As a child, Tsvetaeva read one of the poems addressed to this old woman. In her fullest evocation of her feelings about Pushkin in childhood, "My Pushkin" (1936), Tsvetaeva gives us a set of composite images, of word and sound association that become a sort of memory bank of truth.

> Yes, what you know in childhood you know for a whole lifetime, but also: what you don't know in childhood you don't know for a whole lifetime.
>
> Of what I do know from childhood: Pushkin of all women on earth loved most his own nurse, who was a non-woman.[10]

The myth of Pushkin's devoted nurse who nourished his genius and enabled him to love humanity is given a peculiar twist here. The nurse is faithful, but she is not a woman—just as the wife was picked expressly to betray, while other women were rejected or not taken seriously.

The third woman of the Pushkin myth is the one wholly created by Pushkin: Tatiana in *Eugene Onegin*. The moment in the poem when Tatiana is rejected by Onegin, with its parallel at the end when she rejects his love, is crucial to the romantic myth of Pushkin.[11] Tsvetaeva describes her initial reaction to Tatiana as falling in love with love. She makes the personal observation that her own passion for unhappy, unreciprocated loves stemmed from that nonlove scene. But her major contribution to *Onegin* criticism lies in her Tatiana-oriented (female-oriented) interpretation of the ending, not as the virtuous married woman's rejection of the man she had loved in vain as a girl, but as the triumph of the mature woman "in the enchanted circle of her own loneliness in love,"[12] holding all the trumps in her hand without using them.

For Tsvetaeva as a poet, Pushkin meant not a golden mean to aspire to and emulate but a way of herself being free as a poet. This was true even when she translated his poetry into French in 1936, after most of her own had been written. That same year, in "My Pushkin," she writes of her feelings towards the Tatiana/Onegin relationship: "Neither then nor afterwards did I ever love when there was the kiss of greeting; always when there was the farewell of parting."[13] The self-knowledge about her own creativity in using the end of love is activated retrospectively by a literary myth: Tsvetaeva's *Poema kontsa* (*Poem of the End*) is her *Eugene Onegin*. Freedom from the clarity and harmony of Pushkin's poetry was never a problem for Tsvetaeva; what she had to reckon with was the life of Pushkin and his heroine whose perfection was a constant model for Russian girls. In her prose autobiography, Tsvetaeva revises the life of the poet Pushkin to account for the life of the poet Tsvetaeva. It is a crucial way for her to mark her place in the poetic tradition we shall discuss in the final section of this book.

Female autobiography, so neglected by critics as a mode of writing, forms a tradition in Russia that reacts both to life itself and to the fictional tradition of the heroinic either/or in male fiction. In autobiography, women review the significance of their own lives, usually after most of it has been lived, and they reshape its disappointments into the gains of experience. Their written lives have neither the terrifying finality of the doomed heroine who deviates nor the perfection of the young woman about to marry. By definition, autobiography is a survival story: while survival may include the harshest of exiles, extreme isolation, horrible marriages or even a change of identity, still the narrator's survival to tell her tale is the driving force behind the narrative. Even if she never sees it published, she has written her own reality and named it herself, countering the dominance of other seemingly more powerful namings.

# PART III.
# Women's Poetry in Russia

# 8.

# FROM FOLKLORE
# THROUGH THE NINETEENTH
# CENTURY

The strategy of self-naming by Russian women poets has a long but largely submerged history. While both prose fiction and prose auto-biography trace development of the character or the self in time, in lyric poetry time is compressed into an instant perception. Within the instant, the lyric "I" speaks to the reader/audience with an immediacy rarely felt in other forms. The confessional "I" of prose generally has a story to tell; but while some poetry is narrated, the lyric usually has no mediating voice to come between speaker and audience.

In the case of women's poetry in Russian, the "I" may be marked as female when a woman poet writes the poem. It is marked grammatically in the past tense, and by adjectives and nouns. Occasionally she may choose a masculine "I" and thus a more "neutral," customary form of address; this happens infrequently, but with greater frequency than its reverse, a male poet choosing a female persona. A male "I" is conventional; a female "I" is unusual. (Whether the male "I" used by a female poet is as unmarked as the male "I" used by a male poet poses a problem for which this binary distinction does not allow.)

The poems we will discuss all have as one of their prominent features a calculated use of the female persona. The female lyric "I" has never yet been traced through a body of Russian poetry. Naturally, the poets will have different ways of using this persona. Some reverse the I/you (male subject/female object) dominance of the male lyric. Akhmatova and Tsvetaeva do this powerfully, but with opposite tactics of withdrawal and aggressiveness in their personae. Other poets evoke different strategies for defining the "I." One recurring theme in nearly all the female poets we shall consider is that of the split (or divided, or mirrored) self. As with autobiographical writings by women, conflict is inherent in the text. These conflicts exist within the self, even if imposed from without. We shall also see warnings from the male

world, not unlike the either/or of male fiction; but, again, these male definitions are resisted, and self-definitions involving a less than "perfect" per-
sona/heroine dominate. An ultimate assertiveness exists in the very form of
the lyric: by condensing the conflict into a more demanding form, expression
itself triumphs.

The assertion that craft prevails, made as a direct statement by Pavlova,
Parnok and Tsvetaeva and indirectly by others, is a victory over male namings. It asserts that the poet is a woman. It puts the chisel into the hand of
the sculptress, words into her mind. Thus empowered, she can fashion a
restatement of the love themes, the nature imagery, the mythologies which
form the poetic material of generations of male poets. When these mythologies constitute warnings from the male world—admonitions to a coy mistress, spiteful words to a faithless one—women poets have the means of
direct, unmediated response to conventional warning. But, more important,
they have the terrible perfection of their own art—the power to name without
mediation, directly to define the self.

These resources of lyrical expression were given voice in folk poetry before
women became literate, and continued to be used in the late eighteenth
century when the male poetic tradition was formed in Russia. The first
recognized Russian woman poet, Anna Bunina, wrote in the early part of
the nineteenth century. Among her successors, few are known. Karolina
Pavlova, the most notable Russian woman poet of the nineteenth century,
has not been accorded the stature she deserves. Only in the early twentieth
century do Russian women poets emerge as acknowledged major figures.
But although critics of Russian literature have ignored the links of modern
women poets with their predecessors, such links exist, embedded in the
poetry itself and particularly in poems that name the state of being female
and a poet.

The beginning of Russian poetry's great male tradition is commemorated
by a series of hallowed gestures in which Russian poets pass on the laurel
wreath from one male brow to another. Derzhavin hears Pushkin in his
lyceum days and gives him his blessing. Zhukovsky, after reading Pushkin's
first long poem, bestows his portrait upon the younger poet with the in-
scription: "To the victorious pupil from the vanquished teacher." Lermontov
takes the wreath from the murdered Pushkin by writing "The Death of the
Poet" as a gesture of heroic homage.

The women poets of Russia have no such overt tradition of interconnection.
For the most part separated in their homes, not educated together at lyceums
or universities, having no links with the business world of art—literary journals read by women were owned and edited by men—they rarely met. Still,
they were not unaware of each other, and their references to one another

echo unmistakably across the decades: Pavlova challenges Rostopchina's politics in poetry; Tsvetaeva calls her earliest great collection of verse *Craft* (*Remeslo*) in homage to Pavlova's famous lines about her "holy craft," the writing of poetry. Indeed, the knowledge that such poetry had been written by women could only serve as incentive and inspiration.

There is more to what can be called the tradition of women's poetry than declared friendships, rivalries and influences. The very nature of the lyric, the use of the female "I," can be seen as a vehicle for writing about/by the female self. Poetry about the self is, of course, as much a rhetorical, public gesture as a metaphysical sermon or an epic narration. Formal rules govern the poetic utterance and the poet selects the tone and the image to produce a desired effect. When a woman poet chooses a female voice, a female narrator, an image or myth specific to the female condition, we may refer to a poem as the female lyric. Many we will discuss invoke other women— those whom Pavlova called "mute sisters of my soul"—as alter egos for whom and *with* whom they speak. Female isolation in the autobiographical "I" sought friendships with other women; the lyric female "I" seeks a choral response of other women's voices, if only implied.

The reader should not conclude that a female lyric voice is necessarily more *personally* marked than a specifically male one, or that the resulting poem is somehow more limited or restrictive when Tsvetaeva expresses sexual feelings in her poetry than when Pasternak does. If female readers can accept as plausible the speechless female "you" 's in Pasternak's poetry, then male readers should also be able to recognize the male "you" dominated and defined by Tsvetaeva's female "I."

What the female self requires, as opposed to what the world or her male addressee can provide or will let her have, forms the basis for a disjuncture in the view of both reality and the self in women poets. It does so differently from its obvious analogies in poetry by men. Women poets in Russia consistently attest to feeling alienated from their society not only as poets but also as women. Karolina Pavlova, in her mixed prose/poetic work, *A Double Life*, wrote in detail about the divided self in the person of a young woman deceived by those closest to her and finally severed from her own true voice, that of her poetic dreams. These dreams formed the poetry in her novel. Mirror images, split selves, female selves severed from the male "other" and invoking the other in the form of women—all form recurring patterns in the poetry of Russian women as they do in poetry by Americans like Dickinson and Plath, Sexton and Rich, or Canadians Hébert and Atwood: these patterns are common to female poetry in more than one country.

When did Russian women's poetry begin? The earliest women's poetry in Russia was part of the oral folk tradition. Women chanted and lamented together in the traditional wedding songs which preceded the actual wedding and mourned the young peasant girl's departure from her parental home to a less kind one, the home of her husband and his parents.[1] These songs are structurally typical of Slavic folk songs, with their nature images and their parallel phrasing (often as question and answer or negative statement and positive). Specific places are mentioned, varying imagery is used; but the consideration of the married state as one of some material gain but a basically harder life is a constant. These songs were sung regardless of the individual woman's feelings about her future husband, as part of collective wisdom and tradition. They survived until modernization and the advent of literacy. But their imagery and sentiments have some relation to the upper-class written tradition of the society tale in which marriage or love represents loss of freedom, of the self, of closeness to the natural (free) world. Lack of free will and even betrayal by those closest to the young woman are as inevitable as forces of nature:

> "Ah, mountain ash tree, mountain ash tree,
> My curly haired green darling of the garden,
> When did you sprout, when did you grow up?"
> "Ah, in the spring I sprouted, in the summer I grew up."
> "Ah, when did you grow up, when did you grow big?
> "Ah, I grew big in the precious sun
> The precious sun, and in the dawn."
> "Ah, when did you and why did you bend so early?"
> "Ah, it was not I who wanted to bend,
> It was the deep snows that bent me down,
> The deep snows and the wild winds."
> "Ah, maiden, maiden, why did you marry early?"
> "Ah, it was not I who married early
> But my lord and master who found me a husband,
> And my own mother said I should,
> Ah, my own sister said I should too,
> Ah, my own brothers said I should too,
> Ah, the first to say it was my dear friend Frosenka."[2]

In one song the wearing out of the girl's clothing stands metonymically for the violation of her body:

> "Father, don't make me get married,
> Don't feast your eyes on those high chambers,
> It's not chambers you have to live with, but a man,
> I won't go for dresses, but for wise advice.
> There's many a bright dress out drying on the pole,
> And lying crumpled on the bed,
> Don't make me take off my shoes and my clothes,
> I've no desire to submit yet awhile,

> To get my pretty back bent,
> To get my pretty hands dirty,
> To break my golden rings."

And always the collective experience of the song is stressed, even as the individual is abandoned to her fate:

> Now we'll go up, sisters, up the steep hill,
> Up that steep hill, sisters, in one line we'll go.
> And we'll see, won't we, sisters, if we're all together,
> Or if all our voices are still in tune.
> And we'll call, won't we, sisters, the sun's rising,
> The sun's rising, sisters, and freedom free.
> But tell me where that freedom free has wandered to?
> Freedom free has got tangled in the thick grass,
> Freedom free has got lost in the thick trees,
> Freedom free has got stuck in the black mud,
> Freedom free has been washed over by the rapid river.
> They've shut freedom free behind nine doors,
> They've locked freedom free behind nine locks.
> Sure, there'll be no freedom like with father,
> There'll be no kindness like with mother.

Freedom free, "vol'na volia" as the folk phrasing expressed it, had deeper implications than the merely political for the women poets of Russia. Their personal lives in the most specific sense would be determined by others. The act of writing poetry which explored the self no longer had any collective backing in a society where the sufferings of men in their more varied external world gained primary status. Still the woman's lyric emerged and continued in Russia—first as popular song[3] and later as poetry to be published under its author's own name.

Anna Bunina (1774–1829) was the first woman poet of note in Russia, and the first to support herself by her writing. Her mother had died when she was fourteen months old. She was self-educated and always poor. In 1802, against her relatives' wishes, she went to Petersburg to improve her lot. There she found the protection of Admiral Shishkov, was admitted to his literary circles. Bunina called her first book of verse *The Inexperienced Muse*, although she had begun to write poetry at the age of thirteen. Modesty was the only acceptable mode of self-preservation for a literary woman. Bunina wrote throughout her life, much of which was spent in grave illness. She died of breast cancer after a long and painful struggle. She allied herself with Russia's neoclassicists, Derzhavin being their inspiration, rather than with the newer sentimentalist trend as represented by Karamzin. (Curiously all the sentimentalists were men, discovering their capacity to feel, to love and to be melancholy, rather than women, exploiting what might have been seen as an innate capacity.) Her meditations on death contain not the slightest tinge of emotionalism. Usually, like the "Song of Death" (1812), they are abstract; but one, the remarkable "Sick Woman's May Outing" (1812), blends allegorical symbolism of the journey toward death with specificity of place and inner feeling.

"The Sick Woman's May Outing" ("Maiskaia progulka boliashchei") is composed of ten stanzas of unequal length, amounting to one hundred lines. The regular trochaic tetrameter reflects the outer decorum of a woman walking alone in spring near the banks of the Neva in Petersburg. The speaker immediately and throughout describes the acute pain of her illness in imagery of burning heat, hell (*ad*), and serpent's poison (*iad*). She calls upon God to help her, then tells herself: "Don't delude yourself with fantasies." Her home, her body, have "become repellent as a Tartar." Her perceptions proceed from her bodily sensations. Fleeing the sun, she seeks the shade and praises the beauty of nature. But the fire in her breast persists: "My hell is there, where I tread." She has no one who can help: "I am alone." Just as she comes to this realization, halfway through the poem, its only other human figure appears: another sufferer, an old beggar like a "shadow from the grave," begins to follow her everywhere. She gives him alms, repelled by him for he tells her God is merciful. "Old man, you vomit forth abuse!" she exclaims. "God has turned from me . . . evil is drawn toward me." In the next stanza she catalogs the beauties of the city gilded by the sun, all in vain for her: "I am not the daughter of this nature." In the penultimate stanza the wind from the Neva comes up and it grows cool. Since cool is a positive feature of the poem, the speaker calls for even more: for waves and thunder, and finally for the abyss to swallow her. This baroque imagery is always rooted in a real cry for relief from the burning pain. The final stanza ironically restores calm to the scene. The speaker disappears and we are left with quiet, a mirror-like sea and a cloudless sky: "And in the dark-blue pure firmament/The moon pompously floats by." The total calm of Petersburg's orderly beauty, undisturbed by violent elements, reinforces the alienation of the woman, herself unmentioned at the end, from her own life. The day has turned into night, and her progress is toward a slow death, since not even death has come to relieve her. Her estrangement from life— from the beggar (her fellow man), from the city and nature, even the violent elements, and from God—is total. The inner sickness (woman's body, the reality within it) and the outer, classically ordered world never clash; each exists in separate absoluteness.

A later poem of 1819, "On Parting," considers the paradox that separation, the image of death, is actually worse than death. Next to the words *razluka* (parting) and *smert'* (death), the word most frequently repeated is *minuta* (minute), distantly heralding the semantic fields of Tsvetaeva's poems of instantaneous unity and irrevocable separation: "The Letter" and "Minute."

As with Tsvetaeva, separate lines echo each other, shuffling the word-concepts, the first line of the final quatrain repeats the opening line of the poem:

> Parting is the image of fierce death,
> But death is a hundred times more evil!
> With every minute of existence
> You kill us a hundred times over!

Bunina's poetry is not fully represented in any modern edition. The third volume of the collection of poetry which appeared during her lifetime (*Sobranie stikhotvorenii*, 1819–1821) contains the amusing and pertinent "Conversation Between Me and Women" ("Razgovor Mezhdu Mnoiu i Zhenshchinami") in which a dialogue between the two wittily illustrates the predicament of the female author. The women ask her what she writes about. She answers: "the glorious feats of men." The women complain "and not a word about us!/ . . . why have you learned to write verses?/ . . . Or don't (men) have enough praisers of their own! Or do we have fewer virtues than they?" The poet replies—four lines in a row ending with the stressed syllable *-akh* (alas!)—that they are right, but that men, not they, sit in judgment when authors' wreaths are given out, "and authors' glory is in their hands."

Bunina had praised the excellence of Derzhavin, the finest poet of her age. Without any family, the first professional woman writer of Russia found her peers to be men and gratefully accepted their patronage. Her poetry does not strain at imitation of men: rather Bunina uses what she admired freely, adapting techniques of abstract poetic reasoning to fit her own personal seriousness and wit.

Women poets' words of counsel or explanation addressed to other women are often tinged with irony, stemming from awareness that the woman writer is beyond the pale of ordinary happiness. Anna Akhmatova's lyrics are frequently suffused with this combination of regret, resignation and compensatory pride, as we shall see in the following chapter. A poem of Nadezhda Teplova (1814–1848) called "Advice" (1837) is addressed to a girl, a younger self. It tells her that the poetic vocation is incompatible with happiness: "poetry is a dangerous gift for a girl."

Teplova is known (if at all) to critics as a poet of dreams and mysticism. The escape from earthly self is another frequent theme of many women poets. In the following poem of 1835, "Rebirth" ("Pererozhdenie"), a complete metamorphosis occurs. The flight into space is precisely motivated:

> Farewell, I'll fly away! In the immense distance,

Like morning mist, I'll disappear,
Invisible to the eye, incomprehensible to feeling,
Like the dark riddle of existence.

Your insignificant efforts are laughable,
You cannot reach me:
I'm lighter than air, I've been given wings,
I'm now completely different.

Look: like dust, my chains have fallen away
From this day on a happy fate is mine,—
I'll see the limitless steppes now
I'll cross the boundless ocean.

Farewell, I'll fly away! In its unutterable beauty
Before me are both heaven and the earth:
And much in life has become comprehensible to me,—
I'm now completely different.

Although many of the verbs are in the future tense, the poem's confidence
is based on a change that has already taken place. The poet is already another,
different woman (*drugaia*). The change to another self seems to have been
necessary to escape the "you" who is mentioned briefly. Concentration on
the new self is paramount: the poem's adjectives nearly all contain negative
prefixes or connotations, but they express a lack of the constraints that had
bound her life previously. Most form images of space stretching out, but
the only one which is repeated (*nepostizhima/postizhimo*, lines 3 and 15) has
to do with understanding. The escape from self brings self-comprehension.
The shifting into another self, conveyed through spatial imagery, will be
analyzed as an important feature of Akhmatova's poetry.

Russia's greatest nineteenth-century woman poet, Karolina Pavlova (1807–
1903), repeatedly used images of the self, embedding them in a body of
poetry whose varied themes and forms seem, at first reading, to disguise
the fact that a female self is present in them at all. Often her poems are
allegorical: the poet-craftsman is destroyed by society. Her most extensive
treatment of the feminine condition occurs in her novel *A Double Life*, a mixed
work of prose and poetry, sparing of words like her lyrics, but rich in a peculiarly
female irony, which specifically points to the shallowness of men.

Its heroine, about to be forced into an unhappy marriage, is powerless
and uncomprehending, "used to wearing her mind in a corset,"[4] and increasingly isolated even as she seemingly joins in a life full of the pleasures
of the very rich. Pavlova gives her heroine's soul an outlet in dreams which
occur in verse at the end of each chapter; but by the end of the novel it is
made clear that she will no longer be able to hear the voice of her inner

self. Pavlova has written here about another kind of woman, not a poet but the sort of woman to whom she dedicated the work:

> For you this work of solitude,
> Women, slaves to vanity.
>
> All of you Psyches without wings,
> Mute sisters of my soul!

Pavlova's longest poem about woman, "Quadrille" (1843–1859), has four women narrators who recount life stories of disillusionment, guilt and help-lessness. For Pavlova it is a given that women are not agents of their own destiny: her own life seemed evidence enough. Pavlova's deepest expression of woman's self, her own glimpses into the core of being, go beyond oppres-sion, beyond her own tragically accurate descriptions of women in society. She exchanges resignation and alienation for pride in the meticulousness of craft: the self as woman is remade into the self as woman-poet. As in a poem of September 1839, "Inspiration Has Her Favorites" ("Est' liubimtsy vdokh-novenii"), this is a secret self, not proclaiming its success blatantly, unlike the "mighty bards" who receive rewards and ecstatic comment. The woman poet is not a success. Like other young female friends who appear in a poem written in December of that year, "Da, mnogo bylo nas . . . ," Pavlova's persona is part of a group that no longer exists in the same way. The poem begins: "Yes, there were many of us, youthful female friends," and states categorically that every one has known hardship, "And calls that time unreal,/ And remembers herself, as if she were someone else." The theme of being stranger to one's own former self, which Pavlova asserts as a general condition of womanhood, is one that reappears in full force in the poetry of Anna Akhmatova. A poem of 1855, which begins "I love you, young girls;/I love the sadness of life's spring time" keeps asserting love and remembrance (the verb to remember is repeated in the second stanza anaphorically in three consecutive lines: "I remember . . . /We all remember . . . /We all remem-ber . . . "). But the final stanza turns from the past self, from the "ignorant Eves" who comprise the past selves of women:

> We, who today have insufficient strength
> To bear the present
> Are lowering the veil
> On everything that used to stir our souls,
> And whispering a quiet farewell!

Pavlova's persona often feels disgusted with her own past, trapped in the present and expecting no sympathy from people. In Russian, since the past tense of verbs is gender-marked, when three consecutive lines are dominated

by such verbs, their gender is also felt, as in the poem "O bylom, o pogibshem
. . . "

> The heart is oppressed by the wordless thought
> Of what's past, of what's perished, what's old;
> I have met with much evil in life,
> I have spent much emotion in vain,
> I have sacrificed much to no point.

The poem consists of four such five-line stanzas (Pavlova's verse forms are always classically balanced), but a final extended metaphor occupies the last seven lines, giving the poem's symmetry a counterweight. The speaker compares herself to a gambler who constantly plays and loses, as other fortunate people look on "with an avid, caustic stare" to see whether her luck will change.

One's own past as another state of being does not quite amount to alienation from a former self in Pavlova; rather it is good turned to evil: "Only at times I have a memory/Of my best dream, as if of evil." ("Proshlo spolna . . . ," 1855). Pavlova retains the instinct to take risks, to reach for something better. As expressed in an earlier poem ("V tolpe . . . ," 1845):

> Honor incomprehensible chance!
> He who seeks in vain is perhaps no poorer
> Than he who has found.

These lines would likely have appealed to the adventurous female romanticism of Marina Tsvetaeva. The poem's addressee is, if not another self, then certainly another woman; this woman is not free from that same pain which, the speaker claims, had mastered her in former years and which she still has not conquered.

One of Pavlova's most memorable alter egos is not a woman at all, but the lone figure of a miner in a poem narrated in the past tense, "The Miner" ("Rudokop," 1841). It is an allegory of isolation, in life and in death. The pensive figure of the protagonist, seeking treasure inside the earth, is cut off from the beauties of spring in the earth above. The voice in his dreams tells him that, only when severed from the earth and those close to him, "breathing with a single passion" will he find treasure in the darkness. With apparent ease he "summons forth ore" from the mine. He marries, but lives whole days and nights inside the earth. As counterpoint to his isolation (he no longer speaks directly to the reader) we hear the villagers' rumors that he can sense gold through stone. They glimpse the gleam of "two wolf-like eyes" where he works. Once they find he has not worked for several days and later see him gazing at the stone as if it were foreign matter to him. When it is "no longer night, but not yet day" he stands over the cradle of his sleeping son. His real home, the narrator tells us, is the "dead abyss;" his child will not awaken in his presence. His moment of reckoning is in the nursery: for a moment "the wild gleam of his eyes grew soft." Outside, still alone, while everything sleeps (earth and people are unified, in this poem, and he is estranged from both), he decides "Yes, he will reject the useless gift,/Abandon the craft of darkness." As the words *dar* and *remeslo* are used, the analogy of miner and poet is suggested—work which isolates and confuses night with day, producing treasure at a cost. The analogy is never made explicit. The poem ends with the lonely death of the miner in an avalanche: "the only thing the spirit of the abyss would not give back was its favorite."

The poem is a variation on the Faust legend, on all myths where the hero exchanges life for knowledge or craft. For Pavlova, once one is a poet there is no going back. The keen sense of bleak isolation predominates in the poem. The nursery scene is without pathos (the child merely sleeps); but it marks the poem as belonging to the female tradition of poet and child, which reaches its apogee in Shkapskaia. The analogy of a manual craft with the craft of poetry, unites the poem to twentieth-century poets who use stone as sculptural metaphor. It can also stand more literally for material harder than the human heart. We will see later how Tsvetaeva uses the crevasse for burial of a living soul, using the phrase *ne vydast*, a verb similar to Pavlova's final *ne otdal* in "The Miner," as the expression of no return. What is buried is never given back. The heart, like the earth, keeps its buried treasure.

Many of the key Pavlovian themes are brought together in one of the great poems of Russian literature, "Ty, utselevshii v serdtse nishchem," of 1854. An invocation to her own talent, to her craft, the poem is Pavlova's version of the "prophet" poems of Pushkin and Lermontov; but it also speaks in a voice of human confidence:

> You have stayed whole within my beggared heart,
> I salute you, my sorrowing verse!
> My bright light above the ashes
> Of my blessings and my joys!
> The one thing in this shrine
> That even sacrilege could not touch;
> My misfortune! my enrichment!
> My holy craft!
>
> Awaken then, word fallen silent!
> Sound forth anew from my lips;
> Come down to her you have elected,
> Once more, O fatal grace!
> And soothe the mindless murmur.

> Condemn my entire heart again
> To limitless suffering,
> To endless love!

Pavlova greets her art as something within herself—a self not favored by worldly rewards. Poetry itself becomes a force which condemns the speaker to a double life, of suffering and love. The poem is constructed upon a series of dualities, words which phonetically echo their semantic opposites: "*Uimi bezumnoe roptan'e.*" The three adjectives containing the prefix *bez* (without)—mindless, limitless, endless—ultimately supersede their nouns. The quality of the experience dominates the experience itself; similarly, craft, technique of expression, dominates the subject.

Both the exalted tone of her verse and its emphasis on technique were cruelly denounced by Pavlova's detractors as somehow cold and unfeminine. Both this tone and this virtuosity, are carried even further by Tsvetaeva, who was similarly denounced by her contemporaries. Tsvetaeva entitled her first mature collection of poetry *Craft* (*Remeslo*), echoing her predecessor Karolina Pavlova.[5] Tsvetaeva's poetic power, and her sense of craft, remain unmatched in Russian poetry. She and three other twentieth century women poets—Parnok, Shkapskaia and Akhmatova—are of particular interest to the history of the poetic investigation of the female self in Russia as it continued into the twentieth century.

# 9.

# FOUR MODERN WOMEN POETS

Between Pavlova and the two best-known twentieth-century women poets, Akhmatova and Tsvetaeva, stand others of high quality—some, like Gippius, Parnok, and Shkapskaia, deserve full attention, and are just recently beginning to receive it.[1] In the twenties at least two generations of Russian women poets were publishing their verse: the poets who began writing in the last decade of the nineteenth century (like Gippius) and those born then (like Parnok and Shkapskaia) but who began writing twenty years later. It was the richest age for Russian poetry, and women figured prominently in it, as they had not done in Pushkin's time, during Russia's other, though less stellar, age of poetry. This later period was an age of groupings. It must be understood that the nature of these groups was social as well as poetic. There was a felt kinship among members for however brief a time. The names the groups bear helped win publicity for their members during their lifetimes, as they help the subsequent student of Russian poetry begin to understand a past age. However, the real history of poetry must begin with the actual poetry written, not with labels like symbolist, acmeist, futurist or imagist. Critics have been saddled with these labels, but, interestingly, they have found women poets less classifiable—with the exception of poets whose husbands belonged to a group, as did those of Gippius, Akhmatova and Guro.

A large anthology of twentieth-century poetry, *Russkaia poeziia XX veka*, published in Moscow in 1925 by I.S. Yezhov and E.I. Shamurin, groups poets according to schools, but nearly all the women poets included are in a category called "poets not connected with definite groups." These are: Lokhvitskaia, L'vova, Parnok, Shaginian, Stolitsa, Tsvetaeva, Pavlovich, Krandievskaia, Shkapskaia, Volchanetskaia, Butiagina, Odoevtseva, Inber, Polonskaia, Radlova, and Barkova, or sixteen of the thirty-five poets in that category. Of poets listed as belonging to groups, women comprise two out of nineteen symbolists (Gippius and Solov'eva), one out of ten acmeists (Akhmatova), one out of twelve futurists or imagists (Guro), and no peasant poets or proletarian poets (twelve and thirty-four males are listed, respectively). Whatever the reasons for the existence of groups, and however little they mean in terms of the actual poetry written, the independence of women is striking here. It may have been forced upon them by exclusion: the tone of male assertiveness in the poetry of futurists like Mayakovsky or the quint-essential imagist/peasant poet Esenin, as well as the flamboyantly male-oriented activities of their groups, must have been a discouraging factor.

Among women poets who can be called modern, one manifestation of their modernity is the fact that, with the end of the century, the speaker of the female lyric turns into a more aggressive persona. She makes demands on her interlocutor, and often these demands are sexual. This is nothing new in the history of male poetry, but it forms one striking aspect of modern female poetry. For example, the extremely popular Mirra Lokhvitskaia (1869–1905) wrote verses in which longings were fulfilled, if only meta-phorically. Akhmatova or Tsvetaeva are not unconnected to this "liberated" female tradition, in which sexual and poetic assertiveness are mutually rein-forcing. In a poem written between 1896 and 1898 Lokhvitskaia answers her critics, as other women poets had before her, assuring them that she knows her craft and that its peculiarity has a different, feminine basis:

> I do not know why I'm accused
> Of putting too much fire in my poems
> Of striving toward the living light
> And not wanting to heed the calumny of depression.
>
> Of shining like a Tsaritsa in formal verses
> With a diadem in my luxuriant hair
> Of weaving a necklace of rhymes for myself,
> Of singing of love, and of beauty.
>
> But I will not buy immortality with my death
> And in songs I love resounding songs.
> And my burning, my feminine (zhenstvennyi) verse
> Will not betray the madness of my worthless reveries.
>                    (*Poety 1880–1890-kh godov*, P. 623)

Poets such as Lokhvitskaia also wrote first about Lilith, and poets such as Shkapskaia and Tsvetaeva kept the image alive in new ways: Lilith, the *femme fatale* who, according to rabbinical tradition, was the first wife of Adam, the mother of evil spirits, who preferred to have one hundred of her demon children die each day rather than return to him, became a superior, active force in later poetry by women, after a long life as arch-temptress in poetry by men.

The generation born in the early 1890s was Russia's most gifted and most tragic. Of the four women poets I will discuss—Sofiia Parnok (1885–1933), Mariia Shkapskaia (1891–1952), Anna Akhmatova (1889–1966), and Marina Tsvetaeva (1892–1941)—three lived their entire lives in their native country, and the fourth, Tsvetaeva, returned there to die; yet their recognition there has been limited, considering their talents. Shkapskaia and Parnok had no poetry published after 1925 and 1928, respectively. Akhmatova's second great long poem, *Requiem*, has only now appeared in the Soviet Union; Tsvetaeva's works are published even more rarely than Akhmatova's and often with major, unannounced cuts. The main things these writers had in common was their language, their cultural heritage, and their continued use of the female persona in their poetry. Each was a poet of great skill who chose to write with an unmistakably female voice. How these voices form a significant part of literature by women in the modern age has to be stated variously in each case. Akhmatova and Tsvetaeva are much better known today; Parnok and Shkapskaia are generally totally ignored but are an integral part of the picture of the twenties woman and her poetic persona. Parnok wrote love poetry to other women: one cycle is about Marina Tsvetaeva. Shkapskaia's central love relationship is almost as taboo when used with unconventional intensity: that of mother and child, woman with her own baby. Shkapskaia wrote what should have been considered poetry of the Revolution; Parnok has clearer links with the nineteenth-century classical tradition.

Sofiia Parnok discovered Karolina Pavlova thanks to an edition of Pavlova's works published in 1915 by the symbolist poet Valerii Briusov (*Sobranie sochinenii*, 2 vols. [Moscow, 1915]). Until then Pavlova had been totally forgotten. Briusov had the habit of grouping women poets together regardless of quality. His article "Women-Poets" ("Zhenshchiny-poety"), published in *Dalekie i blizkie* in 1912, added Vil'kina and Galina to recognized poets like Lokhvitskaia, Gippius, Gertsyk, and Teffi. Briusov would later incur Tsvetaeva's defiance and ridicule for his Evening of Poetesses, a gathering of ill-assorted women poets in revolutionary Moscow. After these women poets had read mostly love poems, Tsvetaeva made a point of not doing the expected or the safe thing, and, instead, at this Red gathering, read her poems dedicated to the White Army. Tsvetaeva described this scene in her essay "A Hero of Labor" ("Geroi truda").

Briusov's contribution to the linked history of women's poetry should be taken seriously if only because of his revival of Pavlova. The very year his two-volume edition was published, Sofiia Parnok responded with an important poem "To Karolina Pavlova":

> Once more the fields go sailing—but you can't see, can you!—
> and the dandelion's fluffiness moves my heart.
> Making a dewdrop stir,—but you can't see, can you!—
> a curled-edged leaf trembling.

And the wires sing,—but you can't hear, can you!—
the wires singing over the corn-fields, and
the beat of far-off hoofs,—but you can't hear, can you!—
a late gunshot waking the birch-wood.

Whether it's July or January,—you can't remember, can you:
for you a century's no longer than a day.
Back then your memory was keen,—but you can't remember, can you,
This evening, or this wind, or me!

This poem is a call to a sister-self across the years, with a rhetorical, echoing answer. Not seeing, not hearing, not remembering any longer signals the death of the poet (as we will see in an earlier poem by Akhmatova, also addressed to a sister-self). The responsiveness to details of nature, to specificity of season and place ends with the finality of death. The fact that Pavlova had been a poet is important to the speaker here. The paradox of *not* remembering not the past but the present gives this lyric its peculiar edge, as if the links between one woman poet and another should be intimate enough to destroy time. Pavlova cannot "remember" the speaker; but the poem is devoted to remembering Pavlova, and so much the same thing is achieved.

Pavlova's life of exile and isolation may have meant as much to Parnok as did her poetry. In a poem of 1925, "Fragment" ("Otryvok"), Pavlova is mentioned again as closer than those of the speaker's time. Here the lines echo Pavlova's own voice: "Silence is my only confidant./My doleful voice is dear to no one."

Parnok's addressee, usually another woman, has the quality, when it is not a sexual "other," of being a self reflected in another self. In the poem beginning "I otshumit tot shum . . . " (1927), the use of the masculine addressee (only once indicated by the past tense "bluzhdal") gives an abstract, philosophical quality making it not specifically masculine but rather human. Until gender-marked grammatical categories are systematically studied in Russian women poets, and some statistics tabulated on their use, we cannot have a full understanding of this problem. With Parnok the masculine addressee makes an interesting reversal. It is used here not as camouflage for a homoerotic lyric, but rather as solemn, unmarked lyric exploration of a split self, a theme we have seen and will see again in poetry by women:

The noise will fade and thunder die away,
these ravings of yours in sleep and wakening,
and the delirious cries will be stilled,—
and you will sense that I am calling you.

And there will be silence and blue twilight . . .
And you will start up, longing and grieving,

and suddenly you'll realize that you were wandering in the desert
a hundred miles away from yourself!

The imagery of the prophet receiving disturbing visions has its counterpart
here in sexual fever calmed by the speaker, resulting in a reunion with self.
The validity of passionate wanderings from self is not undercut; but self-
awareness is the ultimate good. Of that, Parnok had much in her life along
with poetry, but the female self-awareness which came first in her life could
only be written about last in her art.

   S. Poliakova in *The Sunset Days of Yore* (*Zakatnye ony dni*) chronicles
the relationship of Tsvetaeva and Parnok, who met in October 1914, when
Tsvetaeva was already married and had a small daughter. Nothing external
seems to have hindered the relationship: the two were free to travel and
live together. When they parted, shortly after an evening important to Tsvetaeva when Kuzmin read his poems and sang, it was Parnok who apparently
found a replacement for Tsvetaeva, robbing her of her pride in being the
first to act.

   Poliakova reasons (always with close textual support) that Tsvetaeva was
affected for life by the break-up and transmuted residual feelings about
Parnok into emotions about others. One of these surrogates is another Sonia,
the heroine of "Povest' o Sonechke," whom Tsvetaeva so emphatically remembers, just as she so emphatically claims not to remember Parnok.

   In an article she wrote in 1924, "B. Pasternak and Others,"[2] Parnok spoke
out courageously and vehemently against the concept of *sovremennost'*, the
fashionable post-revolutionary word for what was considered the positive
quality of contemporary life in the new society, and with which "good" poets
were supposed to infuse their verse. She spoke of the resulting "simulation"
of excitement and of the copying of "new" rhythmical devices (presumably
from Mayakovsky) by less gifted poets. Finally she prophetically named the
four poets who would survive to be the most noted "contemporaries" of the
future: Pasternak, Mandelstam, Tsvetaeva, and Akhmatova. Two of them,
it should be remarked, were women.

   Russians in the nineteenth and twentieth centuries gave the name "the
Russian Sappho" to a variety of women poets like Lokhvitskaia who wrote
about heterosexual love in an aggressive way or who were simply women
who wrote poetry. Parnok really was the Russian Sappho, but the implications of her lesbian lyrics were ignored by her contemporaries. Even the
sexually "free" twenties failed to name love between women. Parnok was
not considered radical in any sense by Russia's professional revolutionaries.
She wrote poetry that was conservative in form and often camouflaged her

true voice. The Russians who emigrated to the West liked her no better, for their own, prudish reasons, which they also applied to Tsvetaeva.

Parnok's contemporary, Mariia Shkapskaia, would seem to fit in better with the post-revolutionary ethos. Her poetry had a public as well as a private voice. Just as Mayakovsky's male persona was both lover and citizen of the new era, so Shkapskaia, who wrote somewhat experimentally as well, used, in addition to a private lyric persona, a public one, universal for the times— that of mother of the child in whom the future resided. But even motherhood was to receive an official, male-originated definition and Shkapskaia did not fit it.

The radiant "heroine-mother," fortress against oppression and upholder of her men-folk, her closeness to female nature always kept somewhat mysterious, continued in Soviet literature as a fundamentally male image. Gorky's female figures tended to mother their men; this was seen as a necessary service to men in hard times. Hard times have never left the official Soviet mentality, as far as the cult of motherhood goes. The strong, motherly woman became the official poster image of the revolution. It was encoded in Soviet law, which deals with women as mothers of Soviet children, fathers and children as a unit being as absent in political legality as they are in fiction.

Mariia Shkapskaia made a different kind of motherhood her primary poetic theme—not radiant motherhood, but rather motherhood guilty, anxious, and, therefore, profound. When Gorky read her collection entitled *Mater Dolorosa* (1921) in 1923, he sent Shkapskaia a letter from Germany, where he was then living, praising her work and saying that she was the first to speak of the meaningful female role. In May 1924, he wrote again from Italy:

> No, I'm no feminist, but for a long time I've been watching two principles at work and have been amazed that one of them, the female one, can't find anyone to express it and never has. It is unjust that mankind is commanded by "the civilizers," it's from this that the truly tragic mess of life's relations comes. And I'm not talking about "woman's softening influence" but about how essential it is for her to understand her role in the world, her governing role and her cultural significance, which is *ipso facto* spiritual. Women have never spoken about this yet.[3]

Through a woman writer, if not through the women characters in his own works, Gorky was looking for something beyond the feminine stereotypes of a previous age; and for him, Shkapskaia might have provided a new female voice, one socially oriented but authentically particularized. Shkapskaia published no poetry in the Soviet Union after 1925 but continued a career in journalism until her death. Writing about the costs of being a woman in the new society never again became a permissible occupation.

The almost universal experience of women in a society whose chief available means of birth control is abortion has always been a taboo subject in art. Shkapskaia describes both the actual operation and the woman's feelings after it in *Mater Dolorosa*. The lines of poetic prose are divided into paragraph-like stanzas with internal rhyme:

> Yes, they say it was necessary . . . And it was horrifying fodder for the rapacious harpies, and my body slowly lost its strength, and the chloroform pacified me and rocked me away.
> And my blood flowed, not drying up—not joyfully, not like the last time, and afterwards the empty cradle did not gladden our confused sight.
> Once again, like pagans, for the life of our children we make human sacrifice. And You, oh Lord, You don't rise from the dead at that crunching of babies' bones!

This first poem indicts the new paganism which, like the old, requires blood sacrifice from women and children. It proceeds from the actual inner experience of the speaker's body and mind. The latter takes longer to heal, for the speaker in the second poem tries to free herself from guilt. She speaks of herself as a mother still:

> Don't come to me in dreams so often, tiny one, don't pass judgment on your mother. For your milk has remained untouched in my breast. For in life—I long ago discovered—there are few places free, your small place is in my heart like a cross.
> Why do you touch my breast at night with your small hand? It's clear that for a guilty mother there's no getting to sleep!

Parallel to the idea that there is not enough space in society for all of human life runs the concept of women's isolation and emptiness. In the next poem, conventionally rhymed, Shkapskaia's speaker is no longer the deprived one but rather the woman who sees deprivation in her "sisters," women who have no children at all (though those who do are "tired"):

> O, my sweet sisters, with unassuageable longing,
> In evening apprehension and in morning tears,
> With such tortured, with such unconquerable,
> With unsatiated greed in your lowered eyes,
>
> No unseen threads bind you to anyone,
> And empty days burn out to dead ash.
> With what envy you, unburdened, stare
> At the tired mother, with a child in her arms.
>
> Life flows swiftly by, without meeting, in separation.
> O, poor ones, how can I help you live,
> And in the dark of evening what sun
> Can I place into your empty hands?

The rhetorical questions at the end imply the helpless feeling encountered in many of Shkapskaia's poems. Women's bonds and priorities, so clear to themselves, pass unnoticed and unfulfilled in the larger world, one from which men are noticeably absent. The important figures in her poetry, the powerful ones, are women. One is Mary, the Sorrowful Mother ("We are all Her children, we are all Her daughters, whether we're dancing in the ballet or standing in line."); another is Eve, also a mother figure, as in the collection *Blood-Ore* (*Krov'-Ruda*, 1922):

> Everything flows from the first mother Eve to days burdened with things, through each new womb, everything joining itself to people new to us.

Religion is akin to birth, coming from the female body and becoming universal.

Russia itself, a woman in so many Russian poems by men, remains within the tradition of poverty-stricken, chaotic wildness; but Shkapskaia's female speaker has a closer relationship with the long-awaited rebirth of her country, that of a more civilized sister. Still, the sisterly relationship is ambiguous, as it is in a poem by Akhmatova to be discussed next. Shkapskaia wrote a poetic cycle in five parts entitled *Russia* (1922) which contains the lines:

> O you, my hempen Russia,
> You are a woman and You are my sister,
> And I keep waiting for you to bear a Messiah
> Towards autumn, at night by the smoky camp-fire.
>
> But you bear only corn, and oats,
> And dark nights, to cater to your wildness,
> And the wood-sprite celebrates christenings in the woods,
> And an evil wind gone wild combs out
> > Straw strands of braids.

There is menace in these lines and, characteristically, Shkapskaia's view of things holds a continual ominousness for women. In what may have been the last poem she wrote, a long poem entitled "Man Goes to the Pamirs" (1925), the cost of human progress is once again counted in female loss:

> Tomorrow's day will be bright and crimson,
> Man has given up his children for that,
> And for that tomorrow, for that holy lie—
> His wife lies under the knife.

Man (*chelovek*) can mean a person of either sex, but here, if he has a wife, he can only be male—this is the poem's irony. The costly striving of man is similar to that of Pavlova's "Miner"; but here the sacrifice to his exploration is not himself, but his children and the women who bear them. The poem's final lines read:

And eternally woman from her own bones
Gives him new children.
Calculate, find out, measure,
Let the beast rear up,
Let the dead world stagnate,—
Man goes to the Pamirs.

The marching rhythm of the lines is undercut by the female irony we have
seen in other women poets. Shkapskaia dedicated two of her books to Elena
Guro and Zinaida Gippius, women poets of an earlier age, using epigraphs
from their poems and those of Akhmatova. Her work seems uniquely revolutionary, using the figure of the mother, a universal one when not senti-
mentalized, as a symbol of bravery in the years of upheaval. Shkapskaia had
no followers, except, in part, the later Akhmatova, who mourned the victims
of a different period of Soviet history. Shkapskaia's female persona is closest
to that of the folk lament, the "original" Russian women called upon to make
personal sacrifice to a larger, incomprehensible and menacing new order.

One is strongly tempted to view Akhmatova and Tsvetaeva as two complementary halves of the human psyche, just as Tolstoy and Dostoevsky have
seemed an either/or alternative in the minds of their readers. Akhmatova's
lyric heroine is *the* poet, speaking with cryptic simplicity of woman's reactions to love or of (and for) her time and her country—always aware of her
symbolic role as mother, lover, witness, tragic actress. Tsvetaeva's lyric heroine is *a* poet, shaping life into words, trying out words for an emotion.
Tsvetaeva, living in actual exile and engaged in actual motherhood, reached
out to other poets, using her poems, essays, and letters as urgent commu-
nications. The selves of the two poets differ radically: Akhmatova is both "I"
and "she," watching herself being changed in order to meet a changed situation; Tsvetaeva meets the impossibility of the situation with her own obstinate self, head-on. Akhmatova's strength is a yielding, collecting strength;
Tsvetaeva's strength is a shattering one.

Anna Akhmatova, early in her career, mastered the public use of a private
persona to great popular effect. She dramatized a weak self, a concessive
self, a "female" self. Her readers identified with it, and her appeal both to
scholars and to the poetry-reading public was immediate. A guarded strength
emerged from Akhmatova's lines, a gathering together of parts of the divided
self—the strategies of the lyric heroine who would become in a harsher era
a symbol of Russia. Akhmatova and those closest to her endured the worst
trials of its history—two world wars, revolution, civil war, and social upheaval, and finally old age and the guilty memory of the survivor. First in
the Red Terror and then in the Stalinist killings, many of those closest to
the poet, her most immediate audience, had been lost. Akhmatova fulfilled

the expectation of others that she would explain this history to its survivors and to the world in her two long poems: *Poem without a Hero* (1940–62) and *Requiem* (1935–40). It is, in part, through dialogue with her own past selves that Akhmatova could juxtapose and unite the pre- and post-revolutionary phases of Russia's twentieth century. The dialogue began with her early verse.

A pattern can be found in Akhmatova's poetry in which the lyric heroine partially triumphs and wholly survives through giving in to a loss, a duty, a memory, to history and time. The self is displaced and replaced by another. We could call this procedure the gains of yielding.

One of the most elusive Akhmatova poems, "Ia prishla tebia smenit', sestra," dated October 24, 1912, puzzled both Akhmatova's friends and, reportedly, the poet herself.[4] It is one of her most striking images of the divided female self:

> —"I have come to take your place, sister,
> At the tall fire of the forest.
> Your hair has turned gray. A tear
> Has dimmed, has misted your eyes.
>
> You no longer understand what the birds sing,
> You notice neither stars nor summer lightning.
>
> And you've not heard the tambourine beat for a long time,
> Though I know you are afraid of quiet.
>
> I have come to take your place, sister,
> At the tall fire of the forest" . . .
>
> —"You have come to bury me.
> Then where is your pick, where your spade?
> You have only a flute in your hands.
> I will not blame you,
> For is it a shame that at some time, long ago,
> Forever my voice fell silent.
>
> Put on my clothes,
> Forget my alarm,
> Let the wind play with your curls.
> You smell of lilacs,
> And you've come by a difficult road,
> To become aglow like the dawn."
>
> And one woman went away, yielding,
> Yielding her place to the other,
> And wandered unsure, as if blind,
> By a path unfamiliar and narrow.

And it still seemed to her that the flame
Was near . . . her hand holds the tambourine . . .
And she is like a white banner,
And she is like a lighthouse beam.

It has often been noted that Akhmatova's early poetry has two major themes: personal love and the act of poetic creation. This poem, however, is not explicitly a love lyric, for it centers on a poignant encounter between two female personae, one of whom expresses tender but firm compassion for the other. Not a lyric exchange between the poet and her muse, it nevertheless suggests something of that relationship as well.

The poem dramatizes an exchange between a strong and a weak persona, almost certainly two aspects of the self; they are close yet distinct. An impersonal narrator appears at the end. The poem, which has the most varied stanzaic arrangement of any of Akhmatova's early works, is worth discussing in detail. It consists of a tripartite argument: assertion (lines 1–10), counterstatement (lines 11–22), and resolution (lines 23–30). The contrast between the two voices of the protagonists is underscored in the first two sections: the five couplets ending in masculine rhymes sound peremptory; the two sestets with aBc aBc rhymes suggest a slower response. There are also some formal similarities between the two voices: sound echoes of "a" and "i" vowels and the unspecified "I" addressing an equally unspecified "you." The final section, consisting of two quatrains with AbAb rhymes, is typographically marked off from the other two.[5] The meter also consists of three parts: five and six foot trochees and two three-beat dolniks.

Within the poem, a movement like a sort of spiritual relay ties the three parts together. The movements of the personae suggest something ritualistic, staged, and inevitable. The ritual of guarding the campfire flame,[6] the flute and the tambourine, and the simile of blindness suggest the Greek poetic tradition.[7] The setting and props of this poem are among Akhmatova's most abstract: its true setting lies within the mind of the poet, a figure in transition and unsure where that transition will lead. Her former, present and future selves remain in contiguous relationship here. One means of defining the delay between one stage and the next is in the references to modes of perception which unify the poem. The senses lag behind awareness. The second persona, speaking first, tells the first persona what she herself eventually admits: that she no longer understands, notices, or hears, and that she fears the silence. The first persona's reply is not only sympathetic but sensually admiring. The perceptual focus that gives the poem its greatest coherence is that of slowly intensifying light: dull or dark images are succeeded by brightness. At the end "she" becomes like light itself. But who is that "she"?

One persona identifies the other as her sister, a word which is strongest when used in any but the generic sense. She surrenders her clothes to the other, making herself vulnerable, completing the ritual. The two seem to lead two phases of the same life. One part of that life is finished; but another part continues, its continuation at first only dimly perceived by the former self. Eventually, both the old and the new selves coexist, the former in a transformed state. The final light image turns outward—flame into light-house beam.

This poem prefigures Akhmatova's later poetry about memory and former selves in time. The way in which it strongly affirms a resolution, which the reader realizes nonetheless to be partial, makes this poem an intriguing and crucial link in the entire corpus of Akhmatova's work, with its deliberate strategies protecting the essence of the female self by asserting her ability to be more than one self, to yield one self to another.

Other early Akhmatova poems, written within a year of each other, may be seen as variations on a theme: the poet-self replacing another earlier self (frequently a lover-self). "To the Muse" ("Muze," 1911) has the lyric heroine yielding joyfully to the Muse, also called a sister. The Muse takes away the ordinary symbol of the ordinary life—a golden ring. The opening lines speak of the Muse's glance as "clear and bright;" in the final quatrain the speaker asserts that the mirror will mock her, saying, "Your gaze is not clear, not bright." Nonetheless, the speaker is given over to the Muse: she has given up not all her former self, but what might have made her happy before. Again the old self overlaps with the new, and the readiness to relinquish the old seems to be an identity-giving mechanism.[8]

Mirrors can mock the emerging self in Akhmatova's poetry—the mirror image being the metaphor for two selves in space. Physical symptoms of distress are pointed out quite plainly by one persona to another in certain poems; they are the characteristics of another self. If they carry over into the present one, this may be seen as paradoxical in view of a new awareness, an inner change or conviction. In "On My Neck a String of Small Beads" ("Na shee melkikh chetok riad," 1913), the persona looking at her mirror image knows that her eyes will never cry again, but most of the poem points to outer symptoms of distress—difficult breathing, unsteady gait, a dis-traught look. The first person is mentioned only three times in an essentially third-person description of the image, a jarring reminder that this uncertain self is "I," even though the "I" is now transformed. The mirror reflects a more real self, a more present self (after "the meeting which didn't happen," the last two words of the poem), but it is the image without the emotion.

The muse of the new self should and can be yielded to, though at first this procedure might seem to threaten loss rather than renewal. The lover, however, is treated in a different way when he threatens the heroine's role as a poet. Here the movement consists once again not of direct confrontation, but of spatial yielding. In the three-quatrain poem beginning "For the last time we met" ("V poslednii raz my vstretilis' togda," January, 1914) the lovers' meeting has the threat of the Neva flooding as its background.

> For the last time we met
> On the embankment where we always met,
> The water was high in the Neva,
> And they feared flooding in the city.
>
> He talked about the summer and about how
> Being a poet is an absurdity for a woman.
> How I remembered the tall house of the Tsars
> And the Peter-Paul fortress!—
>
> Because the air was not at all usual,
> But like a gift from God—as marvellous as that.
> And in that hour was given to me
> The maddest song of all.

"He" is given two lines to speak, two topics which describe him more than they do her. Her reaction exists only in her mind, the inner strength answering the outer attack with implicit silence. She focuses on a different space, tall and solid architecture, the archetypal acmeist metaphor for poetry. Her defiance of his words binds itself metonymically to the buildings' withstanding of the floodwaters. The poem that is given to her finally, arising from a chain of seemingly unconnected associations, corresponds to the frenzy of the Neva. She has now become the other, elemental side of the Petersburg myth as well, totally superseding his casual and falsely rational remark with the triumphantly irrational, like the river flooding the Imperial city. Female "absurdity" joins with the madness of the poet, another myth common to Russian poetry.

The seeming yielding, the resignation which her early contemporaries found so "feminine" in Akhmatova's early poetry, is a tactic of renewal and replacement by the poetic vocation, the writing or receiving of the poem. The poetry itself, documents the way in which consciousness of the former state persists in the memory of the changed persona,[9] often causing two time levels to be juxtaposed in one brief lyric. The early lyrics were precursors of the later poetry about former selves in time-become-history.[10]

A clear example of this strategy in Akhmatova's later work occurs in her cycle of poems, the *Northern Elegies* (*Severnye elegii*), the first four of which were written at different times in the 1940s. They take the form of a conversation between the two voices of a past and present self, here not so much dialogue but rather as inner monologue in blank verse. The elegiac form, loosely interpreted, rationalizes the death of the past self in consolatory irony: it is "for the best." The inevitable is explored, mourned and accepted.

The first elegy begins with the line "Dostoevsky's Russia" and names other Petersburg writers and specific places in present-day Leningrad associated with them. The architecture of the city is itself a work of art, a permanent, if shabby, reminder of the 1870s, an "ancient lithograph/Not first-class, but quite decent." The persona enters the description continually, both as object and as commentator ("Not I alone, but even others have noticed . . . "; "and across from me live Nekrasov and Saltykov"; "I shall never be in Optina again," etc.). Finally, her own mother is introduced toward the end. Proceeding from static description to mobile commentary, the poem ends with leave-taking of a past that exists more in art than in life. (It is dated both "Leningrad, 3 September 1940" and "Tashkent, October 1944"; in Tashkent Akhmatova's poetry frequently recalled Leningrad, which was then under siege.) Spatial and temporal displacement thus unite, and memory, the simultaneity of two existences, replaces the loss.

The second elegy names "my former home" and the anniversary of another loss, a silver wedding not to be celebrated. As is characteristic of her "historical" poetry, the scope widens to include the fact that "all this has happened many times,/And not with me alone—with others also,/And even worse. No, not worse—better." This dialogue with self attempts to reassure or convince the self that historical guilt and pain is shared.

In the third elegy "some woman has occupied my only place, bears my most legal name, having left me a false one." Here the displacement is not by another self; but it results in a similar renewal of her identity as poet (she has made the most of that name). The entire poem alternates between power and displacement: the powerful horizontal metaphor extends from the opening lines.

> This grim age has
> Diverted me, like a river.
> Another life's been substituted for mine. Into a different channel
> It has flowed past the other,
> And I don't know my own banks.

This image both of homelessness and of the abnormal tampering with nature has the peculiarly Akhmatovian double character of bewilderment combined with a limitless strength engendered by despair.

The fourth elegy specifically concerns memory—that of the poet and of ordinary people, her neighbors in the city. The flow of memory parallels the river's current; and the speaker names three stages, which also flow into one another. In the first stage tears flow too, and the house bears traces of its former owners. The house stands here for the old self: it gradually goes through a dream-like transformation (another metamorphosis) until "there are no longer any witnesses to the events/ And no one to weep with, no one to remember with." Finally the speaker's own self undergoes total alienation: "no one knows us—we are strangers." At the bitterest moment, there is a sudden, partial reversal—the same sort of yielding to a changed reality in order to come to an understanding of and with it that we have noted throughout Akhmatova's poetry. The poem ends with the following words:

> We realize: that we could not contain
> That past within the boundaries of our life,
> And it's almost as alien to us
> As to the man next door;
> That we'd no longer recognize the dead;
> And that those from whom God sent us separation
> Have done just fine without us—and even
> That all is for the best . . .

Both futility and resignation are implied in the trailing-off of the banality of the optimistic final line. The relinquishing of the past self here enters the historical dimension: the loss of Russian people in history. Place and memory, space and time, are embodied in the different selves of the poet. The *Elegies* grieve the loss and displacement, but offer as compensation the self's consciousness of its own endurance. Akhmatova has used something reminiscent of the traditional female lament. The female figure as metaphor for the Russian nation is always the female poet-figure in Akhmatova. Here it personified both extreme dislocation and the will (God's mission for her) to record the universal experience in the surviving female self.

Marina Tsvetaeva, because she was never anything but confident of her role as poet ("I am a craftsman and I know my craft"), felt free to choose a wide range of poetic voices from the neutral or masculine to those of deliberate, vigorous femininity. Her lack of heed that her public might find the vigorous female voice too strident, abrasive, hysterical, or immodest constitutes a great part of her appeal to the feminist reader. Her lack of self-regard, the skill with which she inverts strength into vulnerability, marks a good deal of Tsvetaeva's poetic intonation. Her poetry, not yet absorbed into either Russian or nonRussian culture, is beginning to be studied in all its metrical and semantic complexity.[11] A close reading of poems which speak with her female voice will provide further understanding of the structures of her verse and of her unique treatment of the themes we have seen in women's poetry in Russian.

Tsvetaeva used her life primarily to write. Her daughter and others describe how she literally cleared her kitchen table in order to write, having no other space. Her poetry, even when mythically allusive, both uses and rebels against feminine *realia*.[12] Tsvetaeva goes beyond themes and imagery to a totally feminine view of reality. This view begins not with conjunction with a male, but with aloneness—aloneness after intense union, during inadequate union, or prior to union that will never occur. The poet finds this singularity both humanly intolerable and poetically indispensable; the poems integrate these conflicting findings.

Thus the mature Tsvetaeva no longer needs the protective irony we have seen in other women poets. Foregoing irony, she exhorts or declares opposites to be one, absence to be presence, flesh to be spirit. She hits an emotion directly, locating its center within the self. The female self in her poetry is no longer a mirrored self, a split self, or a double self; it is a whole self, one intact, with its own pain and its own ability to recreate it: the "formal feeling" that Emily Dickinson describes as coming "after great pain" applies not to the emotion felt in Tsvetaeva's poetry, but rather to the brilliantly organized poetry itself.

As with other women poets, only some of Tsvetaeva's poems contain a speaker with an explicitly female identity. Whenever the world of her poetry divides into a masculine/feminine opposition, Tsvetaeva allies herself with femininity: Ophelia against Hamlet (one, in defense of Gertrude), Phaedra against Hippolytus, Lilith against Adam, and Helen of Troy against a whole tradition that blames her for the Trojan war. Her heroines of myth and tradition are rescued from their portraits as either destructive or victimized beings—the familiar dual interpretations of masculine tradition—to be reclaimed as new female self-definitions.

Abandonment and power are both regarded by Tsvetaeva as necessary givens, prerequisites to creativity. They no longer exist sequentially (as in Akhmatova) or in opposition. If customary male-female relationships are reversed in Tsvetaeva, with the female calling upon the male to love, care, understand, and obey, there is in her poetry the knowledge that this reversal is as futile as the masculine assertion of power. Only the power of the speaker to reintegrate the two through poetic speech emerges as something saved from the wreckage of emotion or nonemotion.

An early poem of Tsvetaeva, "V gibel'nom foliante" (September 29, 1915), demonstrates several of the mature Tsvetaeva features. The "female" position is advanced against a male order that defines her from the cradle, and against the ultimate male—God—who is spoken back to in his own imperative tones.

> In this fateful folio
> There is nothing seductive for
> Woman—the *Ars Amandi*
> For a woman is the whole earth.

> The heart, staple of all love potions
> Is the surest potion of all.
> Woman from the cradle onward
> Is somebody's mortal sin.

Oh, it's too far to heaven!
Lips are near in the gloom . . .
—God, judge not!—You have not been
A woman on the earth!

Ovid's *The Art of Love*, the Latin title probably restated from poetic memory, gives an idea of how little erudition, and how much culture, Tsvetaeva had. Her Greek myths come from the German retellings of Gustav Schwab, and, more to the point, she uses them as a woman-poet. (Tsvetaeva's sense of word arrangement in the line and the stanza is shown here by the recurrence of the word "woman" in initial position in four lines out of the poem's twelve: in Russian the function of articles and some prepositions is carried by the case endings of the noun.) Thus the challenge to self-definition as well as the latent possibility of defeat inherent in that challenge sets a pattern that will recur in a mature poem like "An Attempt at Jealousy."

The lyrics in the collection *After Russia* (*Posle Rossii*), published in Paris in 1928 but written during the years 1922–1925, form the richest body of work ever published as a book by a Russian poet. Each poem echoes its near and distant neighbors in the collection. Some are put into cycles; the meaning of the Tsvetaeva poetic cycle has yet to be elucidated.

For example, several Ophelia poems were written in 1923: "Ophelia to Hamlet" and "Ophelia in Defense of the Queen" (both February 28), "Hamlet's Dialogue with his Conscience" (June 5) and, finally, a poem of September 28, which was not included in *After Russia* but which is related to the three others. It begins: "Along the embankments, where gray-haired trees/ Follow the traces of Ophelia." Tsvetaeva gave her Ophelia poems a variety of tones; but they are all Ophelia-centered, even when it is Hamlet who speaks, in the poem which begins the second notebook of *After Russia*, "Hamlet's Dialogue with His Conscience":

"She's at the bottom, with the silt
And water-weeds . . . Gone away to sleep
Among them,—but there's no sleep there either!"
"But I did love her
As forty thousand brothers
Couldn't love!"
            "Hamlet!

She's at the bottom, with the silt:
Silt! . . . And the last wreath
Has floated up on river logs . . . "
"But I did love her
As forty thousand . . . "
            "Less
All the same, than a single lover.
She's at the bottom, with the silt".

> "But I did—
> (Bewildered)
> —love her??"

The dwindling of man's love for woman, the inability to reply (in this case not so much to her suicide as to his own self-knowledge, is a common Tsvetaevan theme. Here the poem's structure replaces the spokeswoman for Ophelia's telling action. The lines of Hamlet are taken not directly from Shakespeare's famous graveside speech, but from Polevoi's Russian translation.[13] The whole treatment stands in contrast to traditional male treatments of the theme in Russian poetry—for example Nekrasov's "Ophelia" (1840), which pities Ophelia, who is distraught but beautiful—like a pre-Raphaelite heroine. The Nekrasov poem ends in a lengthy simile comparing woman to nature: Hamlet himself is quite absent. Tsvetaeva's Ophelia is never an object for the reader's pity (a beautiful victim like Poor Liza) and therefore, ultimately, of male self-pity; rather she is a disquieting presence for the reader as for Hamlet, not merely as victim but as agent of her own destruction.

According to tradition, Helen of Troy has the opposite effect from Ophelia—destruction of others rather than self-annihilation. Tsvetaeva's writings bristle with denunciations of the tradition concerning Helen. In "Natal'ia Goncharova" she wrote that "Helen of Troy was the pretext for and not the cause of the Trojan War. . . . "[14] Her most complete reference to Helen is in a poem dated November 11, 1923, that had no title in *After Russia* but was given one by Tsvetaeva in 1940 as she was preparing an edition of her works that never actually appeared. The title "Vzgliad" means "gaze" or "glance," but also "view" or "opinion," and the poem concerns both these things.

> So—Helen had only to gaze above the Trojan
> Roofs! In the stupor of pupils
> Four provinces have been bled white
> And a hundred centuries deprived of hope.
>
> So—Helen only above the marital slaughterhouse
> Had in her mind: by my nakedness
> Four Arabias have become heatless
> And five seas pearlless.
>
> And it was only Helen—don't expect hands to be
> Wrung!—wonders at this swarm
> Of heirs apparent made homeless
> And progenitors rushing to war.
>
> So only Helen—don't expect lips to
> Call!—who was amazed at this ditch

Piled to the top with heirs apparent:
At the sonlessness of a hundred clans.

But no, it is not Helen! Not that twice-married
Plunderess, pestilent draught.
What a treasure-house is wasted
By you, when you look into our eyes—in such a way

As even Helen at her fine supper
Dared not look into the eyes of her slaves:
Her gods.—"Land unmanned by a foreign
Woman! Still crawling like a caterpillar—to your feet!"

The poem's chief device, hyperbole, is used to ridicule the view that the woman caused a major historical tragedy by her glance, her beautiful presence. Neologisms are part of the hyperbole: the words in the final quatrain *obezkrovleno* (bled white) and *obeznadezheno* (deprived of hope) are formed according to Russian rules of word-formation, but are not in the language. Others arise according to this example, all meaning "un-," "-less," or "deprived of" and all giving a sarcastic intonation to the poem. The name Elena occupies the same place in every quatrain, but its semantic position changes as the myth is exploded.

Ophelia and Helen stand for variations of the female self, but they also exist primarily in the world of myth. In other poems Tsvetaeva begins with self and uses myth only as backdrop to female self-definition through the highly disciplined and crafted poetic response to a painful emotion of love irretrievably ended. These poems culminate in the restoration, though partial or transmuted, of the speaker's self. This they have in common with Akhmatova and with some of Emily Dickinson's poetry ("Power is only pain—/Stranded, thro' Discipline, . . . " Dickinson wrote circa 1861). Two poems from *After Russia*, "Crevasse" ("Rasshchelina" of June 17, 1923) and "An Attempt at Jealousy" ("Popytka revnosti" of November 19, 1924) give a specifically female frame of reference to Tsvetaeva's shattering strategies that open an impasse and reform an absence into a presence. The controlling voice is that of a woman who selects images of both female mythic and female bodily significance.[15] Both poems proceed from a painful sensation of loss and take an attitude that refuses to settle for less (or for loss). The poems echo and expand upon the words of Montaigne chosen by Tsvetaeva as the epigraph to the "Second Notebook" (and used again as an epigraph to the essay "Poet on Critic" ("Poet o kritike") in 1926: "J'en ay assez de peu . . . J'en ay assez d'un. J'en ay assez de pas un." It is the forcefulness of the poetic attitude taken to reverse an emotional finality imposed by a man upon a woman that unifies these two poems, each of which echoes other poems in *After Russia* in different ways.[16] The first poem is a virtually unknown

masterpiece; the second is familiar to anyone acquainted with any of Tsvetaeva's poetry.

"Crevasse" begins with a flat statement of an ending and asserts the impossibility of further knowledge, in an impersonal manner:

> How this incident ended
> Neither friendship nor love can learn.
> With each day you respond more dully
> With each day you are lost more deeply.
>
> So, you're no longer upset by anything,
> —Only a tree shifts its branches—
> You've fallen into an icy crevasse—
> Into my chest that was *so* smashed against you!
>
> From the treasury of simulacra
> Here's a riddle for you at random:
> In me as in a crystal coffin you
> Sleep, in me as in a deep wound you
>
> Sleep,—tight is the ice cut!
> Ice is jealous of its dead men:
> Ring—armour—seal—and girdle . . .
> Beyond return and beyond recall.
>
> In vain you curse Helen, widows!
> It's not the flame of red Helen's
> Troy! It's the icy crevasse's
> Blue, in the depths of which you are resting . . .
>
> I, having coupled with you like Etna
> With Empedocles . . . Sleep, dreamer!
> And tell the servants that it's futile:
> The chest will not give up its dead men.

The chest stands metonymically for the "I" in the poem, and a glacial crevasse
is the poem's central metaphor for this (wounded) part of the body. Distance
and disappearance, in time and space, usually conceived of as lateral and
outward, are transferred by the poem to the vertical plane, a thrust downward (into the crevasse) and inward (into the chest). The addressee has
become literally "unmoved," frozen; by contrast, a tree moves slightly. The
chest, still impersonal at the end of the second quatrain, has been hurt, and
pain is expressed by the italicized *so* and by the exclamation mark. In the
third quatrain the tone shifts, as the speaker fully assumes the role of defining
the situation: she poses a riddle from the storehouse of similes at her com-
mand (her power is implied both by her ability to select from many images
and by her ability to speak in images at all). The riddle states the I/you

relationship two ways: you sleep in me in a crystal coffin/a deep wound. The first simile reverses the well-known fairy-tale image of Snow White. As we remember, the Prince wishes to possess the beauty in her glass coffin even though he believes her to be dead.[17] Preserved in ice or crystal, the beloved has become an object. The second image, the deep wound, the icy cut, both overlaps and contrasts with the deathly serenity of the first. Line 14 summarizes the theme of possession (by the personification of ice, making jealousy impersonal). It also contains a threat: the ice will not let go. The next line is a catalogue of the personal effects of a dead knight, as if a funeral were taking place. These are the last means of identifying him, metonymic remains of his person. The ring, coat of mail, seal, and girdle are all round (or made of ring-shaped parts); all hold or seal in. The absence is now stated positively, for the speaker has shifted the loss into her own self, where no one else can find it. In the last two quatrains, two other myths are reversed by the speaker. Helen of Troy is not to blame for the Trojan War. It is not the flame of war but the blue of glacial ice, its opposite in temperature but its twin in intensity, that the emotion is compared to. Finally, Empedocles' legendary death-leap into Etna[18] is rephrased with Etna (female and geological, like the glacier, but hot—the passion before it turned to iciness) being the active force of union. The indicative "you sleep" becomes an imperative "sleep!" as the speaker gains total control of the situation, telling those close to the addressee that they search in vain. The final line of the poem imposes a finality of possession in the speaker's own terms: the chest will not give up its dead men. The plural signifies a general rule. The future tense appears for the first time (an earlier variant had "to the end of ages" in line 10; but a future finality is more effective at the end). Like Tsvetaeva's *Poem of the End*, "Crevasse" begins with the beginning of the end and finishes with the end of the end, with its literal incorporation (into the corpus of poetry and the physical body of the poet).

Thus, the theme of physical loss of a lover/friend made into eternal, spiritual (metaphorically physical) possession is reinforced by a triple feminist reversal of the conventional myths which tell us that: (1) a woman, Snow-White, is made into a dead object for all eyes; (2) a woman, Helen of Troy, wreaks destruction; and (3) a man, Empedocles, takes an active plunge into physical annihilation and immortal glory. The poem, like so many of Tsvetaeva's lyrics, is built upon paradox. The heat of passion becomes the ice of possession. The direct association is made on the level of imagery: the juxtaposition of geological images of ice/crystal and flame/volcano. The speaker's loss of the lover/friend has paradoxically shifted into its opposite: *she* will never lose *him*.

Imagery of the geological crevasse keeps yielding place throughout the poem to its anatomical "literal" explanation. In bodily terms, the imagery is sexual and a reversal of a birth process. He sleeps in her (like a baby), but he will never be born; the pain of his breaking into a crack in her body results in his total absorption by her. The word *propast'*—to fall through, to be lost—becomes a pun, similar to the womb/tomb pun of English poetry.

Having metonymically located pain in one part of her body, the speaker is free to name it. The effect of this poem is that of a horrible deadening of pain intensified to the point at which it is transmuted into the power of possession. But the poem remains static at that point: I possess you (but you are dead); I won't release you (but you are my pain).

The sound structure of the poem activates the intersecting semantic fields at every level. "Crevasse" is constructed of many parallels: only six of the poem's twenty-four lines contain no parallels. These parallels lend an incantational dignity to the lines, and they also recall certain other poetic genres: a negative simile (it is not one thing; it is another), the Slavic folk epic, the repetition of the verb "to sleep," a lullaby. On the lexical level, words shift their meaning within a single stanza ("tak" in the second stanza is italicized to indicate a new meaning). The words move slightly higher than in ordinary speech (words like *ogn'* or *koye* are archaic/poetic), so that when the word *grud* is used, it tends to connote "breast" or "heart" while still keeping its anatomical literalness.

The poem's elliptical syntax, characteristic of Tsvetaeva, here provides verbal mimicry of the glacial gap/chest/wound imagery. Every quatrain but the third (the riddle-posing one) contains a negative statement: the crevasse is empty space. Verbs are omitted altogether or else pulled apart from their subject by an intervening metaphor ("you in me as in a crystal coffin/Sleep"). Enjambements span separate lines in the third and fifth stanzas and jump stanzas, from the third to the fourth. Grammatical disjunctures reflect the unbridged death/life, fire/ice, absence/presence oppositions which inform the poem.

In the second poem, some of the same devices (anaphora, enjambement) are used more repetitively, as constants; while the imagery (a constant in "Crevasse") fluctuates widely.

### An Attempt at Jealousy

How's your life with the other one—
Easier?—A stroke of the oar!—
Like the coastline
Does it take long for the memory to recede

Of me, a floating island
(In the sky—not on the waters!)
Souls, souls! you should be sisters,
Never lovers—you!

How's your life with an *ordinary*
Woman? *Without* deities?
Now that you've dethroned your Queen
(Having stepped down yourself).

How's your life—do you fuss—
Do you shiver? How do you feel when you get up?
How do you deal with the tax
Of deathless vulgarity, poor man?

"Convulsions and irregular heartbeat—
I've had enough! I'll rent my own place".
How's your life with anyone—
My own chosen one!

More compatible and more palatable
The food? If it palls—don't complain . . .
How's your life with an imitation—
You who have trampled upon Sinai!

How's your life with a local
Stranger? Point-blank—do you love her?
Or does shame, like Zeus' reins,
Lash at your forehead?

How's your life—your health—
How've you been? Are you managing to sing?
How do you deal with the ulcer
Of deathless conscience, poor man?

How's your life with goods
From the market? Is the price steep?
After Carrara marble
How's your life with plaster

Dust? (From a solid block was hewn
A god—and smashed to bits!)
How's your life with one of a hundred-thousand—
You, who have known Lilith!

Are you sated with the newest thing
From the market? Having cooled to magic,
How's your life with an earthly
Woman, without a sixth

Sense? Well, let's hear it: are you happy?
No? In a shallow bottomless pit—
How's your life, my darling? Harder than,
Just like, mine with another man?

Like "Crevasse," "An Attempt at Jealousy" also takes place *after* the event has occurred, beginning and ending in an inexplicable present. Here the speaker attempts to redefine the situation, giving a hyperbolic explanation to a rather banal turn of events. She reverses "You have left me for another woman and I'm miserable" into the defiantly wishful "You are miserable with her and here's a reminder of who *I* am"! Tsvetaeva accomplishes this tour de force by the magic of ritual vituperation. She shows her skill by saying the same thing in numerous ways (much like a medieval sermon). The poem keeps leading off with the same rhetorical question ("How's your life"?) posed eleven times in twelve stanzas, all but the second one. We—and he—get no relief, presumably because she has none. Jealousy is a rhetorical question, getting and needing no answer; it supplies its own.

This poem, too, begins with a movement away (laterally rather than downward): the stroke of the oars followed by a two-beat line suggesting a slow pull, a three-beat and finally three four-beat lines as the pace quickens. The poem's meter is as regular as its returning refrain: trochaic tetrameter, the first and fourth ictus always stressed, the fourth line of all stanzas but three omitting the stress on the third ictus, the masculine endings of the second and fourth lines reinforcing the question or exclamation marks they frequently end with and delivering a double punch with the stressed first syllable of the next line.

Reflexive verbs and adjective/noun combinations in the instrumental (both similes and accompaniments) also dominate the poem; the only direct object accusative, by way of contrast, occurs in the two lines spoken by the departing lover, "I will rent a house." These words, uttered as a quote by the speaker, have the mocking irony of words flung up a stairway being thrown back down. They are also simple in comparison with her baroque circumlocutions, and they reinforce the idea that maybe this simple man belongs with a "simple woman" rather than with the speaker.

Given the essential sameness of its stanzaic structure, the poem is a marvel of variety. The hyperbolic language, once begun, must maintain its pitch and even appear to be stepping it up. Tsvetaeva accomplishes this feat by piling metaphor upon metaphor and by varying the breaks in line and stanza that form the boundary between two questions (although there is a tendency for the second line in each quatrain to have the greatest number of such breaks, even these are varied). The first and last lines of the poem link up with their final words (*s drugoiu/s drugim*) underlining the circular reasoning of the questions.

Part of the variety within the tight framework stems from the formal structure of address (the use of the formal pronoun *vy*, the reflexive verbs and high-toned Church Slavonic lexicon) combined with a colloquial prying into extremely intimate moments of life. This creates an element of humorous backlash important to the total effect of the poem. Hyperbole is commonly used humorously. The speaker calls herself a Queen, Carrara marble, Lilith. Tsvetaeva, in letters, identified herself with Lilith, as opposed to wifely other women, Eves. The other woman is simple, earthy, vulgar, largely defined by hyperbolic contrast to herself. The man is ironically pitied, sarcastically and blasphemously called "my chosen one" (in the context of other Biblical references, the implication is that the speaker is God); but at the end, when he is called simply *milyi*, dear, the tone shifts suddenly from the metaphorical plane to the "real" one. He is still loved; she is living with another man and still loving him. Our desire to laugh along with the speaker as she redefines the all-too-definable is suddenly broken with a return to the original feeling, love.

How can the title be explained? First of all, this is an attempt at jealousy by someone who fails at the end: the other woman doesn't really exist for her; only the man does. Second, the "attempt" can be seen as an *exercice de style*; much like Wallace Stevens's "Thirteen Ways of Looking at a Black-bird," it demonstrates the poet's skill in saying the same thing in different ways, expressing the simultaneous as sequential. The speaker can even change metaphor in midstream when she redefines the floating island as being in the sky. Nothing verbal is technically impossible to her. The rhetoric of vituperative jealousy has famous precedents in the history of the art: Catullus and Shakespeare come readily to mind. A deliberately crude and blasphemous female lyric voice, exulting in its own sense of freedom in being unladylike, is not to be found until the twentieth century.

One of Tsvetaeva's later poems again shows a sense of space invaded, obstructed, partitioned off. This poem, entitled "The Naiad" ("Naiada," August 1, 1928), is complex and elusive: though its main theme seems to be repeated, only the concept of between-ness is constant; the invaded premises change as do the addressees. Here we translate *grud'* as "breast," rather than "chest" to signal its figurative as well as its anatomical qualities.

> Pass me by, pass me by,
> Free body, fish's body!!
> Between me and the wave,
> Between my breast and the swell is a
>
> Third thing, the malicious barrier
> To friendship naked and proud:
> The hundred-pood tribute
> To that minor trifle: sex.
>
> I recognize you, wedge,
> Whatever your name might be:

In the sea there's a weave, in a field a fence
The eternal third thing in any love!

Isn't the right to build stone cells
Enough for human malice?
Isn't the trembling weave of the sea
Enough for the mermaid?

Aren't the inexhaustible riches
Of Father Ocean enough for her?
His foam her marvellous bonnet?
His wave her marvellous tent?

I recognize you, reptile,
Whatever your name might be:
In the sea a weave, in grief a glance,—
The eternal third thing in any love!

How shall I accept you, battle,
Given me by the depths,
If between me—and the wave:
Between my breast—and the breast of . . .

—O Nereid! Wave!
We need nothing
Which is not I, not she
Not wave, not naiad!

I recognize you, coffin,
Whatever your name might be:
In a faith it's the church, in a church it's the priest,—
The eternal third thing in any love!

The baker, the stoker,—
Marriage with no third person between!
They hide the fat (rich men's woe)
For the pure—there are no clothes!

The cry of Black Sea forelocked sailors:
Fellows, go to it naked!
We go naked into the sea and into love,
Like the warriors at Perekop go

into the battle . . .
The ripple of sailors'
Nipples.—"So long, Comrade!"
. . . Into the bullet a helmet, into the storm a roof:
The eternal third thing in any love!

)

Seacoasts of vagrants,
Vows without church altars!
How can I enter into you, marriage,
If between me—and myself—is

What? Well, that nose in the shade,
That age-old spy—
One's own. All there could possibly be—
What? It's everything if it's something:

I recognize you, debbil,
Whatever your name might be:
Today a nose, tomorrow a promontory,
The eternal third thing in any love!

The mother full of pride,
Above her the flourishing sprig,
Hurry up and die!
Tomorrow a third will worm in!

I recognize you, death,
Whatever your name might be:
In my son it's his growth, in a plum it's the worm:
The eternal third thing in any love.

The speaker of the poem is sometimes an actress in the drama and sometimes a namer, who "recognizes" the interferers. She is female in the first instance and not gender-linked in the second. The object comes "between me and the wave" and later "between me and myself." The interposing object, the chief actor of the poem, is variously named by the speaker as: a wedge, a reptile, a coffin, a devil (the Ukrainian word is used), and, finally, death. All are monosyllabic words in Russian and all but the last of these thrusting penetrators or dividers are masculine nouns. They have little in common per se, except their ability to come *between*. Other interfering forces go *into* or reside *in* and carry the quality of thirdness: these too are masculine nouns, except for *tkan'* (a net or woven fabric, possibly a bathing suit here). Even growth in a son is not part of life, but an ally of death, interfering in the love of mother and son.

The mermaid partakes of two natures and can merge with the sea, without fear of interference; but although the speaker swims in the same sea and though she is capable of naming the interfering agents, she is female-mortal, rather than female-immortal, and therefore subject to defeat. Mother feeling would be constant, but the son grows and so this love, too, will be defeated, just like the one in the refrain. Any pure experience, even that of the self (the female self who, like her spiritual analogue, the mermaid, can swim) will be blocked. The very nose on one's face is, as in Gogol's tale, one's own enemy, a probing betrayer. With death, in the final stanza, the final kinship of self and self-destroyer is established. The mermaid appears at the beginning of the poem and later disappears from the speaker's self-identity as she goes deeper into nonlife, nonfreedom, nonunity.

Tsvetaeva has carried the female imagery we have identified as the split self to its ultimate position as the enemy of all creation. Her poetry, women's poetry at its most female and universal, is the model for future Russian poetry by women. It is a model evoked rather than technically exploited. Tsvetaeva has had no real successors among women poets so far. She, of all women writers, travels farthest into her own female myth reversals, anger, romanticisms, into the female voices buried within her, and into a terrible perfection of craft in *After Russia* and in many poems preceding and following it. Her elliptical style, like that of Emily Dickinson, should elicit endless serious involvement on the part of the reader when we learn to leave aside our fascination with these poets' lives.

# CONCLUSIONS . . .
# AND CONTINUATIONS

This study has attempted initially to intercept and decode the most powerful messages Russian women writers received from Russian literature, the messages sent from male writers who shaped and dominated the tradition. Not surprisingly, men—both writers and literary bureaucrats—have continued to shape and dominate the Russian literary tradition to the present day. Following the revolution of 1917, which proclaimed full equality for women, policies varied as to women's economic and social roles; however, the aim consistently articulated by the Soviet government was that women should be equal to men.[1] Nevertheless, despite these stated aims, Soviet women even today do not rise to the top of what are essentially male hierarchies in the public spheres, such as the Party, the military, the foreign service, the KGB, the professions, or the Writers' Union. Still, the idea of equality in one form or another continues to be asserted as Soviet policy. As regards the private sphere, the sphere in which Russian literature is located (home, love, family, and self), not only has there been no revolution, there has been almost total silence.[2] Both government policy and private attitudes place responsibility for the home and for children either solely with women or with women and society, which means that men are not encouraged to share in these responsibilities. In the personal and domestic spheres, Russian society has changed far less than any other developed nation. Discussions of women's economic, political, and social life remain separate from any discussion of the role of men in the private sphere. There is, instead, a concern that men are becoming "feminized" (i.e., passive, weak). The reasons for Soviet women's lack of progress have been discussed only in the context of the society's greater good. One work of literature consisting of such an examination of the interrelationship of a woman's life at work and at home is Natal'ia Baranskaia's "A Week Like Any Other" ("Nedelia kak nedelia," *Novyi mir*, No. 11, 1969, pp. 23–55). It is perhaps the most overtly woman-centered literary text published in the USSR since the 1930s. Its heroine tells her story because she must answer a questionnaire about women: thus the imprint of wider social concern gives "legitimacy" to the telling of one woman's harried daily life.

The messages being sent today by the men who dominate literature not only do not differ from the message in the society as a whole—that women, whatever their work outside, are particularly well-suited to life in the personal and domestic spheres—these messages by the most powerful writers of Russian literature actually confirm and advance notions of woman's otherness. The images of terrible perfection have, since the thirties, been even more boldly imprinted on Soviet women in fiction. In works critical of Soviet society in other respects, women's mysterious strengths are the redeeming force. The torments women endure are described in terms of heterosexual love and caring motherhood, while, as in the nineteenth century, men follow in the wake of women's emotion but have the capability to think politically, historically, creatively. We shall comment on Russia's most famous (anti-Soviet in a nonfeminist political sense) post-war novel, *Dr. Zhivago*, and the Soviet-published, universally acclaimed work of V. Rasputin as examples of the persistence of male fictions of women in otherwise quite different works, one stressing the individuality of the artist (Pasternak) and the other the communality of Russian moral life (Rasputin).

Women writers are faced once again with these male definitions as the most powerful cultural determinants. As previously, they concentrate on the private sphere without, in fiction, dwelling on redefinitions of the self in any feminist or non-male-defined sense. The struggles of daily life take precedence over the naming of a female life. Yet, in autobiographies by women there again seems to be greater breadth of self-definition. Two central works of this century from the Soviet Union, the autobiographies of Nadezhda Mandelstam and Evgeniia Ginzburg, surpass any other chronicles of the Stalinist age save that of Solzhenitsyn in recovering events of that era. Nothing in fiction matches these "lives;" but occasionally fiction uses autobiographical narrative strategies (and perhaps events) to advantage. Two writers, I. Grekova and R. Zernova, have written small masterpieces with distinctly autobiographical frames of reference, to be discussed below. There are now other autobiographical works being published[3] which may confirm our thesis that this is still a more viable form for Russian women writers than fiction. Of our major nineteenth-century female memoirists, only Durova saw her autobiography published during her lifetime. What works lie buried today we can only hope that time will tell.

Poetry, to a lesser extent than in the symbolist and modernist ages, continues to render some direct expression of the female self. There are references to Tsvetaeva by women poets (Akhmadulina, for example), but only Joseph Brodsky has used the poetic riches Tsvetaeva mined from the Russian language by violating poetic norms of that language to a similar degree. Within a more conservative poetic framework, themes of isolation, the experience of loss, the split self and the sister self that we have traced in previous women poets continue to appear, as we shall see in two interesting, but little-known poets, Vladimirova and Shvarts. Only sporadically, then, have Russian women been writing scripts of their own: the situation in past Russian literature described in our study seems not to have undergone any fundamental change in recent years.

The mystery of female strength seems most absurd in works pretending to philosophical and historical truth, especially in the twentieth century; yet these persist. In *Doctor Zhivago*, Boris Pasternak, a poet who chose not to continue his own modernistic prose style of the 1920s, founders in a sea of metaphor, of improbability without irony, and of male self-pity. Pasternak's grand sweep of history takes him, in the space of a single phrase (using the Max Hayward and Manya Harari translation [London, 1958] throughout since it has been more widely read than the Russian text) "from the obscure fate of these spread-out bodies to the riddle of life and death itself" (III, 2). Such prose continually explains its own mystery, asserting the mysterious with confidence.

One of the chief mysteries promoted in this novel is that of female nature. Lara is "a living indictment of the age," an inspiration both to her revolutionary husband and to her anti-revolutionary lover who, toward the end of the novel, meet and discuss her, congratulating themselves on the one thing they can agree on. Lara manages to be the ideal of several men. She says to Zhivago, "struggling with tears . . . 'You were given wings to fly above the clouds, but I'm a woman, mine are given me to stay close to the ground and to shelter my young.' He was deeply moved by everything she said, but he didn't show it, lest he give way to his emotions." As he sends Lara off to freedom without him in the arms of her former violator, Zhivago, in one of several voyeuristic passages, even imagines Lara thinking about him, "her absurd, obstinate Yurochka" (XIV, 13). Zhivago seems to know a lot about life, being a poet, and this includes a certain knowledge of women. He sees what they cannot see: themselves. As he remarks to Lara: "How much more painful must it be [to love] to a woman and to be the current, and to inspire love" (XIV, 3). Zhivago has three wives—one from each class: upper, middle, and lower. Their attraction for him is based on a common denominator of domesticity in spite of hard times. The novel opens with the death of the hero's mother. Soon Russia wouldn't mother her citizens either, but:

> Coming home at night, hungry and tired, he found Lara busy at her domestic chores, cooking or washing. In this prosaic, weekday aspect of her being, dishevelled, with her sleeves rolled and her skirts tucked up, she almost frightened him by her regal attractiveness, more breath-taking than if he had found her on the point of going to a ball, taller in high-heeled shoes and in a long low-cut gown with a sweeping rustling skirt. (XIII, 15.)

The extended almost-metaphor of a Gogolian fantasy woman blends finely with kitchen realism. But for Yura's third, proletarian, wife, the description is on an appropriately lower level:

> It was from this water-carrying on a Sunday that a friendship sprang up between the doctor and Marina. She would often come and help him with his housework. One day she stayed with him and did not again go back to the lodge. Thus she became Yurii Andreievich's (the formal name she would call him) third wife, though he was not divorced from the first . . . (XV, 6.)

Zhivago's first wife, Tonia, is class-bound as her husband is not. Even the scene where she gives birth is governed by the author's knowledge of how women of her class do give birth, in what circumstances, rather than by any attempt to project her feelings from within. There is no inner voice, as Tolstoy imagined for Anna Karenina, although the scene is full of Tolstoy-like estrangement of the hero's feelings and sensations. The cries, the physical suffering, and the lack of reflection on the part of the woman are made to exist solely within the male receiver who is the father. To him is transferred the childbirth experience, which he reconverts into Art.

Tonia Zhivago gives birth in a Moscow hospital, attended by the head gynecologist, who "was of mammoth size, and always responded to questions by shrugging his shoulders and staring at the ceiling." As the episode is bracketed by a successful diagnosis of another case by Dr. Zhivago himself, the reader is first led to feel some outrage that *he* (not she) is being treated with less than respect, because of his professional status. After the birth he is prevented at first from seeing his wife, lest he upset her. The indignant reader is overtaken by the saintly protagonist who, tired though he is, has very definite and characteristically modest thoughts on the meaning of the childbirth experience: "Father—son; he did not see why he should be proud of this unearned fatherhood, he felt that his son was a gift out of the blue."

The reader, like the hero, is kept at a distance from Tonia both during and after the birth. The closest we are admitted to her experience is when by mistake the door "had been left half-open, he heard Tonia's heart-rending screams." She screams in Anna Karenina-like metaphor: "like the victims of an accident dragged with crushed limbs from under the wheels of a train." The first transference is made into male blood, that of Zhivago. Pasternak is more delicately symbolic when describing *couvade* than Hemingway in the famous story of the Indian husband who slits his throat when his wife gives birth: "Biting his knuckle until he drew blood, he went over to the window."

The second, artistic transference of the female experience to the male domain occurs a few paragraphs later when Zhivago is allowed to look at his wife *on condition that she does not see him.* Here the voyeuristic act which we have noted in earlier male fictions is instantly transformed into metaphor. Indeed, Tonia becomes the writer's ultimate metaphor, a writing desk. "She lay fairly high. Yurii Andreievich, exaggerating everything in his excitement, thought that she was lying, say, at the level of one of those desks at which you write standing up." The female body, overseen, inscribed on, is next metaphorised into a ship that has just unloaded its cargo in one of the novel's many beautiful poetic digressions, an extended simile which ends with words absolving reader and husband of all guilt for their distance and self-distancing: "And as no one had explored the country where she was registered, no one knew the language in which to speak to her."

Zhivago's later reflections on pregnancy and childbirth, in the "Varykino" chapter, exclude even the slightest intrusion of gross reality. The knowing husband merely writes in his journal that he feels Tonia is pregnant, though she herself "doesn't believe it." Tonia then becomes abstracted into "a woman" and "the woman": "A woman's face changes at such a time. It isn't that she becomes less attractive, but her appearance is no longer quite under her control." Thus deprived of identity, "the woman" can move fully into the spiritual realm: "It has always seemed to me that every conception is immaculate," writes Zhivago, "and that this dogma, concerning the Mother of God, expresses the idea of all motherhood." Tonia/Woman has become an icon. The concept of male irrelevancy, which reinforces the main idea of the novel that Dr. Zhivago's true responsibility lies elsewhere, in his artistic mission, is repeated: "the man's part is as irrelevant as if he had never had anything to do with it, as though the whole thing had dropped from heaven." The woman "alone, in silence and humility, . . . feeds and rears the child." Thus the hours of childbirth are extended into a lifetime of separation of the sexes. Man the artist has been freed. The section ends with an epiphany, Biblical quotation, and Pasternakian commentary: "all women are mothers of great men—it isn't their fault if life disappoints them later."

The circle has been closed: from an actual birth to the birth of a great man, who describes the birth process and especially its meaning to the distracted and abstracted mother and to mankind. Tonia reified becomes woman deified under Zhivago-Pasternak's artistic doctoring of reality and the husbandly role. *Doctor Zhivago* seems to have been received as a par-

ticularly powerful naming of women's reality, except by Anna Akhmatova.[4]
With minor changes it could become a Soviet novel.

Contemporary Russian literature has split into two streams; yet whether
published in the Soviet Union or outside, it retains certain common features
of language and tradition. One of these concerns the images of women as
they appear today. In the Soviet Union the most acclaimed writers of prose
fiction are still male.[5] They write within a realistic framework and their
heroines generally reflect the projections of male consciousness we have
seen in nineteenth-century works which idealize women, when not either
pitying or castigating them for materialism. Today, women characters continue to function as repositories of collective Russian wisdom, especially if
they live in the village and are very old. Solzhenitsyn's story "Matriona's
Home" and novellas of the Siberian writer Valentin Rasputin like "Farewell
to Matera" (1976) and "The Final Hour" (1970) have much in common: their
descriptions of very old women rooted in the countryside and in Russianness
carry powerful moral messages, but ones having little to do with women per
se. Younger heroines tend to carry instinct and devotion to a man to self-
destructive extremes, neutralizing any sexual threat.

In his novella *Live and Remember* (*Zhivi i pomni*, 1975), the most talented
Soviet Russian prose writer, Valentin Rasputin, portrays the heroine Nastyona as dying for her deserter-husband. Keeping the secret he had sworn
her to (he threatens to return to get her even from beyond the grave), she
throws herself into the Siberian river Angara with their unborn child rather
than reveal the fact that Andrei has returned to the vicinity of their village.
The tremendous strain of concealment and survival on both husband and
wife produces a different effect on each. Andrei becomes a wild animal,
learning to howl like a wolf and killing a calf in front of its mother. Nastyona,
an orphan whose very name was given her by her father-in-law, takes her
husband's guilt upon herself. Thus she resolves the potentially interesting
conflict the author has set up between duty to the narrow family (husband,
unborn child) and duty to the larger family (husband's relatives, village,
nation). Nastyona's whole life has been predicated on giving "more love and
care than she would receive—that's why she was a woman" (chapter 11).
The author approves of such a womanly role (so does a reader like Viktor
Nekrasov, writing from the emigration[6]). Nastyona's inner monologues are
close to the authorial narrative, for Rasputin believes in the connectedness
of people to each other and to the land as the greatest good. Though tragic
in this case, the instinctive assuming of human burdens by women is seen
by the author as natural, like their need to bear children: "from generation
to generation each woman got by on her instincts, with blind, passionate

and uncertain spells, and as if that wasn't enough, then she killed herself with the same old guilt." (chapter 9) Andrei says to Nastyona that there is no way he can pay her back, that he can never live up to her. But it is she who must die: perfection once again claims its terrible price.

That contemporary women writers of Russia generally write about urban life should not come as a surprise when one grasps the full implications of the patriarchal tradition of "village prose." Female prose writers like I. Grekova and Natal'ia Baranskaia have inherited the society tale tradition, which even today often means the ironic detailing of social confinement and spiritual resignation for women. Soviet heroines were supposed to have been free and equal; but the post-heroic age for Russian woman was heralded in the 1920s in Aleksei Tolstoi's "The Viper," where the former revolutionary fighter is reduced to battling fluffier ladies in the communal kitchen. Excluded by tradition and ideology from what seems to be the most powerful current in Soviet literature today, women writers have once again found it difficult to create heroines as radiantly virtuous as those of male writers. Their view of the "ordinary" woman is small scale and quietly despairing. When a good writer like Grekova tries her hand at the Russian heroine, the result is wooden.

I. Grekova's "The Hotel Manager" (1975),[7] really a short novel, has a heroine whose ability to adapt and endure while keeping her moral value system intact comes to us straight from the Russian nineteenth century. The novel doesn't ever ask the question "Why do women have to be so much better than men?," but rather assumes that since men have hard lives and are prone to drink, deception and self-deception, women's superiority is necessary for human survival. The heroine, symbolically named Vera (Faith), lives through all the major upheavals of Soviet history (excepting the collectivization and the purges—none of her friends or neighbors disappears). She loyally survives a difficult marriage with the isolation it brings, remaining virtually unscathed.

Vera, daughter of a strong mother and weak father, grows up by the Black Sea and finally returns there as a widow to begin an independent life. Her married life, shown in flashback, has consisted of utter devotion to a high-ranking military man who gives her what she most wants, "love," or rather words of love and extravagant romantic gestures. He extracts in return a perfect devotion to household, and service with a smile. Yet from this obviously unprogressive marriage Vera transfers her skills to manage a larger establishment, a seaside hotel.

Although satisfaction in work is continually asserted in this novel, work itself is not depicted in detail. The food Vera prepares and serves is described as if by a restaurant critic; the process of making it and of washing up afterwards is omitted. No kitchen realism mars the positive effect, as her husband would say.

The novel, like its heroine, wears a smile and is thus an eminent example of women's fiction as Socialist Realism, upbeat no matter what is actually mentioned. Vera's husband forces her to have an abortion, but she raises other people's children, experiencing maternal bliss of the highest order until they go away. Her mother is wonderful and strong. Her best woman friend is eccentric but lovable, as is an actress-friend in later life. A final love-affair, with a man she can see only three or four times a year because he is married to a cripple, is described as mature perfection.

The author of this fantasy in the realist/idealistic mode is a woman brilliantly successful at two professions. Under her real name, Yelena Sergeyevna Ventsel, she is a professor of mathematics and Doctor of Sciences. At the age of nearly fifty she began to be published as a writer of fiction in the major Moscow journals. Her pseudonym, I. Grekova, is a mathematical pun, "Mme X." Probably her best story was written in 1962. "The Ladies' Hairdresser" has a heroine more like its author, highly placed and middle-aged, with two sons and a hectic urban life that has its satisfactions and annoyances. She meets another genuinely admirable professional, a young male hairdresser, devoted to his art. Although the story makes clear that they are of different classes, they establish real rapport, for they have their professional honesty in common. Whether autobiographical or not, this story is closer to its author's reality.

Another story of particularly high craft, Ruf' Zernova's "Elizabeth Arden" (as yet untranslated) also describes an autobiographically presented experience in a beauty salon, but this time in the context of the Stalinist terror. Zernova, an established writer in the Soviet Union, has published her finest and most feminist collection since emigrating to the West. She explains its title, *Women's Stories (Zhenskie rasskazy)* and defends the notion of the "distinctiveness" (*svoeobrazie*) of literature "written by women about women"[8] in the preface. Zernova cites Akhmatova, Ginzburg, and Nadezhda Mandelstam as examples of the preservation and transmission of what was the true reality of Russia. Although they are called "stories," Zernova's best works in this collection are both historically specific and autobiographically narrated. "Elizabeth Arden" (a name even more redolent of fantasy-glamor to Russians) takes place during the years 1948–1949. The months preceding Zernova's (the narrator's) own arrest are given body and atmosphere.

Like her two great predecessors, Nadezhda Mandelstam and Evgeniia Ginzburg, Zernova combines the personal with the common fate, but she does so differently. Mandelstam centers her narrative on the figure of her poet-husband, almost effacing herself except as a voice. Ginzburg is present largely as human being among others in the whirlwind. Both direct their female narrative attention outward, apologizing in places for wanting a pair of silk stockings (Mandelstam) or giving mothering care to male prisoners who are motherless and wifeless (Ginzburg). Zernova barely mentions her husband and children, although clearly they are close to her. A housekeeper, a cosmetician, and a friend who composes an underground song are her secondary protagonists, her alter egos.

Zernova seems at ease with the fact that in writing about her self as a woman she can be writing about Russia. The more self-absorbed her narrative, the more the reader feels the pathos of the individual young female city-dwelling person doomed to enter the world of prison and labor-camps. The first sentence ("In 1948 we became rich") already contains all the ironies of a short period of relative ease before the arrest with which the "story" ends, but which is recalled throughout. The reader, like the author, knows what will happen and yet accompanies the author on small pleasurable forays into Leningrad life during most of the narrative, as well as backward into a warm and irretrievable Jewish Odessa.

The central series of forays takes place in Leningrad's high-class hotel, the European. The author spends her free time and money with a woman cosmetician who cares for her, in the same way as Simonovna, her peasant housekeeper, cares for her children. The narrator describes the delicious feeling of facial masks and creams on her dry skin, the fingers that massage her skin, and the mysteriously obtained Arden products she is allowed to take home before the course of treatment ends as doom closes in on both women. The woman, whom she names Elizabeth Arden, tells her not to frown, for "the face should always be at peace." The hotel functions primarily for foreigners and high officials. The male "working" world bangs away, removing radiators in the next room. Peace and delight are a female conspiracy to live an intimate and pleasing life.

There is much more to this story in very few pages—the evening gatherings, the author's gradual awareness of anti-Semitism, private family jokes—but its central image is that of the blue-eyed cosmetician claiming to be sixty and looking like forty, arrested just before the author and dreamed of by her until her own release. The fragility of life and beauty and the ability of women to care for themselves and each other in an atmosphere in which one is robbed of one's true identity, in which people "turn out to be" enemies of the people or spies or cosmopolitans, instead of the people one knew, compose the inner/outer (female-intimate/male-official) axis of the memoir/ fiction.

The awareness of other women's lives marks the autobiographical writings of Nadezhda Mandelstam as well:

> Thinking about *this*, I forgot myself and what had happened to me personally
> and even that I was writing about my own life, not somebody else's. The fact
> is that there was nothing exceptional about my case. There were untold num-
> bers of women like myself roaming the country—mute, cowed creatures, some
> with children, some without . . .[9]

The autobiography that actually describes in detail women in prison, women
in labor camps, women in every degree of brutalized existence is the work
of Evgeniia Ginzburg (1904–77). *Journey into the Whirlwind* and *Within the
Whirlwind* were published in English in 1967 and 1981 respectively (the
Russian editions, called *Krutoi marshrut* I and II were published in Italy in
1967 and 1979). As with Mandelstam, Ginzburg's second volume is fiercer,
more revealing of intimate emotion, as the act of writing without hope of
publication in her own country pushed each writer further into the region
of the self. While Mandelstam rarely uses her self-as-woman, Ginzburg remains true to an old humanitarian ideal of woman as the one who must not
only endure but do so without extremes of anger or self-pity. Thus, we can
view her volumes as a real version of a real Russian heroine, preserving the
self through selflessness. For example, to survive she must try not to think
about her own children because it is unbearable; but when she thinks of her
fellow prisoners it is as mothers or members of destroyed families. She writes
of an older prisoner: "My mother was eight years younger than this woman,
but it was unbearable to think of her in the same situation."[10]

How different her attitude toward the meaning of her own life from that
of Solzhenitsyn, who incarnates ultimate male autobiographical certainty:

> I have done many things in my life that conflicted with the great aims I had
> set myself—and something has always set me on the true path again. I have
> become so used to this, come to rely on it so much, that the only task I need
> set myself is to interpret as clearly and quickly as I can each major event in
> my life.[11]

Ginzburg, while describing the most abject inhumanities, also seeks and
finds the human spirit: this is her "great aim," but it is performed rather
than stated. Her continual forging of links with other human beings, a skill
she had exercised in her previous life as teacher, mother, and Party member,
gave life to others and surviving strength to herself.

When she was arrested in 1937, Ginzburg was thirty-two, the mother of
two small boys, an idealistic Party worker and the wife of a highly placed
Communist, who was to be arrested shortly afterward. Eighteen years later
she was released. She remarried, a doctor she had met in the camps, Anton
Walter, a Crimean German and a Catholic. Ginzburg's elder son died during
the siege of Leningrad. Her surviving son is the popular writer Vasily Aksyonov, who left the USSR in 1980. The story of their reunion in Magadan

after her first, short-lived release, followed by her rearrest, is told factually by Ginzburg in *Within the Whirlwind* and, fictively, by Aksyonov in *The Burn (Ozhog)*. Both accounts are among the most moving pieces of writing in Russian literature. Ginzburg is arrested in front of her own six-year-old pupils. She insists on going to her son's school. The seventeen-year-old, who had lost his mother at four, is told by their "security" escort to stop crying. Ginzburg writes that as she was driven away, "I raised my eyes in the direction of our window and saw that Vasya had moved the table away and had his face glued to the glass. This image would haunt me in prison like a deathly visitation. Even now, after a period of so many years, I find it painful to write about." Infusing such tragedy with dignity is the author's great achievement.

Although her two volumes of prison and camp memoirs were never published in the USSR, an earlier set of memoirs appeared in the journal *Youth (Yunost')* in 1965 (No. 11, pp. 87–99) and 1966 (No. 8, pp. 77–92). The first installment ("Edinaia trudovaia") describes the early days of her Soviet schooling, during the two years following the revolution when Ginzburg was one of the "children of the transitional years." The second part ("Studenty dvadtsatykh godov") is darker in tone: Ginzburg describes, in the midst of the positive ideals of the new generation, the increasing misery of her fellows, who were fed according to the class their parents belonged to. Genia and her schoolfriend see the corpse of a peasant woman whose six-year-old daughter tells her two smaller brothers to stop crying, that mother will soon wake up and feed them. Ginzburg feels shame at her friend's idealistic outburst against her mother, who tells her daughter to study medicine instead of social sciences which never fed anyone. (Later Ginzburg would give her own son the same advice.) The descriptions of her school and the University of Kazan have real historical interest; but their human interest is always primary. The narrator already possesses the conscience we find in her memoirs of a later period.

*Journey into the Whirlwind* describes Ginzburg's life from 1934 through 1939. From the first chapter, the author's powers of narrative compression, ironic detail, and hushed, tense dialogue are evident. Her memory of who people were and how they acted in a well-delineated situation makes her the ideal eyewitness when the very aim of existence had become to survive and remember. The first sentence of the book begins with true historical understanding: "The year 1937 began . . . at the end of 1934"—i.e., that the mass arrests began with Kirov's murder. Leaving her two children "breathing evenly in their sleep," Ginzburg is summoned from her normal existence in Kazan by a 4 A.M. phone call to a 6 A.M. meeting and from there to a factory to repeat words received from above about Kirov's death.

On this occasion, as always in Ginzburg's memoirs, there are those who understand more and those who understand less. These other actors in the Soviet tragedy are always characterized precisely and unforgettably; it is part of Ginzburg's greatness to rescue from oblivion people who lived in times when all lives were meaningful precisely because they were being destroyed.

The memoirs are a continual initiation into the deepening horrors of a changed situation for a Communist who had been accustomed to the rewards and responsibilities of what had seemed to be a position of trust. The implication that other whole groups had not been trusted and had indeed been destroyed and that those currently in power would be the next to die is only the first of many realizations. The first of her close associates to go, a man named Elvov, expressed sorrow in early 1935 that she might suffer from association with him. She was astonished; the first test of her "unshakable political naivete" comes with his arrest that night. And so the opening chapters lead us at an almost leisurely pace into events central to twentieth-century history.

The last year of her freedom is spent amid practical warnings to get lost in the countryside from her wise but ignored mother-in-law, and frequent trips to Moscow, where her appeal is reviewed. The wife of a still important Party member, she stays in comfortable hotel surroundings and is driven in an official car. She sees Stalin at Gorky's funeral, as she is still in the official ranks of mourners from the Writers' Union.

Her conversations with other "marked" people, fellow-petitioners for justice, are conveyed in the same terse, tense dialogue used throughout the memoirs. The world inside prisons, railway cars and labor camps has its own forms of communication, information-sharing that leads to attempted understanding and survival. Dialogue with the male accusers and inquisitors is also carefully reproduced in all the absurdity of its horror.

The year 1937 begins with the sort of telling incident that Ginzburg uses for dramatic irony throughout: she loses her gold watch in the snow, and she and her husband are unable to find it. They and their children see in the year at a ruling-class resort where nine-tenths of the arrogant people "were doomed, and within months nearly all of them were to exchange their comfortable suites for bunks at the Butyrki prison." Their children, experts in identifying the makes of foreign cars, would be put into special children's homes and (Ginzburg shades her sentence gradually from ironic reversal to Gogolian lunacy) "even their chauffeurs were pulled in for complicity in something or other."

Inside first the prison, then the boxcar to Siberia, then the camps, Ginzburg takes the reader on a "precipitous journey" of horror that killed millions who took it. The author herself is saved from death at various moments only by chance, which she sometimes calls "a miracle." In part she attracts miracles by her generosity toward others. Eventually becoming a nurse, she eases pain and suffering, distributing what little medicine there was, finding herbs in the *taiga* for the homeopathic remedies of a doctor-prisoner, Dr. Walter, and often just taking a fellow-prisoner into her arms.

The links forged between the innocent women of the camps and the grotesque world of female criminals form one remarkable counterpoint. The portrait of the Elgen camp commandant, Valentina Zimmerman, completes the picture: "Zimmerman never let pass a single incident that came to her notice." The author speculates on the developmental psychology of this stern, fanatical, and incorruptible punisher of the "guilty" and finally admits, "It is beyond me." She has given us more understanding of cold self-justifying evil in female form than we may ever find elsewhere.

Some portraits take on a symbolism beyond their bearers' own existence. Ginzburg writes of Dr. Walter: "I wanted to show through his image that the victim of inhumanity can remain the bearer of all that is good." The many other life stories she recounts serve as pieces in a huge mosaic of the millions in the "gulag archipelago" during all those years. The second volume, *Within the Whirlwind*, begins with a group of children born in the camps, speechless, loveless little animals, some of whom occasionally see their mothers or can learn briefly to take care of a puppy before it grows into one of the dogs that will guard them. Ginzburg then focuses, in unbearable detail, on a dying five-month-old girl.

These descriptions culminate in that most fragile of families Ginzburg constructs in Magadan. Some of the most fascinating sections of the book involve her "civilian" life in Magadan: the *beau monde* parading on Stalin Street, the ladies in silver-fox furs, and the terror of those just released from the adjacent world of the camps, soon to return to it.

The second volume ends with her return in 1955 to Moscow, where she is given a rehabilitation certificate with the words: "Please note that if you lose it, it will not be replaced." What the author calls her "inner censor," which accompanied her hope that the first volume would be published in Russia, disappears from the tone of the second volume. Without the aid of heavy irony, everything is told. The writing is the only possible rehabilitation certificate for the phenomenon it describes.

Incredibly, had Nadezhda Mandelstam and Evgeniia Ginzburg remained what can only be called "at home"—with the husbands who had originally shared their lives—these memoirs, and probably any other works by them, would never have been written. Their own terrible isolation over a period of many years made writers of them, as it had been the case with Dashkova, Durova, and Sokhanskaia.

Like autobiography, poetry by Russian women continues to thrive, in Moscow, Leningrad, Paris, Tel Aviv, New York, and elsewhere. The tradition of the specifically female lyric, the direct description of a woman's state of being, has flourished in the Soviet-published lyrics of, for example, Bella Akhmadulina and on the pages of emigre journals. Previously unpublished poetry kept in secret diaries during her imprisonment and afterward by Olga Berggol'ts (1910–1975), who enjoyed a successful career as an established Soviet writer, has only recently appeared in an emigre publication.[12]

Two younger women poets, Liia Vladimirova and Elena Shvarts, use an emphatically female voice in some of their poetry. In her poem "In the Theater" ("V teatre"),[13] Vladimirova continues the female tradition of the split self, at the same time poetically commenting on the famous Hamlet poem of Pasternak:

> I'm in the hall. And I'm onstage.
> Playing two parts. I act, I look.
> I'm forced to my knees.
> I'm in my upholstered seat.
>
> And so many faithful admirers
> Of mine have arrived from all over
> To catch sight of the three-act miracle,
> The tragedy "Land of the Living" . . .
>
> From the hall the applause doesn't stop.
> Actress, play us some pain!
> Timelessness lets us out
> For an hour, an instant, a part.
>
> Work! Anguish! Miracle-making!
> In all this the flaw can be seen.
> The actress without any acting
> Burns under a layer of cream.
>
> The play is a little drawn out,
> But acted with brilliance and wit,
> Though the feeling and fire of the prologue
> Are not given us to repeat.
>
> And, near the finale, I'm crying
> And can't see the action at all;
> I weep as I follow my footsteps
> Outside through the dark of the hall.

The tragic role of the hero has been skillfully adapted here to suit the female

persona. Tsvetaeva confronted the same split theatrical image in her poem
"Curtain" ("Zanaves," 1923), but resolved it by having the persona actually
become the partitioning curtain. Women poets co-opt and reinterpret male
images, as we have seen. They also give contemporary meaning to female
figures of the past. In Vladimirova's poetry Deborah and Yaroslavna represent the Jewish and Russian female past. Akhmatova and Tsvetaeva are
frequently recalled as well.

Perhaps the most striking image by one Russian woman writer of another
was evoked by the virtually unpublished Leningrad poet Elena Shvarts,
writing in her twenties;[14] it concerns Princess Dashkova in her old age. We
have seen Kliuchevskii's account of Dashkova's degradation, mocking the
Enlightenment she represented. The poem follows its details, but argues
with its thesis:

### The Old Age of Princess Dashkova

Princess Dashkova presides no more
At the Academy on the Isle
In her old age
She's left for Moscow.
Who will pity the rats?
Who will pity the rats?
For a rat, you know,
Neither reaps nor sows,
And is not a thing of beauty.
Hey, rats, run
Fast
Into that house on the corner
Onto the roof, into the drain
But all the same you're too late—
Your patron is in her grave.
A wake. In the kitchen gossiping, gossiping.
No one, but no one weeps for her.
"A small rat brings morning greetings to her bed,
It squeaks something in her ear,
She returns the compliment,
And lifts some sugar to its snout
With her white hand.
Her son died.
She buried him without a tear—
God gave, God took away,
Not for us to judge, they say.
But Mashenka, the rat, pinched her tail
She cried so hard and boxed the servants' ears all day."
Consciousness dims,

The icon-lamp smokes,
Voltaire and Rousseau
In far-away tombs.
Yes, old age is freedom
You do what you please
Then why are you crying
What are you muttering for?
"Are these the coffin's walls
Or the walls of a cradle?
Now a rat is over me
In a black and knitted shawl.
Dearest, how much you look
Like Grandma—you're as tender
And you mix solace with tears
Just the way she did."
The rat rocks the tidy coffin
Touches the poor yellow shoulders
Its words incomprehensible
Like grownup talk to children
The fool blows his tin whistle
Live on until that day
When you bind up grave and cradle
In fantastic, evil play.

Shvarts makes Dashkova into a universal prototype of female old age. Her behavior is a travesty of the maternal instinct: why expect maternal tenderness from an abandoned female, on the edge of the grave? Kliuchevskii mocks the contrast between Voltaire and Rousseau (the French enlightenment) and Dashkova (the Russian one), whereas Shvarts emphasizes the phenomenon of Russia's most outstanding female cultural figure, forgotten by all near death. The use of the second person singular pronoun addresses both Dashkova and the reader: all of us share the total isolation of an old woman.

Shvarts hardly idealizes her subject. The poem speaks not of woman's wisdom and spirituality but of her senile willfulness. Yet the portrait is more authentic in its view of the freedom of the total outcast, woman who has nothing left to lose, than are the abstract portrayals of Russian womanhood that have persisted in the masculine tradition.

Can it be said that there is a feminine tradition in Russian literature? The conscious echoing of one female voice by another, especially in poetry, has been a recurrent theme of our exploration of women's writing in Russia. In this poem by Elena Shvarts, the subject is Dashkova; but the rhetorical quality of poetic voice echoes that of Tsvetaeva. In the Vladimirova poem the thematic link is Pasternakian, but the withdrawing persona and the

neutral diction are reminiscent of Akhmatova. Akhmadulina refers to Tsvetaeva in three poems of her newest collection, *Taina* (1983). Even without
their echoes, many poems by Russian women use feminine attitudes, female
personae, and female imagery. Whether women's voices will emerge more
clearly in prose fiction remains to be seen; but their eminence in autobiography and poetry is bound to continue. Considered as a whole, feminine
writing provides an alternative perspective on Russian literature as it has
been traditionally viewed.

It is fitting to end with Shvarts's poem on Dashkova, for it summarizes
many of our major points: women's writing as obscurely (if at all) published
and unmentioned by critics; women's writing as self-referential, often ex-
ploring the self in other women; women's writing as self-defining in defiance
of male namings; and women's writing as powerful in its craft, world-creating
and word-creating.

Women writers in Russia are still in large part bound to the dominant
male definitions of their culture: real-life heroines who have endured trials
the nineteenth century barely guessed at have often written paler versions
of themselves in fiction published after passing the male censors, governmental and editorial. No doubt the attempts of a feminist critic from a different world to ferret out the counter-statements in seemingly traditional
texts that may exist and to find other texts with other values will not meet
with deafening applause from most Russians. But, to use Osip Mandelstam's
metaphor, the message women writers have put into bottles and set adrift
will eventually reach a farther shore than that of their homeland. It has been
the purpose of this book to hasten that process.

# NOTES

## Introduction

1. Dorothy Atkinson, "Society and the Sexes in the Russian Past," *Women in Russia*, ed. Dorothy Atkinson, Alexander Dallin, and Gail Lapidus (Stanford, 1977); Gail Warshofsky Lapidus, *Women in Soviet Society* (Berkeley and Los Angeles, 1978); Richard Stites, *The Women's Liberation Movement in Russia* (Princeton, 1978); Barbara Alpern Engel and Clifford N. Rosenthal, ed. and trans., *Five Sisters: Women Against the Tsar* (New York, 1975); Barbara Alpern Engel, *Mothers and Daughters: Women of the Intelligentsia in Nineteenth-Century Russia* (Cambridge, 1983); Rose L. Glickman, *Russian Factory Women: Workplace and Society 1880–1914* (Berkeley and Los Angeles, 1984); Linda Edmondson, *Feminism in Russia,1900–1917* (London, 1984).

2. Bibliographies and detailed lists of women writers in Russia are currently being compiled. As a beginning, see Barbara Heldt, "Russian Literature," in *Women in Print 1: Opportunities for Women's Studies in Language and Literature* (MLA Publications, New York, 1982), pp.149–154, with a bibliography by Sandra M. Thomson, pp. 155–157. A comprehensive annotated list of nineteenth-century Russian women authors is being prepared by Mary Zirin (*Russian Women Writers, 1830–1890*).

3. See the use of these terms in Annis Pratt, *Archetypal Patterns in Women's Fiction* (Bloomington, 1981).

4. See my introduction to and translation of Karolina Pavlova, *A Double Life* (Ann Arbor, 1978; reprinted, Berkeley, 1986).

5. The work of M. M. Bakhtin, especially his "Avtor i geroi v esteticheskoi deiatel' nosti," *Estetika slovesnogo tvorchestva* (Moscow, 1979), pp. 7–180, is useful background. His concept of "fate" and the "I-for-myself" hero led me to think of differences between male and female authors: for the latter, fate emanates from society rather than from society plus the self. The Bakhtinian concept of the classical hero's being (*bytie*) is most easily applied to male authors in Russian fiction. The best commonsense defense of referentiality in fiction is Gerald Graff's *Literature against Itself* (Chicago, 1979).

6. "Feminist Criticism in the Wilderness," in Elizabeth Abel, ed., *Writing and Sexual Difference* (Chicago, 1982), p. 16.

7. Rosalind Coward, *Patriarchal Precedents* (London, 1983), pp.12–13. See also the discussion of Hegel in Genevieve Lloyd, *The Man of Reason* (Minneapolis, 1984), *passim*, especially pp. 39, 70–73. This book is also the best discussion of how the formation of the concept of self in male thought has excluded, or defined itself in opposition to, the female.

8. Luce Irigaray, "Ce sexe qui n'en est pas un," *New French Feminisms*, ed. Elaine Marks and Isabelle Courtivron (Amherst, Mass., 1980), p. 104.

9. Mary Louise Pratt, *Toward a Speech Act Theory of Literary Discourse* (Bloomington, 1977), p. 95.

## 1. The Russian Heroine

1. See Ann Douglas, *The Feminization of American Culture* (New York, 1978).

2. See Vera Sandomirsky Dunham, "The Strong-Woman Motif," in Cyril E. Black, ed., *The Transformation of Russian Society* (Cambridge, Mass., 1960), pp.459–483.

This well argued piece rightly stresses the "lack of unity between heroines and heroes" (p. 481); however, I disagree that "the large number of artistically convincing heroines stands in contrast with the stilted heroes" (p.459). If anything, the opposite is true. The definitive study of the Soviet heroine, Xenia Gasiorowska, *Women in Soviet Fiction, 1917–1964* (Madison, 1968), also contains many illuminating comments about the prerevolutionary heroine.

3. B. Tomashevskii, *Teoriia literatury* (Moscow-Leningrad, 1928), p.154.

4. *Fantasticheskii mir Abrama Tertsa* (New York, 1967), p. 426.

5. Ibid., p.427.

6. Carl Proffer, "The Similes of Pushkin and Lermontov," *Russian Literature Triquarterly*, No.3 (Spring 1972), p. 159.

7. Eva Kagan-Kans, *Hamlet and Don Quixote: Turgenev's Ambivalent Vision* (The Hague, 1975). Turgenev "obliterated the distinction between the idealized young girl and the predatory woman, revealing his conception of the female element as essentially destructive" (p. 49). A "tenacious will" (p. 51) characterizes both. The author further demonstrates how logically they become phantoms in the later works, following their lack of distinctness in earlier ones.

8. Edmund Heier, "Elements of Physiognomy and Pathognomy in the Works of I. S. Turgenev (Turgenev and Lavater)," *Slavistische Beitrage*, Band 116 (Munchen, 1977), pp. 7–52. This excellent study of portraiture in Turgenev explains why the face receives the most attention and how Turgenev combines description with commentary. Heier's examples are limited to depictions of male characters. An earlier study of the female romantic portrait stresses that "The authorial 'I' never remains indifferent to the exterior looks of his heroine." See M. G. Davidovich, "Zhenskii portret u russkikh romantikov pervoi poloviny XIX veka," p. 88, in A. I. Beletskii, ed., *Russkii romantizm* (Leningrad, 1927). I would maintain that it would be difficult to find a case of authorial indifference to female portraiture in all of Russian realism.

9. D. I. Pisarev, "Zhenskie tipy v romanakh i povestiakh Pisemskogo, Turgeneva i Goncharova, " *Sochineniia*, I (Moscow, 1955), p. 238.

10. Richard Freeborn discusses the "different social experience" of hero and heroine in *Turgenev: The Novelist's Novelist* (Oxford, 1960), p.54 and *passim*.

11. V. Rozanov (1856–1919) described this phenomenon: "The universal 'I don't want to' of the male in regard to the female and of the female in regard to the male has been studied only recently." See "The Third Sex," *Four Faces of Rozanov*, trans. and intro. Spencer E. Roberts (New York, 1978), p.67. Goncharov has been omitted from this study because of the good discussion along similar lines in Carolina De Maegd-Soëp, *The Emancipation of Women in Russian Literature and Society* (Ghent, 1978), p. 151–195.

12. *Zhenshchina v russkoi khudozhestvennoi literature XIX veka* (1823–1876), p. 1.

13. Ibid., p. 2.

14. *The Trilogy of Alexander Sukhovo-Kobylin*, trans. Harold B. Segel (New York, 1969), p. 212.

15. E. Likhacheva, *Materialy dlia istorii zhenskago obrazovaniia v Rossii (1828–1856)* (St. Petersburg, 1895), p. 152.

16. D. I. Pisarev, *Polnoe sobranie v shesti tomakh*, IV, (St. Petersburg, 1894), pp. 447–448.

### 2. Misogyny and the Power of Silence

1. Joan Grossman, "Feminine Images in Old Russian Literature and Art," *California Slavic Studies* (XI, 1980), pp. 33–70, gives a good survey of the entire period from the Christianization of Rus' to the mid-seventeenth century, mentioning images

of women as saintly, wise, and heroic, as well as condemnatory works. Grossman shows that the division into Church misogyny and folkloric positive figures cannot be clearly made; she stresses the male authorship of all genres except embroidery and bridal laments.

2. "The Formidable Woman: Portrait and Original," *Russian Literature Triquarterly*, No. 9 (1974), pp. 433–453. This issue of *RLT* presents a range of texts and criticism on women in Russian literature.

3. See D. S. Likhachev, "Sotsial' nye osnovy stilia 'Moleniia Daniila Zatochnika'," in *Trudy otdela drevnerusskoi literatury*, X (Leningrad 1954), pp. 106–119, and M. O. Skripil', "Slovo Daniila Zatochnika," in *Trudy*, XI (Leningrad, 1955), pp. 72–95, for differing views on this text and its author, none of which substantially affects our argument. The recent book by Likhachev and A. M. Panchenko, *'Smekhovoi mir' drevnei Rusi* (Leningrad, 1976), in discussing the *Molenie*, claims that making fun of one's wife is a form of laughter at oneself, of buffoonery (p. 31). This seems to us an overly complacent view, especially as the speaker here has no wife.

4. See the texts in *Russian Literature Triquarterly*, No. 14 (1976), pp.416–429. See also William H. Hopkins, "Lermontov's Hussar Poems," in ibid., pp.36–47.

5. *Harvard Slavic Studies* (Cambridge, Mass., 1970), pp. 81–107. Essential reading on this subject is Olga Matich, "A Typology of Fallen Women in Nineteenth-Century Russian Literature," *American Contributions to the Ninth International Congress of Slavists*, Vol.2, ed. P. Debreczeny (Columbus, Ohio, 1983), pp. 325–343.

6. I have avoided juxtaposing art to biography by calling the lyric "I" the "speaker" or "narrator," not the author. The case of Nekrasov as the kept man of working women (including a prostitute) and the degrader of Avdotia Panaeva (with whom he lived for seventeen years and whose memoirs are a good example of repression of the self)—and the peculiar relationship of his situation to some of his lyrics is discussed by Richard Gregg, "A Brackish Hippocrene: Nekrasov, Panaeva, and the 'Prose in Love'," *Slavic Review* (December, 1975), pp. 731–751.

7. I have cited the David Magarshack translation of *The Idiot* (Penguin Publishers, 1956) throughout.

### 3. Tolstoy's Path toward Feminism

1. Most of this chapter appeared in *American Contributions to the Eighth International Congress of Slavists*, Vol 2, ed. V. Terras (Columbus, Ohio, 1978), pp. 523–535.

2. For an excellent account of how Tolstoy reworked factual material into fictional images in "Family Happiness," see O. I. Nikiforova, *Issledovaniia po psikhologii khudozhestvennogo tvorchestva* (Moscow, 1972) pp. 119–137.

3. L. N. Tolstoy, *Polnoe sobranie sochinenii* (Moscow and Leningrad, 1929–1959), 5, p. 313.

4. "A person equal to me" is closer to the more neutral Russian *"eto byl ravnyi mne chelovek"* than the more explicit J. D. Duff version: "he was a man on my level."

5. Tolstoy, 27, p. 596.

6. *Ibid.*, p. 563.

7. Tolstoy noted in his diary the intention to put more love and sympathy for the wife into his story, but after seven revisions she is only slightly more fully developed (Ibid., p. 578).

8. Tolstoy, 60, p. 127.

### 4. "Woman Is Everywhere Passive"

1. In the commentary to his edition of Chekhov's letters, Simon Karlinsky devotes several pages to a discussion of Chekhov's non-Victorian attitudes toward women and

the lack of any trace of the double sexual standard in the writings of the mature Chekhov. Simon Karlinsky, ed., *Anton Chekhov's Life and Thought: Selected Letters and Commentary* (Berkeley, 1973).

2. In another variant of the story, the narrator gives much more weight to his memory of the newly-wedded Agafya and compares her to a moth drawn to the flame. Chekhov saw fit to cut any extended reference to Agafya's past in the final version, as well as any lyrical narrative passage relating directly to her which might lead to an easy sympathy or cliché about fatal attraction. *Polnoe sobranie sochinenii i pisem. Sochineniia*, V (Moscow, 1976), p. 493.

3. Until very recently Chekhov's readers tended to see Olenka's devotion as a positive quality, while disagreeing about the author's attitude towards his heroine. A friend of Chekhov's reported in a letter that a woman he knew thought that Chekhov "looked at woman with too much humor, making her good to the point of stupidity, having nothing of her own": quoted in A. S. Melkova, "Tvorcheskaia sud'ba rasskaza 'Duschechka'," *V tvorcheskoi laboratorii Chekhova*, ed. L. D. Opul'skaia *et al.* (Moscow, 1974), p. 79. Other women, upon reading the story, wrote Chekhov "angry letters" presumably for the same reason (Ibid., p. 81). Leo Tolstoy rendered a famous opinion that Chekhov had "praised what he had wanted to curse," that he had put into a comic story a heroine who was ultimately an ideal of womanly love, for "Men are not able to deal with . . . matters of love, of complete giving of oneself to the loved one, which good women have done, do and will do so well and naturally." L. N. Tolstoy, *Polnoe sobranie sochinenii*, vol.41 (Moscow, 1957), pp. 375–376. See also V. Ia. Lakshin, *Tolstoi i Chekhov* (Moscow, 1963), pp. 94–115.

On May 4, 1940, F. Scott Fitzgerald wrote to his wife Zelda in her insane asylum: "I hope you're happy. I wish you read books (you know those things that look like blocks but come apart on one side). I mean loads of books and not just early Hebrew metaphysics. If you did I'd advise you to try some more short stories. You never could plot for shocks but you might try something along the line of Gogol's 'The Cloak' or Chekhov's 'The Darling' ": Andrew Turnbull, ed., *The Letters of F. Scott Fitzgerald* (New York, 1963), pp. 115–116.

Renato Poggioli, agreeing with Tolstoy about Olenka's ultimate goodness, writes: "Olenka is poor in spirit and pure in heart, and this is why life curses her three times, only to bless her forever, at the end." He likens her to Psyche: *The Phoenix and the Spider* (Cambridge, Mass., 1957), pp. 124–130. Thomas Winner takes issue with Poggioli, calling Olenka part satire but nonetheless "capable of love, even though it is submissive and possessive": *Chekhov and His Prose* (New York, 1966), pp. 210–216. This is the most balanced reading of the story.

Recent critics have given us a darker and, to my mind, better interpretation: Karl Kramer underlines Olenka's negative effect on those close to her and their "resistance to her attentions: *The Chameleon and the Dream* (The Hague, 1970), p. 161. Psychiatrist Michael A. Sperber writes of Olenka's "problem," symptomatic of what Helene Deutsch termed the "as if" personality, which uses "multiple identifications . . . to form an ego in order to make up for the absence of one": "The 'As If' Personality and Anton Chekhov's 'The Darling,' " *The Psychoanalytic Review* (Spring, 1971), pp. 14–21. Finally, Virginia Llewellyn Smith relates "The Darling" to Chekhov's general view of women in love: "For women love is something assumed rather than felt, a kind of acquisition prompted by custom, like an article of clothing": *Anton Chekhov and the Lady with the Dog* (London, 1973), thus bringing us back to Chekhov's early women readers' perception of his misogynistic intent.

4. Letter of January 27, 1899, to Suvorin, *Polnoe sobranie sochinenii*, XVIII (Moscow, 1949), p. 45.

5. A. S. Melkova (op. cit.) gives us a painstakingly researched but still sketchy outline of the story's genesis in earlier Chekhovian writings. Two other works on

Chekhov's notebooks are similarly inconclusive: S. Balukhatyi, "Zapisnye knizhki Chekhova," *Literaturnaia ucheba*, 1934, No.2, p. 58, and Z. Papernyi, *Zapisnye knizhki Chekhova* (Moscow, 1976), pp. 297–312.

6. See Barbara Heldt, "Chekhov (and Flaubert) on Female Devotion," *Ulbandus Review*, Vol. 2, No. 2, pp. 166–174, in which part of the section on "The Darling" first appeared.

7. I am grateful to Simon Karlinsky for providing me with a copy of this virtually unknown play, rediscovered by him: N. Minskii, *Al'ma* (St. Petersburg, 1900), previously mentioned in Karlinsky's "Russia's Gay Literature and History (11th–20th Centuries)," *Gay Sunshine*, No.29/30 (San Francisco, 1976).

8. For an important reevaluation of the influence of Nietzsche on Russian writers, and on Gorky in particular, see Betty Y. Forman, "Nietzsche and Gorky in the 1890's: The Case for an Early Influence," *Western Philosophical Systems in Russian Literature*, ed. A. Mlikotin (Los Angeles, 1979), pp. 153–164.

9. Noted in Jeffrey Brooks, "Readers and Reading at the End of the Tsarist Era," in *Literature and Society in Imperial Russia (1800–1917)*, ed. William M. Todd III (Stanford, 1978), pp. 97–150. This extremely valuable study discusses the popularity of women's fiction after 1905 (pp. 116–117).

10. Alexander Herzen, *Who is to Blame?*, tr. R. Busch and T. Yedlin (Edmonton, Alberta, 1982), p. 40.

11. See L. S. Herrmann, *George Sand and the Nineteenth-Century Russian Novel: The Quest for a Heroine*, unpublished Ph. D. thesis, Columbia, 1979; M. B. Nielsen, "The Concept of Love and the Conflict of the Individual versus Society in Elena A. Gan's *Sud sveta*," *Scando-Slavica* 24, 1978, pp. 125–138; and Y. Harussi, "Hinweis auf Elena Gan (1814–1841)," *Zeitschrift für slavische Philologie*, XLII, 2, 1981, pp. 242–260.

12. A. Beletskii, "Turgenev i russkie pisatel'nitsy. 1830–1860–kh godov," *Pratsy v piati tomakh* (Kiev, 1966), IV, p. 301.

13. Shoshana Felman, "Rereading Femininity," *Yale French Studies*, No. 62 (1981), p. 21. Quoted in Teresa de Lauretis, *Alice Doesn't: Feminism, Semiotics, Cinema* (Bloomington, 1984), p. 111.

### 5. Public and Private Lives

1. See the articles in *New Literary History*, 9, No. 1 (Autumn, 1977); the collection by James Olney, *Autobiography: Essays Theoretical and Critical* (Princeton, 1980); and the introduction to Avram Fleishman, *Figures of Autobiography* (Berkeley, 1983), for an overview of many of the critical works in this rapidly growing area. An excellent bibliography of books and articles from 1980 to 1985 can be found in *a/b. Auto/Biography Studies* (December, 1985), pp. 12–26.

2. See the volumes of *Istoriia dorevoliutsionnoi Rossii v dnevnikakh i vospominaniiakh*, ed. P. A. Zaionchkovskii (Moscow, 1976—) for books and journal publications, and *Vospominaniia i dnevniki XVIII-XX vv.*, ed. S. V. Zhitomirskaia (Moscow, 1976), for holdings in the manuscript division of the Lenin Library.

3. Domna C. Stanton, "Autogynography: Is the Subject Different?" in *The Female Autograph*, ed. D. Stanton, *New York Literary Forum* 12–13 (New York, 1984), p. 16. The entire collection is of value, as is the other major collection on the subject: Estelle C. Jelinek, ed., *Women's Autobiography: Essays in Criticism* (Bloomington, 1980).

4. Durova's memoirs dealing with her childhood years have recently appeared in excellent English translation by Mary Fleming Zirin in *The Female Autograph*, pp. 119–141. Zirin's translation of Durova's memoir, *Kavalerist-devitsa: Proisshestvie*

*v Rossii (The Cavalry Maiden: It Happened in Russia)* (St. Petersburg, 1836) will be published in 1988 by Indiana University Press.

5. Patricia Meyer Spacks, "Selves in Hiding," in Jelinek, p. 113.

6. Sofya Kovalevskaya, *A Russian Childhood* (New York, 1978). See Beatrice Stillman's fine introduction. The definitive biography of Kovalevskaia is: Ann Hibner Koblitz, *A Convergence of Lives* (Basel and Boston, 1983).

7. Aleksandr Nikitenko, *The Diary of a Russian Censor*, ed. and trans. Helen Saltz Jacobson (Amherst, 1975), pp. 83–84.

8. Ibid., p. 282 and *passim*.

9. Alexander Herzen, *My Past and Thoughts*, ed. Dwight Macdonald (New York, 1973), p. 438.

10. Catherine the Great, *Memoirs* (New York, 1955), p. 60.

11. Vera Figner, *Memoirs of a Revolutionist* (New York, 1927), pp. 16–17.

12. Ibid., p. 21.

13. The English edition is closest to the original, and all my quotations are taken from it: *The Memoirs of Princess Dashkov*, trans. and ed. Kyril Fitzlyon (London, 1958). The French edition by Pascal Pontremoli was taken from the French translation, not from the French text in the Manuscript Room of the British Library. For a critical bibliography of works about Dashkova, see the review of L. Ia. Lozinskaia, *Vo glave dvukh akademii* (Moscow, 1978), by A. G. Cross in *Study Group on Eighteenth-Century Russia Newsletter* No. 6 (September, 1978), pp. 71–76. An interesting unpublished thesis is R. A. Longmire, "Princess Dashkova and the Intellectual Life of Eighteenth-Century Russia" (M.A., University of London, 1955).

14. Marc Raeff, *Origins of the Russian Intelligentsia* (New York, 1966), p. 102. See also J. L. Black, "Educating Women in Eighteenth-Century Russia: Myths and Realities," *Canadian Slavonic Papers* XX, No. 1 (March, 1978), pp. 23–43, and the excellent study by Carol S. Nash, "Educating New Mothers: Women and the Enlightenment in Russia," *History of Education Quarterly* (Fall, 1981), pp. 301–316.

15. Hans Rogger, *National Consciousness in Eighteenth-Century Russia* (Cambridge, Mass., 1960), *passim*.

16. V. O. Kliuchevskii, *Sochineniia*, V (Moscow, 1958), p. 176.

17. *Sobranie sochinenii*, XII (Moscow, 1957), p. 361.

18. The best account of Dashkova's stay in Britain is found in A. G. Cross, *"By the Banks of the Thames": Russians in Eighteenth-Century Britain* (Newtonville, Mass., 1980), pp. 131–134, 235–240.

19. Richard Wortman, introduction to Derzhavin's *Zapiski* (reprint; Cambridge, Mass., 1973), p. 3.

20. See M. F. Shugurov, "Miss Vil'mot i kniaginia Dashkova," *Russkii arkhiv*, III, No. 1 (1880), pp. 150–217. Dashkova outlived her son and became reconciled with her daughter-in-law. See V. V. Ogarkov, *E. R. Dashkova: Biograficheskii ocherk* (St. Petersburg, 1893).

21. In her book *Vo glave dvukh akademii* (Moscow, 1978), the only full-length monograph on Dashkova, L. Ia. Lozinskaia argues in passing that she is an "example of Russian sentimentalism with its characteristic striving toward self-knowledge and non-acceptance of ossified norms of life" (p. 114). But Dashkova's tastes were formed by French classicism, and she was herself a classical author. Her five-act comedy, "Toisekov, ili chelovek bezkharakternyi," has the protagonist loudly and petulantly lamenting his "unhappy union" with a wife who has gallicized their household. To this common Russian theme she adds mockery of the husband's indecisiveness and penchant for shifting the blame.

## 6. Mothers and Daughters

1. Barbara Alpern Engel, "Mothers and Daughters: Family Patterns and the Female Intelligentsia," in D. L. Ransel, ed., *The Family in Imperial Russia* (Urbana,

Illinois, 1978), p. 44. Since completing this study, I have read Engel's *Mothers and Daughters: Women of the Intelligentsia in Nineteenth-Century Russia* (Cambridge, 1983). With its focus on discontent and rebellion measured in historical decades and its use of women's writings to illuminate their lives and activities, it provides many parallel findings which complement my approach. Her discussion of Labzina overlaps with mine; otherwise we focus on different kinds of self-expression and therefore on different women. Engel's conclusion is that the ethic of moral perfection led women away from specific women's issues and toward a more general social concern. As activists, she notes, women radicals were sustained by friendships with other women, just like many of the women writers I discuss.

2. A. E. Labzina, *Vospominaniia* (St. Petersburg, 1914; reprinted, Newtonville, Mass., 1974), p. 21.

3. E. N. Vodovozova, *Na zare zhizni* (Moscow-Leningrad, 1934), Vol. I, p. 54.

4. Ibid., p. 342.

5. The same abridged version of *Zapiski kavalerist-devitsy* has appeared four times since the sixties (Kazan', 1960; Moscow, 1962; Kazan', 1966; Kazan', 1979). The full version was published twice in 1836 (*Sovremennik*, 2, pp. 53–132 and 2 vols, Petersburg); the first Soviet edition appeared in 1983. An "addendum," *Dobavlenie k "Devitse-kavalerist"*, was published in Moscow in 1839. Part of the section on Durova in this book appeared in *History Today* (February, 1985), pp. 24–27.

6. Sandra M. Gilbert, "Costumes of the Mind: Transvestism as Metaphor in Modern Literature," *Writing and Sexual Difference*, ed. Elizabeth Abel (Chicago, 1982), p. 217.

## 7. The Emerging Writer

1. *Russkoe obozrenie*, 1896, Nos. 6–12.

2. (Bremen, 1977). These have been translated by Lucy Vogel as "Facts and Myths about Blok and Myself" in *Blok: An Anthology of Essays and Memoirs* (Ann Arbor, 1982), pp. 8–63. The translations used here are my own.

3. Marina Tsvetaeva, *A Captive Spirit: Selected Prose*, ed. and trans. J. M. King (Ann Arbor, 1980), p. 235.

4. Ibid., p. 237.

5. Anna Akhmatova, *O Pushkine* (Leningrad, 1977), p. 188.

6. Ibid., p. 110.

7. See R. A. Budagov, "Kak rasskazala Marina Tsvetaeva o zhene A. S. Pushkina," *Russkaia rech'* 11 (1977), pp. 19–23.

8. Marina Tsvetaeva, *Moi Pushkin* (Moscow, 1967). All quotations from "Natal'ia Goncharova" are translated from pages 200–205 of this edition.

9. Ibid., p. 236.

10. Tsvetaeva, *A Captive Spirit*, p. 349.

11. For an excellent reevaluation of this myth, see Richard Gregg, "Rhetoric in Tat'jana's Last Speech: The Camouflage that Reveals," *SEEJ*, Vol. 25, No. 1 (1981), pp. 1–12.

12. Tsvetaeva, *A Captive Spirit*, p. 337.

13. Ibid., p. 336.

## 8. From Folklore through the Nineteenth Century

1. For a description of the potential abuse such a move entailed, including the patriarch's right to sexual intercourse with his daughters-in-law, called *snokhachestvo*, see Glickman, pp. 28ff.

2. *Lirika russkoi svad'by* (Leningrad, 1973). The quotations used in this section are translations of nos. 20, 28 (in part), and 185 in that order.

3. In his preface to *Russkie poetessy XIX veka* (Moscow, 1979), N. Bannikov

discusses the disputed origins of Russian poetry sung and written by women. His collection forms a small anthology of poetry of the eighteenth and nineteenth centuries, drawn by and large from separate volumes of poets in the Poet's Library series, Biblioteka poeta. Our selections, unless otherwise noted, are drawn from the latter and from the entire volume devoted to Karolina Pavlova, the only woman poet before the twentieth century to have her own volume: *Polnoe sobranie stikhotvorenii* (Moscow and Leningrad, 1964). The women poets are grouped as follows in the Biblioteka poeta: *Poety 1790–1810* (Leningrad, 1971) (Bunina and Volkova); *Poety 1820–1830*, Vol. 1 (Leningrad, 1972) (Teplova); *Poety 1840–1850* (Leningrad, 1972) (Rostopchina, Khvoshchinskaia, and Zhadovskaia); *Poety 1880–1890* (Leningrad, 1972) (Chiumina and Lokhvitskaia). Bannikov's volume includes Zubova, Sandunova, Volkonskaia, Gotovtsova, Barykova, Figner, Solov'eva, Galina, and Shepkina-Kupernik.

4. Karolina Pavlova, *A Double Life*, p. 26. The introduction to this edition chronicles Pavlova's exile and mistreatment by her contemporaries, which I will not discuss here.

5. Tsvetaeva decided to remove the actual epigraph of Pavlova's lines at the time of publication, "not wishing, according to my custom, to facilitate anything for the reader, respecting the reader," as she wrote in a letter to Bakhrakh. Quoted in Simon Karlinsky, *Marina Cvetaeva: Her Life and Art* (Berkeley, 1966), p. 193. Simon Karlinsky's *Marina Tsvetaeva: The Women, Her World and Her Poetry* (Cambridge, 1985) provides a superb analysis of Tsvetaeva's links to other women throughout her life.

### 9. Four Modern Women Poets

1. Illuminating works on Gippius and Parnok in particular have been published recently in the West. Zinaida Gippius has remained completely unpublished in the Soviet Union for political reasons. On Gippius see: Simon Karlinsky, "Who Was Zinaida Gippius?" Introduction to Vladimir Zlobin, *A Difficult Soul* (Berkeley, 1980); Olga Matich, *Paradox in the Religious Poetry of Zinaida Gippius* (Munich, 1972); Temira Pachmuss's numerous publications of and on Gippius's works; and her anthology *Women Writers in Russian Modernism* (Urbana, 1978). Parnok, unpublished since the twenties, has now reappeared in a definitive edition in the West, the Ardis collection edited by S. Poliakova: Sofiia Parnok, *Sobranie stikhotvorenii* (Ann Arbor, 1979). See also Poliakova's *Zakatnye ony dni: Tsvetaeva i Parnok* (Ann Arbor, 1983) and an article by Rima Shore: "Remembering Sophia Parnok (1885–1933)," *Conditions*, 6, 1980, pp. 177–93, with translations of eight poems (pp. 171–75). Karlinsky and Shore give sensitive descriptions of the sexuality of Gippius and Parnok, respectively, while Poliakova illuminates the sexual friendship between Parnok and Tsvetaeva. Without this, an understanding of their poetry is impossible. The poetry of Mariia Shkapskaia had not been published since 1925, until the appearance of a recent Western edition called *Stikhi* (London, 1979), with introductory articles by the editors, Boris Filippov and Evgeniia Zhiglevich. My translations of Shkapskaia have been made from this edition, and those of Parnok from the Ardis edition cited above.

2. Sofia Parnok, "B. Pasternak i drugie," *Russkii sovremennik*, Kniga pervaia (Moscow and Leningrad, 1924), pp. 307–11.

3. "Dva pis'ma. Publikatsiia Arkhiva A. M. Gor'kogo," *Rabotnitsa*, No. 3, 1968, p. 1.

4. Lidiia Chukovskaia writes of a meeting with Akhmatova on October 18, 1939, during which her poetry was discussed: "I complained that I didn't understand one poem: 'Ia prishla tebia smenit', sestra.' 'I don't understand it either,' answered Anna Akhmatova. 'You have hit the mark. It's the only poem of mine that I myself could

never understand.' " Lidiia Chukovskaia, *Zapiski ob Anne Akhmatovoi*, I (Paris, 1976), p. 51.

5. I quote the Struve edition: Anna Akhmatova, *Sochineniia*, I (London, 1967), pp. 94–95. The Biblioteka poeta edition—Anna Akhmatova, *Stikhotvoreniia i poemy* (Leningrad, 1976), pp. 76–77—sets the last eight lines as six plus two, following the manuscript of *Beg Vremeni*. However, all earlier editions (*Chetki* of Petersburg, 1913; Berlin, 1913; and Petrograd, 1923, as well as *Iz shesti knig*, Leningrad, 1940) have two quatrains. The other Akhmatova lyric poems quoted are based on texts from the Biblioteka poeta edition. Translations of selected lyrics by Walter Arndt, of *Requiem* by Robin Kemball, and of *Poem without a Hero* by Carl Proffer are in Anna Akhmatova, *Selected Poems* (Ann Arbor, 1976).

6. In another lyric, "Ne budem pit' iz odnogo stakana" (1913), the "koster" occupies a similar but less literal place as somewhere that "neither oblivion nor fear dares touch" in the relationship of two people who understand and love each other but live separate lives. The "koster" is mentioned in the penultimate couplet only rhetorically stressed by the preceding words "O, est' " and by the strong enjambement (separating two complements of a verb), and therefore carries an emotional weight greater than that of the final couplet which contains an ironic undercut to the purity of the fire image. The poem describes separation, with assertions of unity and longing throughout. The mind acknowledges and possesses what the body cannot have, as in "Ia prishla . . ."

7. For a discussion of Akhmatova's use of classical heroines as doubles, which does not mention this poem, see: T. V. Tsiv'ian, "Antichnye geroini—zerkala Akhmatovoi," *Russian Literature* 7/8 (1974), 103–119. An interesting analysis of "Ia prishla . . ." interprets the narrow path as the spiritual one, giving a religious interpretation to the poem. See W. Rosslyn, *The Prince, the Fool and the Nunnery: The Religious Theme in the Early Poetry of Anna Akhmatova* (Letchworth, 1981), pp. 110–113.

8. In a later Muse poem ("Muza", 1924) the Muse herself gives her one-syllable answer—"I"—to a longer question of the poet. Here there is no doubt that the heroine is a poet of the stature of Dante, but even so she waits and is stripped of her coverings (similarly to the giving over of the clothes in "Ia prishla . . ."). The poet of 1924 even more vigorously accepts the price she will pay ("What are honors, youth, and freedom before the dear guest with reed-pipes in her hand?").

9. Akhmatova called this process a metamorphosis in "Kak belyi kamen' v glubine kolodtsa" (1916).

10. Kees Verheul, *The Theme of Time in the Poetry of Anna Axmatova* (The Hague, 1971), deals with the continuity of this subject. Sam N. Driver, *Anna Akhmatova* (New York, 1972), discusses "the stance or point of view of the *persona*—somehow apart from herself, observing herself" (p. 62).

11. See the following articles of G. S. Smith: "Logaoedic Metres in the Lyric Poetry of M. Tsvetayeva," *Slavonic and East European Review*, LIII, 132 (1975), pp. 330–54; "Versification and Composition in M. Cvetaeva's *Pereuločki*," *IJSLP*, 20 (1975), pp. 122–53; "The Versification of M. Tsvetaeva's Lyric Poetry, 1922–23," *Essays in Poetics*, I, 2 (1976), pp. 21–50; "M. Cvetaeva's *Poema gory*: An Analysis," *Russian Literature*, VI, 4 (1978), pp. 365–88; "Characters and Narrative Modes in M. Tsvetaeva's *Tsar'-devitsa*," *Oxford Slavonic Papers*, NS XII (1979), pp. 117–34; "Compound Meters in the Poetry of M. Cvetaeva," *Russian Literature*, VIII (1980), pp. 103–23.

12. See the excellent discussion of the development of Tsvetaeva's female poetic representations in: Antonina Filonov Gove, "The Feminine Stereotype and Beyond: Role Conflict and Resolution in the Poetics of Marina Tsvetaeva," *Slavic Review* (June, 1977), pp. 231–255. The Russica edition of Tsvetaeva, *Stikhotvoreniia i poemy*,

Vols. I–V (New York, 1980– ), will be the most complete edition when Vol. V appears. I base all texts on that edition unless otherwise noted.

13. See Ju. Levin, "Russkie perevody Shekspira," *Masterstvo perevoda* (Moscow, 1968), p. 301.

14. Ibid.

15. My discussion of these poems is based on my article: "Two Poems by Marina Tsvetayeva from *Posle Rossii*," *Modern Language Review*, Vol. 77, No. 3 (1982), pp. 679–687.

16. "Rasshchelina" has many such echoes: the poems addressed to Boris Pasternak, which emphasize distance and silence (see especially "Pedal'," which repeats the word "glushe"); the poems that sound like lullabies in part ("Nochnogo gostia," "Svetlo-serebrianaia tsvel'," "Kolybel'naia"); poems that mention Helen of Troy ("S etoi gory," the first poem in "Dvoe," "Tak-tol'ko Elena"); and poems that repeat certain concepts verbatim like "Ty vo mne" ("Daby ty menia ne videl—") or "Sokrovishchnitsa podobii" (the tenth poem in the "Provoda" cycle). Four poems written in the same month as "Rasshchelina" seem to have a particular connection to it: "Rano eshche" which uses imagery of wounds and ices; "Zanaves" in which the speaker mediates between the addressee and others; "Sakhara," the closest of all in its imagery of someone buried in sand, rather than ice; and "Rakovina" which ends in opposite fashion, with the chest opening up to permit a rebirth. Similar imagery is used later (in 1934) by Tsvetaeva to describe the loss of a beloved friend, the actress Sonia Holliday: "Not: Sonechka has died for me and not: love has died—Sonia has died from my life, that is, has entirely gone within, into that mountain, into that cave, into which she so prophetically feared to fall [propast']." "Povest' o Sonechke," *Neizdannoe* (Paris, 1976), p. 348.

17. This fairy-tale, Germanic rather than Slavic in origin, was reworked by Pushkin in his "Skazka o mertvoi tsarevne," which contains the lines "I v khrustal'nom grobe tom/Spit tsarevna vechnym snom." Pushkin is a likely source for Tsvetaeva's image, although Grimm cannot be excluded. The conscious reworking of an image of female passivity into one of male passivity and moral numbness is similar to the Ophelia/Hamlet poems.

18. According to legend, this act was intended to convince his friends that he had become a god. See Diogenes Laertius VIII, 67–61. The more widely-read *Ars Poetica* of Horace is likely to have put the story of Empedocles' death into circulation in Russia. It contains the lines (453ff): "Siculique poetae/narrabo interitum. Deus immortalis haberi/dum cupit Empedocles, ardentem frigidus Aetnam/insiluit. Sit ius liceatque perire poetis!" Compare also two poetic reworkings of the legend: Matthew Arnold's "Empedocles on Etna" and Hölderlin's "Empedokles." (Hölderlin was used as the epigraph to *Poema gory*, written by Tsvetaeva in January 1924.)

## Conclusions . . . and Continuations

1. Lapidus, *Women in Soviet Society*, and *Women, Work, and Family in the Soviet Union* (New York, 1982).

2. The breaking of this silence and the reasons for it can be found in Tatyana Mamonova, ed., *Women and Russia* (Boston, 1984).

3. See the interesting review essay on recent female autobiographies: Laura Engelstein, "In a Female Voice," *Slavic Review* (Spring, 1985), pp. 104–107.

4. Aside from politically based Soviet criticisms, Anna Akhmatova is reported to have made some scathing comments about the novel when it appeared, calling it "bad, except for the landscapes . . . a Gogolian failure, like the second volume of *Dead Souls*." See Lidiia Chukovskaia, *Zapiski ob Anne Akhmatovoi*, II (Paris, 1980), p. 259.

5. See Geoffrey Hosking, *Beyond Socialist Realism: Soviet Fiction since Ivan Denisovich* (London, 1980).

6. In a recent interview ("Beseda s Viktorom Nekrasovym," *Strelets* 3 (985), p. 39) V. Nekrasov, highly critical of most literature published in the Soviet Union, calls "Live and Remember" the best novella of Rasputin and "a sort of hymn to woman's love and faithfulness. It is on the level of Nekrasov's 'Russian Women'." Female sacrifice remains in vogue.

7. See I. Grekova, *Russian Women: Two Stories*, trans. M. Petrov and intro. M. Friedberg (New York, 1983) for translations of "The Ladies' Hairdresser" (1962) and "The Hotel Manager" (1975). They are published in Russian in I. Grekova, *Kafedra* (Moscow, 1983).

8. Ruf' Zernova, *Zhenskie rasskazy* (Ann Arbor, 1981), p. 5.

9. Nadezhda Mandelstam, *Hope Abandoned* (New York, 1974), p. 3.

10. All quotations are from Eugenia Ginzburg, *Journey into the Whirlwind* (New York, 1967), and *Within the Whirlwind* (New York, 1981).

11. *The Oak and the Calf*, tr. Harry Willetts (New York, 1979), p. 111.

12. *Vremia i my*, 57 (1980), pp. 283–291.

13. "V teatre" was first published in *Vremia i my*, 9 (1976), pp. 103–104.

14. "Starost' kniagii [sic] Dashkovoi" was published in the student newspaper of Tartu University: *Tartu Riiklik Ulikool*, 5 (May 25, 1973).

# INDEX

Editor: Susan Harlow
Book designer: Joan Cavanagh
Jacket designer: Joan Cavanagh
Production coordinator: Harriet Curry
Typefaces: Caledonia, Cochin Display
Printer: J. Jarrett Engineering
Binder: Braun-Brumfield, Inc.

BARBARA HELDT teaches Russian and Comparative Literature and Women's Studies at the University of British Columbia in Vancouver, Canada. She is the author of *Koz'ma Prutkov: The Art of Parody*, has translated Karolina Pavlova's *A Double Life*, and co-edited (with Gerald Graff) W. B. Scott's *Parodies, Et Cetera, and Stuff*.